myoclonic seizures

The preparation and publication of this Excerpta Medica monograph was made possible by a grant from Hoffmann-La Roche Inc., Nutley, New Jersey 07110

myoclonic seizures

Editor

Maurice H. Charlton
*The University of Rochester School of Medicine and Dentistry,
and Strong Memorial Hospital, Rochester, N.Y.*

Excerpta Medica 1975

International Congress Series No. 307
ISBN 90 219 0244 3
Library of Congress Catalog Card Number 73-87381

Excerpta Medica Offices
Amsterdam Keizersgracht 305
Geneva   17-19, chemin du Champ d'Anier
London   Chandos House, 2 Queen Anne Street
Princeton Nassau Building, 228 Alexander Street

Typeset in The Netherlands by Van Gorcum, Assen
Printed in the U.S.A.

Contributors

Maurice H. Charlton, M.D.
University of Rochester School of
  Medicine and Dentistry and
  Strong Memorial Hospital,
Rochester, N.Y.

Donald F. Farrell, M.D.
Division of Neurology,
University of Washington School of
  Medicine,
Seattle, Wash.

A. M. Halliday, M.D.
Medical Research Council,
Institute of Neurology,
National Hospital,
London, U.K.

Marcel Kinsbourne, M.D.
Department of Pediatrics,
Duke University Medical Center,
Durham, N.C.

Gary J. Myers, M.D.
Department of Pediatrics and Neurology,
The University of Rochester School of
  Medicine and Dentistry and
  Strong Memorial Hospital,
Rochester, N.Y.

David B. Rosenfield, M.D.
Division of Neurology,
Duke University Medical Center,
Durham, N.C.

Larry Schneck, M.D.
Department of Psychiatry,
Kingsbrook Jewish Medical Center,
Brooklyn, N.Y.

Dhruva G. Sulibhavi, M.D.
Department of Neurology,
Kingsbrook Jewish Medical Center,
Brooklyn, N.Y.

Phillip D. Swanson, M.D.
Division of Neurology,
University of Washington School of
  Medicine,
Seattle, Wash.

Contents

Introduction

The thrust of much recent literature on epilepsy has been towards more precise classification by means of clinical, electroencephalographic and pharmacologic criteria. It might therefore seem that one is swimming against the current in devoting a book to 'Myoclonus', heterogeneous in its clinical manifestations, in its gravity and its electrophysiologic features. However, the range of conditions which may produce myoclonus makes an attempt at differential diagnosis doubly important with regard to continuing care of the patient. In addition, the myoclonic epilepsies, however different from each other, present a common problem in therapy, either in refractoriness or in the need for the physician to employ drugs different from the more familiar anticonvulsants.

The subdivision of the chapters is based on an attempt to help in differential diagnosis and treatment, while at the same time dealing with some underlying biochemical and neurophysiologic mechanisms, and touching on differences of approach as they are found in the literature of different countries. It has seemed to the editor preferable to allow some overlap in authors' references, rather than be ruthlessly surgical with their texts.

The editor wishes to thank the individual contributors for their efforts, the staff of Excerpta Medica for their guidance, and Mrs. Helena Vatter for secretarial assistance.

M. H. Charlton
Editor

The neurophysiology of myoclonic jerking — a reappraisal

A. M. HALLIDAY

Institute of Neurology, National Hospital, Queen Square, London, U.K.

The term myoclonus has become attached clinically to a number of distinct and only distantly related phenomena, which have only one thing in common. They are all involuntary jerks of the muscle unassociated with any obvious change in consciousness. The term was first used by Seeligmüller (1886),[70] but it derives from the name 'paramyoclonus multiplex', coined by Friedreich (1881)[32] to describe the generalised, brief and rapid involuntary jerking of the musculature in a 50-year-old patient of his. This patient had the jerking for 11 years before he died, without ever having had a fit, and there was no family history of epilepsy. He had sought medical care for a chronic lung infection, and the discovery of the jerking was quite incidental.

Many healthy people have a few isolated myoclonic jerks when going off to sleep at night, but such sudden, brief, lightning-like jerks occur much more frequently in epileptic patients, especially in the morning, commonly for the first half hour or so after waking. In some patients myoclonic jerking occurs throughout the day and may build up in frequency and severity, sometimes over several days, in the prodromal stage leading up to a major attack. It is so common among the idiopathic group of epilepsies that it has earned a place in Lennox's petit mal triad, along with absences and akinetic attacks (Lennox, 1945).[54] This association of myoclonus with epilepsy has been well known for over a century. Russell Reynolds (1861)[68] found that it occurred in over half of his epileptic patients. He called it 'clonic spasms'. Muskens (1928)[63] found a similar incidence in his series of 400 epileptic patients. Myoclonus as a minor phenomenon is therefore very common and of little significance. But there are certain clinical conditions in which it dominates the picture, and among the more important of these are the progressive myoclonic epilepsies and benign essential myoclonus. The jerks characteristic of these syndromes are brief and irregular, and vary from moment to moment both in amplitude and site of occurrence. This non-rhythmical jerking is typically sensitive to stimulation and to the influence of voluntary activity or arousal, and it disappears during sleep. Many of the jerks are associated with extremely brief, hypersynchronous discharges in the electromyogram (Fig. 1). This type of myoclonus is the same as that labelled 'pyramidal' in an earlier review by the author (Halliday, 1967b),[43] but there is now further evidence to be considered below, which establishes that this type of jerking can occur independently

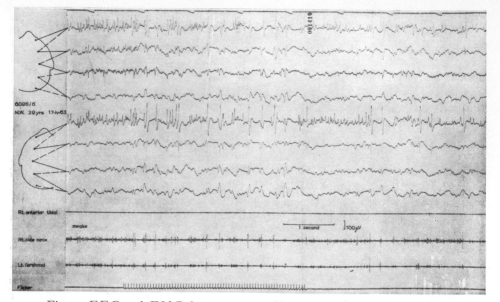

Fig. 1. EEG and EMG from a 29-year-old woman with progressive myoclonic epilepsy during flash stimulation at 18 per second. Generalised, irregular, high-voltage spike discharges are seen in the record, and these are exacerbated during the period of flicker stimulation (indicated in the lower channel). Brief hypersynchronous muscle action potentials, associated with lightning-like myoclonic jerks, are recorded from the right side of the neck and synchronously from the left forehead. Many of these show a close temporal correspondence with the high voltage spikes in the EEG.

of the integrity of the corticospinal tract, and this label is therefore no longer appropriate.

A quite distinct type of myoclonic jerking, characterised by its rhythmical or pseudo-rhythmical character, occurs in some viral infections of the nervous system, and can also be encountered in association with localised lesions of the spinal cord. This rhythmical jerking was that labelled 'segmental' by Halliday (1967*b*).[43] In contrast to the irregular type of myoclonus already described, it is usually unaffected by sensory stimulation, arousal or voluntary activity. Moreover, it persists typically during sleep and even during deep coma. Many of these features of segmental myoclonus are shared by palatal myoclonus (Nathanson, 1956).[65] It is the purpose of this chapter to review the evidence as to the nature of these two contrasted types of myoclonic jerking: the irregular, variable, stimulus-sensitive jerking typical of myoclonic epilepsy and the rhythmical, invariable, insensitive myoclonus typical of local lesions of the cord or brainstem. The third type of myoclonus mentioned by Halliday (1967*b*),[43] and labelled 'extrapyramidal', will not be considered further here. It consists essentially of fragments of involuntary movements, more familiar as forming part of a well-developed extrapyramidal syndrome.

EEG CHANGES IN MYOCLONIC EPILEPSY

The association between abnormal cortical potentials and myoclonic jerking was first demonstrated by Grinker et al. (1938).[38] They reported 2 members of a family with myoclonic epilepsy in whom there were bursts of high voltage spike potentials followed by slow waves occurring in the electroencephalogram synchronously with the muscle jerks. The propositus and her aunt showed the full syndrome, but the patient's father had had muscular jerking, especially of the face, without major seizures. There was epilepsy unassociated with myoclonus elsewhere in the family. When off medication the patient exhibited a characteristic 'building-up' of the myoclonus over some 2 to 4 days, culminating in a major fit. At first the twitchings were confined to the face, but these got progressively more frequent and violent and spread to the limbs, where they caused gross movements. Following the major fit the myoclonus disappeared for a few hours and then began again, gradually increasing in intensity, to build up over the next few days into a further fit. This cycle repeated itself indefinitely so long as the patient was off medication.

Dawson (1946)[21] studied the relationship between the EEG and the muscle action potentials in 2 non-familial myoclonic epileptics, who showed a similar prodromal increase in generalised, irregular myoclonic jerking of the skeletal musculature. He found the same pattern of cortical spikes and spike-and-slow-wave complexes in the EEG, and showed that, at the height of the attack, there was a close correspondence between the cortical spikes and the muscle jerks. He also studied a third patient with myoclonic jerking associated with a regular 3-per-second spike and wave discharge, in whom the temporal relationship was much less constant. Dawson observed that, while in a fully developed jerk the flexors and extensors discharged simultaneously, there was a preferential innervation of the flexor muscles, as evidenced by their earlier recruitment during a train of cortical spikes and the slower time course in the decay of their facilitation. He demonstrated that there was definite evidence of increased spinal reflex excitability in the periods between the spontaneous jerks, as a tendon tap elicited a second late burst response in the muscle following the tendon jerk.

Since these original observations the association of myoclonic jerking and abnormal cortical spike discharges has been repeatedly recorded on other patients (Halliday, 1967b).[43] Halliday (1967c),[44] reviewing the clinical literature, found that the electroencephalogram in progressive myoclonic epilepsy showed the same abnormal features irrespective of the underlying pathology. It was characterised by diffuse spike or polyspike potentials with or without a following slow wave superimposed on a disturbed background activity of irregular slow waves, sometimes admixed with faster rhythms (Figs. 1-4). Periodic runs of high voltage slow wave discharges were also very characteristic. The myoclonic jerking in these cases is characteristically rapid, irregular, arrhythmic, and lightning-like, and is associated with hypersynchronous action potentials in the EMG. It usually affects the face and the limbs, and may also less commonly involve the muscles of the trunk. It ceases during deep sleep and is very susceptible to any alerting influence, such as an emotional upset. It is exacerbated by voluntary movements (Fig. 4).

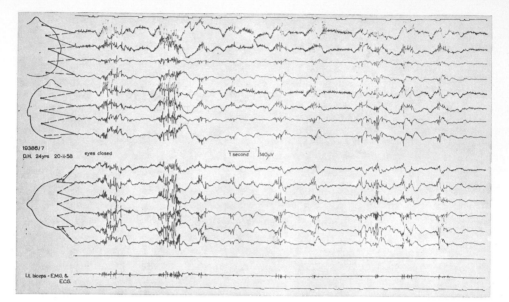

Fig. 2. Simultaneous EEG and EMG from the left biceps in a 24-year-old woman with progressive myoclonic epilepsy of the lipidotic type. Bilateral, high-voltage, polyspike bursts are seen, some of which are followed by a slow wave. Bursts of musle action potentials in the left biceps channel, associated with myoclonic jerks of the arm, are synchronous with the cerebral polyspike bursts.

One of the more puzzling features of the generalised myoclonus of progressive myoclonic epilepsy is the conflicting observations which have been reported on the association between the cortical spikes and the muscular jerks. Many publications have stressed the accurate one-to-one relationship between cortical spike and jerk, which is very clearly seen in many cases when the myoclonus is severe (Figs. 1 and 2). Halliday (1967b),[43] in reviewing the early literature, has collected a large number of instances illustrating this close association. Equally, however, it is often difficult to find such a correlation, or this correlation may vary from time to time in a single patient (Figs. 3 and 4).[79] Furthermore, as Dawson (1946)[21] emphasized, not all types of myoclonic epilepsy show spike discharges in the EEG accompanying the muscle jerks. This absence of an abnormal EEG discharge in some types of myoclonus is even clearer in the case of benign essential myoclonus, where the EEG is usually normal (Halliday, 1967c; Halliday and Halliday, 1970).[44,45] This demonstrates that the EEG abnormalities are not an essential or invariable concomitant of the generalised, irregular type of myoclonus.

FOCAL JERKING (EPILEPSIA PARTIALIS CONTINUANS)

In contrast to generalised myoclonus, with its variable and varying distribution, focal jerking, limited to one group of associated muscles, is characteristic of the

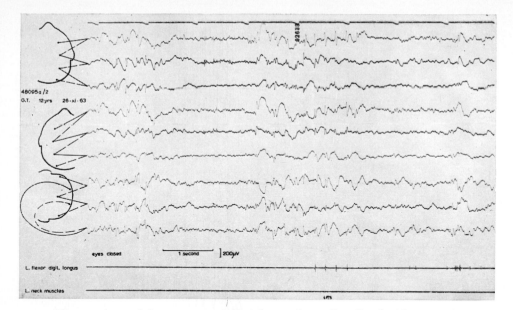

Fig. 3. A record from a 12-year-old girl, one of two sibs affected with progressive myoclonic epilepsy of the system degeneration type (Halliday, 1967c).[44] Paroxysms of high voltage slow waves are superimposed on a disturbed background. Many of the slow waves have a well-marked preceding spike. In the second paroxysm a series of high-voltage spikes appear with maximum amplitude in the right frontal area and four of these are associated with hypersynchronous action potentials in the left flexor digitorum longus. Many of the other spikes, however, are unassociated with obvious discharges in the muscles recorded, and there are some small hypersynchronous muscle action potentials towards the end of the record unassociated with any obvious cerebral disturbance. Compare Fig. 4.

cases of epilepsia partialis continuans of Kojevnikov (1895).[49] The jerking remains localised to the initially affected part, unless it spreads by orderly Jacksonian march to culminate in a grand mal attack. The jerks may be associated either with focal cortical spikes in the contralateral Rolandic region or with a focal sinusoidal discharge at about 30-per-second in the Rolandic area which may be unilateral or bilateral, although sometimes only a blunt wave is found (Juul-Jensen and Denny-Brown, 1966)[47] and many cases show no apparent EEG correlates. In cases of localised jerking, the site of the cortical discharge has closely followed the expected somatotopic arrangement in the contralateral Rolandic area. It is invariably contralateral and nearer the midline if the lower limb is the one affected. Dawson (1947b)[23] studied a patient with focal 'myoclonic' jerking of both legs, associated with a rapid 'spike' discharge with a frequency of 30-per-second in the Rolandic area near the midline. Van Bogaert et al. (1950)[78] described 2 patients with 'myoclonic' jerking of the left side associated with a high voltage negative spike in the right parietal region. Kugelberg and Widén (1954)[50] reported a woman of 26 with attacks of unilateral jerking in the right

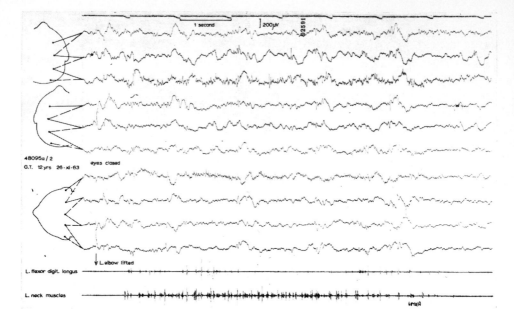

Fig. 4. The same patient as Fig. 3. A voluntary movement (raising the left elbow) produces a violent outburst of jerking both of the head and the left upper limb. The jerks are associated with brief hypersynchronous action potentials in the EMG. The EEG shows a disturbed background with irregular high-voltage slow waves and a few scattered spike potentials, but there are no spike discharges corresponding to the muscle jerks.

foot, who had a spike focus at the upper end of the Rolandic strip in the left hemisphere; each spike was followed by a discharge in the right anterior tibial muscle occurring 27 to 34 msec later, and the amplitude of the cortical and muscle discharge varied in parallel with each other. Halliday (1967*b*)[43] recorded a 32-year-old man with localised jerking of the left leg, which could be evoked by local tactile stimulation or arousal, and was associated with a focal 27-per-sec sinusoidal discharge at the upper end of the contralateral Rolandic area (Fig. 5). Naghiu and Bogdan (1969)[64] describe a 24-year-old man who had had continuous localised 'myoclonic seizures' of the first 2 fingers of the right hand since the age of one. There were central spikes of 150 to 200 μV on the left side in the EEG. The movements were increased by emotion or effort, but, in spite of having been present for over 20 years, had only once become generalised into a major seizure. Buser et al. (1971)[15] have recently studied a patient with focal jerking of the right foot since the age of 24, who, after a grand mal attack at the age of 33, developed similar jerks in the left foot. On X-ray he had dilatation of the left ventricular atrium and marked pooling of air over the convexity. There was complete asynchrony between the myoclonus in the left and right foot, and the EEG exhibited only rare single spikes or spike bursts in the region of the vertex,

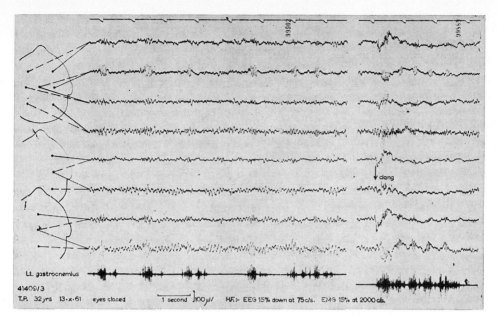

Fig. 5. A focal sinusoidal rhythm at about 30/sec localised at the upper end of the right Rolandic area in a 32-year-old man with focal jerking of the left lower limb. There is a close correspondence between many of the muscle discharges and the accompanying cerebral discharge. The jerking could be evoked by light tactile stimulation of the left lower limb or by an arousal stimulus, as in the right-hand record.

sometimes associated with slow theta activity. There was no relation between the scalp-recorded spikes and the muscle jerks, but stereotactically implanted electrodes revealed large asynchronous spikes in the left paracentral lobe which had a strict temporal relationship to the jerks in the right foot.

ENHANCED SOMATOSENSORY RESPONSES IN MYOCLONIC EPILEPSY

Dawson (1947b)[23] first reported that abnormal cortical potentials could be evoked in the Rolandic area by stimulation of the peripheral nerves in the contralateral arm or leg of his patient. He found that these potentials appeared to be part of an abnormal enhancement of much smaller responses which could be evoked in healthy subjects, but which were only a fifth to a tenth the size of those in his myoclonic patient (Dawson, 1947a).[22] These responses have been shown to originate in the cortex of the Rolandic gyrus, and are increased, not only in many patients with epilepsia partialis continuans, but in association with the jerking of progressive myoclonic epilepsy (Halliday, 1965, 1967a,b).[41,42,43] The response which can be recorded from the scalp appears to depend entirely on afferent impulses passing up the posterior column/medial lemniscus pathway. At spinal cord level, lesions of the antero-lateral column pathways producing loss of pain and temperature sensibility leave both early and late components of the response unaffected, while the incidence of abnormal responses correlates very highly with impairment of joint position sense (Halliday and Wakefield, 1963; Giblin, 1964).[46,35] The response from the lower limb has been shown to be unaffected by spinal tractotomy, producing a loss of pain and temperature sensation below T6, and stimulation of the dorsal columns at operation produced responses very similar to those evoked by peripheral stimulation (Larson et al., 1966).[53] In spite of suggestions that the later components of the response may travel to the cortex by non-specific pathways of the medial brainstem and thalamus, the evidence is against this (Williamson et al., 1970; Goff et al., 1971).[80,36] All components of the cortical response are affected by thalamic lesions involving VPL, the specific relay nucleus (Domino et al., 1965; Tamura, 1972).[28,75] Moreover, it has been shown by Stohr and Goldring (1969)[74] that local excision of the hand area in the post-central gyrus permanently abolishes the response to stimulation of the contralateral median nerve. Exploring the field of the response with transcranial electrodes, they found that all the components appeared to be generated exclusively in the primary somatic cortex. There is thus good evidence identifying the afferent pathway and generator area concerned in this response.

This is not to say that the response necessarily comes from the post-central, rather than the pre-central gyrus. Dawson (1947b)[23] found that the maximum response in his myoclonic patient appeared to be coming from a point 3 cm in front of the central sulcus, whereas the normal response was maximal over the central sulcus itself. The relationship of the scalp electrode to the underlying cortex was verified at post mortem, so that the result can be accepted with considerable confidence. It looks, therefore, as if the abnormally large myoclonic response may have been coming from the motor cortex rather than the sensory strip. Goldring et al. (1969)[37] have recorded responses evoked by median nerve stimulation in the motor cortex of 6 out of 18 patients undergoing surgery. These responses had the same latency as those recorded from the sensory cortex, but electrical stimulation of the point on the cortex from which they were recorded produced only movement and not paraesthesiae. As the potentials were not delayed relative to the sensory evoked response, it appears that there is a direct pathway going independently to the motor strip, a conclusion which is in line with the results of animal experiments (Woolsey, 1958).[81]

Enhanced somatosensory responses are characteristically found in patients with progressive myoclonic epilepsy at the time when they are jerking (Halliday, 1967a, b)[42,43] but not in patients with hereditary essential myoclonus (Halliday and Halliday, 1970).[45] They are often found in patients with focal epilepsia partialis continuans (Dawson, 1947b; Kugelberg and Widén, 1954)[23,50] but not invariably so (Halliday, 1967b).[43]

There are thus several puzzling and apparently conflicting features about the association of abnormal cerebral discharges and the brief, irregular myoclonic jerking which exists in its generalised form in progressive myoclonic epilepsy and in a more local, somatotopically limited form in epilepsia partialis continuans. New light has recently been thrown on this problem, however, by the study of some experimentally-produced myoclonic states in animals.

THE EXPERIMENTAL STUDY OF
MYOCLONIC STATES IN ANIMALS

Myoclonic jerking can be produced in animals by a variety of means, including chloralose anaesthesia (Adrian and Moruzzi, 1939),[1] intraventricular tubocurarine (Carmichael et al., 1962),[17] intraperitoneal catecholamines (Angel and Dawson, 1964),[10] chronic decortication (Denny-Brown, 1968),[27] and mesial thalamectomy (Milhorat, 1967).[62] Of particular importance are the findings of Cesa-Bianchi et al. (1967),[19] who demonstrated that a myoclonic syndrome can be produced by implantations of cobalt in the lower brainstem, and of Zuckermann and Glaser (1972)[82] who have shown that myoclonic jerking can be produced in the cat by the intravenous infusion of urea and is accompanied by a characteristic epileptiform discharge in nucleus ventricularis gigantocellularis of the medullary reticular formation. In these experimental myoclonic states (with the obvious exception of decortication) the myoclonus is associated with abnormal discharges in the EEG of essentially the same type as those seen clinically in progressive myoclonic epilepsy.

MYOCLONIC JERKING IN THE CAT UNDER
CHLORALOSE ANAESTHESIA

Adrian and Moruzzi (1939),[1] in their classical study of the relationship between the discharges in the motor cortex and the descending impulses in the pyramidal tract, noted that chloralose produced a combination of deep anaesthesia and stimulus-sensitive myoclonic jerking involving all four limbs and the trunk. Any abrupt stimulus such as a light tap on one of the feet, or even on the table near the animal, was sufficient to evoke a jerk. The reaction fatigued if repeated at short intervals and varied from time to time without obvious cause. Adrian and Moruzzi concluded that this touch-evoked response was a cortical reaction, because it was abolished by ablation of the cortex and could be reversibly suppressed by temporary occlusion of the carotids. Each jerk was accompanied by an abrupt potential wave in the motor area and a corresponding discharge of impulses down the pyramidal tract. The latency of the touch-evoked jerk was remarkably constant from one animal to another. Comparing latencies in the cuneate nucleus and the pyramidal decussation, they concluded that only about half the delay between the ascending and descending volley could be accounted for by the time taken in the conduction of impulses to and from the cortex. There was something like 10 msec unaccounted for, although with tactile stimulation of the hind foot this value was occasionally much larger. It could also be increased by repetitive stimulation at short intervals. The descending pyramidal discharge in response to tactile stimulation was still seen in deep chloralose anaesthesia when no overt muscular response occurred.

This stimulus-sensitive myoclonus produced by chloralose was further studied by Alvord and Fuortes (1954),[4] who showed that the generalised jerk response was abolished caudal to an acute spinal cord transection, and that supra-spinal structures were therefore necessary for its development. Many different kinds of stimulus were effective, provided that their application was abrupt. Sudden changes in illumination (e.g., a light turned on or off), sudden, sharp, but not necessarily loud, sounds such as clicks or hand-claps, or light taps or puffs of air on any part of the body, were often sufficient. Like Adrian and Moruzzi, they noted that there was often great fluctuation in the responsiveness of the animal which defied experimental control. In the generalised jerk, which resembled a startle response, the eyelids closed, the head flexed ventrally and the forelegs abducted and flexed. In the extremities the movements usually involved the more proximal muscles of the shoulder and the pelvic girdles. There was often dilation of the pupils. The reaction was rather stereotyped, regardless of the stimulus, but occasionally one or other of the muscular contractions either did not occur or was replaced by an opposite movement of the neck, back or extremities. In the accompanying EMG discharge both extensors and flexors were activated simultaneously, even where the initial movement of the limbs was a flexion. The discharge occurred in muscles of all areas, and was not limited to the area stimulated, but the latency was longer in the muscles supplied by the more caudal segments, and was also increased when the stimulus was applied more caudally. This, and the absence of the response in the spinal preparation, could be explained by the conduction delays to and from a supra-spinal centre, as suggested by Adrian and Moruzzi. Alvord and Fuortes found that stimulation of group I fibres was not sufficient to produce the chloralose jerk; the afferent volley appeared to be carried in group II or III fibres.

Examination showed that even subliminal stimuli might greatly influence the response to a succeeding stimulus. In general there was a period of facilitation lasting 20 to 30 msec, followed by a period of inhibition, lasting up to 300 msec. If the afferent volleys elicited by the conditioning and test stimuli entered the CNS at the same segments, they yielded maximum facilitation when simultaneously applied. If entering at different segments, maximum facilitation occurred when the more caudal stimulus was made to precede the more rostral one by an appropriate interval.

Adrian and Moruzzi (1939)[1] had concluded that the chloralose jerk was a reaction involving the motor cortex and was due to a sudden discharge of impulses in the pyramidal fibres, but it was later shown that it could still be recorded after decortication, thus establishing that the cortex was not necessary for its elaboration (Alvord and Whitlock, 1954; Ascher et al., 1963).[5,12] It also survived bilateral section of the pyramidal tracts at medullary level (Ascher et al., 1963).[12]

MYOCLONUS FOLLOWING CHRONIC CORTICAL ABLATIONS IN THE MONKEY

The studies of Denny-Brown (1968)[27] in the monkey confirm that the integrity of the precentral gyrus and the pyramidal tract is not necessary for the occurrence of myoclonus. Irregular, brief, stimulus-sensitive myoclonic jerking developed about 3 or 4 weeks after ablation of either the post-central or pre-central cortex. Scratching with a pin was a particularly effective stimulus, but the jerking also occurred spontaneously at the commencement of a new movement. The jerks were accompanied by very brief discharges in the EMG, involving the proximal flexors of the limbs bilaterally and the extensors of the neck. The latency was some 10 msec longer in the thigh muscles than in those of the arm. It was characteristic of the myoclonus following cortical lesions that it usually required repetitive stimulation, but once evoked it was explosive, frequently repetitive but short-lasting. There was often a second burst when a steady stimulus came to an end. The myoclonus was particularly marked following complete bilateral decortication.

THE ROLE OF THE SPINO-BULBAR-SPINAL REFLEX IN STIMULUS-SENSITIVE MYOCLONUS

There is evidence that the myoclonic response is mediated by the spino-bulbar-spinal reflex, which depends on sensory impulses, some of which cross the spinal cord at the level of entry, passing up bilaterally in the ventral quadrants to relay in the nucleus reticularis gigantocellularis of the medial medullary reticular formation and descending in the reticulo-spinal tract to terminate on the inter-neurones of the spinal cord at all levels (Shimamura and Livingston, 1963; Shimamura and Aoki, 1969; Brodal, 1969).[72,71,14]

Shimamura and Livingston have demonstrated that a transverse lesion, extending some 2 mm from the midline at the level of the obex, and in depth as far as the pyramid, completely blocks the spino-bulbar-spinal reflex on the same side. This lesion spares many of the descending pathways, including the pyramidal, rubro-spinal, the lateral reticulo-spinal and the vestibular spinal pathways. Denny-Brown (1968)[27] showed that the same small lesion abolishes the myoclonus on the ipsilateral side in a decorticate animal.

The myoclonus in the decorticate animal is facilitated by ablation of the cerebellum or section of the posterior column, so that these structures do not form part of the essential mechanism. Denny-Brown (1968)[27] concludes that this stimulus-sensitive type of myoclonus is a release phenomenon, resulting from the loss of control exerted by the superior levels which modify the effects of diffuse sensory input on the medial reticular formation of the medulla.

The nucleus reticularis gigantocellularis is the central point of a spino-bulbar-spinal mechanism producing widespread facilitation of the alpha motoneurones, particularly of the flexors. The input may be cutaneous or proprioceptive, but involves fibres of group II or smaller. There is some evidence that a large proportion of the afferent fibres may be part of a nociceptive system (Casey, 1969).[18] The neurones are excited by somatic stimuli from all parts of the body. The large cells of the nucleus gigantocellularis lie in the medial two-thirds of the medullary reticular formation. There is no evidence of somatotopic organisation within the nucleus. In addition to acting on the motoneurones, apparently via internuncials, the reticulo-spinal projections influence the central transmission of sensory impulses. The nucleus receives a massive influx of direct spinoreticular fibres which ascend in the ventro-lateral funiculus intermingled with the spinothalamic fibres. It is also acted upon by cerebellar afferents from the fastigial nucleus and by corticoreticular fibres, the majority of which derive from the central 'sensorimotor' region (Brodal, 1969).[14] The most caudally placed cells send axones only downwards to the spinal cord, but the axones of many of the more rostrally placed neurons divide into two, one branch descending to the cord and the other ascending to end in the medial thalamic nuclei. Not all the reticulo-spinal projection originates in the medulla. There is a second area of origin of the reticulo-spinal fibres in the pons, but no fibres to the cord appear to come from the mesencephalic reticular formation. The pontine reticular fibres, unlike the medullary ones, descend almost exclusively ipsilaterally. The pontine region also receives a large afferent projection from the sensorimotor cortex. There is some evidence suggesting that the pontine region may be especially implicated in the myoclonic jerking associated with the episodes of rapid eye movements during desynchronised sleep (Scherrer, 1968).[69]

INFLUENCE OF THE CORTEX ON MYOCLONUS

Although the stimulus-sensitive myoclonic jerking seen in cats under chloralose survives removal of the cortex or decerebration and depends on the spino-bulbar-spinal reflex pathway, Ascher has shown that the Rolandic cortex plays an active part in its production in the intact animal (Ascher et al., 1963; Ascher, 1966).[12,11] There appears to be a cortical reflex superimposed on the spino-bulbar-spinal reflex. Depression or facilitation of a local area of cortex in S1 by the topical application of potassium chloride or strychnine depresses or enhances the general-ised motor response to stimulation of the corresponding area on the contralateral side of the body. The response to stimulation of other areas, or of the same area on the ipsilateral side, is not affected. The effect therefore is somatotopically organised as regards the input, but generalised as regards the motor output. The modification of the jerk affects both sides of the body equally at all levels from cervical to sacral ventral roots. Evidently, the corticofugal impulses have access to a motor system providing generalised non-somatotopic effects. This is borne out by the fact that electrical stimulation of S1 under chloralose anaesthe-sia can elicit generalised motor responses. There seems little doubt that this pathway involves the cortical projection to the pontine and medullary reticular formation, and in particular the projection to the nucleus reticularis giganto-cellularis which mediates the spino-bulbo-spinal reflex. Brodal (1969)[14] has pointed out that the cortical projection of fibres to this nucleus comes predo-minantly from the Rolandic areas and provides an alternative pathway from the cerebral cortex to the spinal cord.

Ascher (1966)[11] has shown that the afferent impulses responsible for this cortically-mediated reflex travel to the cortex by the lemniscal pathway. Inter-ruption of this pathway at any level (by section of the dorsal quadrants of the cord, cooling of the ventro-basal complex of the thalamus, or depression or ablation of S1) leads to the depression of the response following stimulation of the corresponding peripheral areas. He concluded that lemniscal impulses arrive at the primary sensory cortex and are reflected down to converge with the spino-bulbar-spinal impulses which produce the motor jerk in the absence of the cortex. Facilitation or depression of the visual or auditory areas of the cortex has a similar influence on the chloralose response to inputs in these modalities, without affecting the response to other modalities (Ascher et al., 1963).[12] But although the primary auditory area exerts a specific facilitatory control upon their amplitude in the intact animal, the jerks evoked by auditory clicks are not abolished by bilateral removal of the cortex. They may be reversibly suppressed, however, by blocking of the inferior colliculus. Such blocking also abolishes the jerk in response to electrical stimulation of the auditory cortex. It therefore appears that the inferior colliculus acts as an intermediary for the jerks produced by the auditory stimulation (Buser et al., 1966).[16]

MODULATION OF THE LEMNISCAL VOLLEY BY A NON-SPECIFIC CONVERGENT AFFERENT SYSTEM

This work has shown that there are generalised motor responses, evoked by local stimulation, depending on impulses passing up the lemniscal pathways to the sensorimotor cortex. In these responses, the sensory input is somatotopically organised, and the motor output generalised. Dawson and his co-workers have further shown that the size of the afferent volley within the lemniscal pathway can be influenced as it passes through the thalamic relay nucleus by stimulation over a wide area of the body (Dawson et al., 1959, 1963; Angel and Dawson, 1961, 1963).[24,25,8,9] This implies the existence of a powerful, convergent, non-specific system on the input side as well. The thalamic post-synaptic response to a test stimulus in the specific sensory relay nucleus of the thalamus is increased if the animal is pinched, rubbed or stimulated electrically on any part of the body before the test stimulus is applied. Angel (1964, 1969)[6,7] found that these changes were associated with modulation of cell firing in the reticular nucleus of the thalamus and in the dorsomedial part of the ventral thalamic nucleus. Some of the non-specific thalamic units, which had a high rate of spontaneous firing, were slowed by the conditioning stimulus; in others the firing rate was increased. Angel has suggested that the former may exert an inhibitory action, and the latter an excitatory one, on the specific units of the ventrobasal nucleus. The conditioning stimulus which influences these non-specific units does not fire the cells of the specific relay nucleus unless it is applied in the small contralateral receptive field subserved by this specific unit. After a train of conditioning stimuli the non-specific units may continue firing for 2 or 3 seconds, and this firing is paralleled by the change in size of the specific evoked potential, either in the specific thalamic relay nucleus or in the sensory cortex. The ascending impulses responsible for the firing of the non-specific units ascend in the ventral columns of the spinal cord contralateral to the applied stimulus. The effect is abolished if the ventral quadrant is sectioned on this side, but not if the dorsal columns are cut on the same side as the stimulus.

There are thus ascending non-specific convergent pathways modulating the transmission within the dorsal column lemniscal system and travelling via the ventrolateral columns of the cord. Albe-Fessard and Bowsher (1965)[3] have recorded long-latency convergent responses in the medial nuclei of the monkey thalamus under chloralose. They noted that they could only be evoked by brusque, although not necessarily noxious, natural stimuli, and never by the phasic hair movements or light touch of the sort that were found to evoke somatotopic responses in the specific nucleus. It seems possible that both the spino-bulbar and spino-thalamic non-specific projections may share common pathways, particularly in view of the known projection of the medullary and pontine reticular formation to the midline thalamic structures.

The picture that emerges is of a two-tiered system, in which a highly somato-topically organised cortical response system is interconnected and integrated on both its input and output sides with a non-somatotopically organised generalised system, providing for the influence of sensory input over a wide area and for a generalised motor response covering all spinal segments. Moreover the efferent pathway also provides for the modulation of the sensory input over a wide area, not only at thalamic, but at spinal level. The biological value of such a system, in relation to the startle response, is obvious. It provides a mechanism for the immediate 'alerting' of all motoneurones, no matter where a stimulus impinges. The effective stimulus may or may not be noxious (e.g. a scratch), but will be most effective if it is sudden. Brusqueness is a more important stimulus characteristic than mere intensity in this system. On the motor side the fully generalised jerk is indistinguishable from the startle response described by Landis and Hunt (1939).[52] This pattern of generalised flexion, particularly affecting the proximal muscles, is reminiscent of the 'lightning jerks' seen in their fully-fledged form in infantile myoclonus. The scattered, irregular jerks of adult myoclonic epilepsy presumably represent a fragmented and disorganised functioning of the same basic mechanism. This may explain why both infantile and adult myoclonus, although so different in the character of their jerks, are both often accompanied by very similar spike and slow wave discharges in the EEG.

THE EFFECT OF THALAMIC LESIONS ON MYOCLONUS

Denny-Brown (1968)[27] established in one rhesus monkey that stimulus-sensitive myoclonus could still occur after bilateral removal of both the cortex and the thalamus. This shows that the thalamus, like the cortex, is not essential to the occurrence of myoclonus. He found, however, that thalamic lesions could produce the same sort of stimulus-sensitive myoclonus as was seen after decortication, if the thalamic lesions were massive and bilateral. Milhorat (1967)[62] was able to produce myoclonic jerking confined to the opposite side of the body by even unilateral mesial thalamectomy in 20 adult rhesus monkeys. In half the animals the brief, irregular jerks occurred spontaneously, but in the remainder it could easily be evoked by the injection of small doses of pentylenetetrazole. The jerks were more frequent in the arm than in the leg, and involved mainly the distal musculature. The face was rarely involved, and laryngeal, pharyngeal and palatal myoclonus were not seen. The irregular jerks tended to occur in short bursts of 3 to 5 contractions, associated with polyspike discharges in the con-tralateral EEG. The unilateral medial thalamic lesions produced a characteristic EEG abnormality in all animals, with high voltage slow and sharp waves accompanied by bursts of spikes, usually confined to the hemisphere on the lesioned side. The myoclonus was enhanced during drowsiness or light sleep, but was not seen during deep sleep. With bilateral lesions, the EEG showed bilateral high voltage slow waves and spikes. Although the jerks in the EMG were generally synchronous with the paroxysmal bursts of spikes in the EEG, this was not invariable; either event also occurred independently. Synchronous EEG and EMG spikes were very reproducible, however, after sensory stimulation, such as a loud handclap or other startling stimulus. Lateral thalamectomy did not produce myoclonus or any of the characteristic EEG changes, and abolished the myoclonus following medial thalamectomy where this was already present. The authors concluded from post-mortem histology that the essential lesion common to all animals exhibiting the myoclonus involved the intralaminar or non-specific thalamic nuclei (centromedianum, parafascicularis, the central lateral nucleus and the paracentral nucleus) and the medial nuclei including the median dorsal nucleus. Since the enhanced response in the more laterally situated specific relay nucleus, studied by Angel (1964, 1969),[6,7] is known to be associated with myoclonic jerking when it exceeds a certain size, it may be that the effect of medial thalamectomy in these experiments is partly due to the loss of the tonic inhibitory influence on the specific pathways following destruction of the more medially placed non-specific thalamic nuclei.

MYOCLONUS FOLLOWING COBALT IMPLANTATIONS IN THE BRAINSTEM

Cesa-Bianchi et al. (1967)[19] have shown that cobalt introduced into the region of the medullary or pontine reticular formation in the cat produces diffuse myoclonic jerking of the facial, cervical and flexor mucles accompanied by characteristic changes in the EEG. There is a slowing and increase in amplitude of the background rhythm on which are superimposed either high-voltage spikes, isolated or in bursts, or irregular bilateral spike and wave complexes. The changes were particularly evident during relaxed wakefulness and synchronised sleep. The myoclonic jerks were associated with spikes in the EEG, and both phenomena could easily be triggered by sudden sensory stimuli, such as handclaps. These changes developed within 24 hours of the cobalt implant. In most animals they faded away in 4 to 6 days, leaving only a little diffuse theta in the EEG. In some animals, however, the jerking and abnormal EEG discharges markedly increased after 3 or 4 days, and they developed generalised attacks of myoclonic type. In these animals high voltage spikes and atypical spike-and-wave complexes appeared spontaneously in the EEG associated with synchronous jerks in the muscles. The entire attack could last 40 to 60 seconds. It was frequently brought on by sudden sensory stimulation (e.g., gently tapping the legs or the tail, handclaps or whistling).

The convulsive threshold to intramuscular pentetrazole (which had been tested before the implantation) was always lowered by cobalt in the lower brainstem. The animals with cobalt in this region showed a marked reduction of postural tone, with an increase in flexor tone in all limbs. The sleep-wakefulness cycle was also profoundly disturbed. With bilateral implants of cobalt in the pons the episodes of desynchronised sleep practically disappeared for several days. Desynchronised sleep could still occur with implants in the medulla, but was sometimes interrupted by episodes of hypersynchronous EEG potentials.

Cobalt in the most rostral part of the pons could be as effective as in the medulla in producing the large amplitude, hypersynchronous spikes and irregular spike-and-wave complexes in the EEG, accompanied by myoclonic jerking. However, the generalised attacks seen after more caudal implantation were never observed. Implantations of cobalt in the mesencephalic tegmentum, on the other hand, were either without effect on the EEG or induced only minor transient changes. The normal sleep pattern was unaltered.

Introduction of cobalt into the midline thalamic nuclei produced changes not unlike those seen with pontine or medullary implantation. Within 24 hours, the background activity in the EEG was slowed and increased in amplitude. Hypersynchronous, high-voltage spikes and atypical bilateral spike-and-wave complexes appeared. These were particularly marked during times of relaxed wakefulness or slow wave sleep, and were usually associated with myoclonic jerks of the facial, cervical and forelimb flexor muscles. The abnormal potentials again lasted about 4 to 5 days and progressively faded away within a week. In some animals the thalamic implants induced fast spike discharges in the EEG, particularly during periods of EEG desynchronisation, either in wakefulness or desynchronised sleep. In the latter case they occurred particularly in association with the rapid eye movements. In some animals with thalamic implants the abnormal discharges could generalise into an epileptic fit. Sensory stimuli might trigger these fits, but could never block them.

The type of generalised myoclonic jerking observed in these experiments was in sharp distinction to the localised, contralateral jerking and Jacksonian epilepsy produced by local cobalt implants in the sensorimotor cortex. This closely resembled the type of jerking occurring clinically in the epilepsia partialis continuans of Kojevnikov.

These experiments are important in establishing that irritative foci in the lower brainstem are capable of causing marked EEG changes of the type seen in myoclonic epilepsy accompanied by widespread irregular jerking in the skeletal musculature. Mesencephalic foci did not produce the myoclonus or the EEG spike discharges. It was only when the cobalt was introduced into a limited area of the brainstem in the caudo-pontine and rostro-bulbar regions that the typical EEG changes accompanied by myoclonus were produced. These regions are known to have a diffuse synchronising effect on the EEG, and both EEG and myoclonic manifestations were facilitated by the appearance of slow wave sleep. The synchronous appearance of electrical and motor phenomena suggests that the brainstem structures involved by the epileptogenic focus have simultaneous ascending and descending actions on the EEG and the spinal motoneurones respectively. This is consistent with the anatomical data which show that the reticular neurones from the pontine and bulbar regions send their axones down to the spinal cord and also up to the thalamic diffuse system. There are no direct descending pathways from the mesencephalic tegmentum, which is an ineffective site for the production of the myoclonic syndrome. It therefore appears that the synchronising structures of the medulla and pons are involved in this type of myoclonic epilepsy. The ability of cobalt implants in the midline thalamic nuclei to produce a very similar picture suggests a close functional interconnection between some midline thalamic nuclei and the lower brainstem structures.

UREA-INDUCED MYOCLONIC SEIZURES

Zuckermann and Glaser (1972)[82] have found that it is possible to produce a myoclonic syndrome in cats by the intravenous infusion of urea. Myoclonus is, of course, a well known complication of clinical uremia (Locke et al., 1961; Tyler, 1968).[57,76] Jerks associated with a period of electrical silence in the EMG, synchronous in a number of associated muscles (asterixis), are particularly common and produce the characteristic 'flapping' tremulousness. Zuckermann and Glaser found that the jerking in uremic cats was associated with spike discharges in the nucleus gigantocellularis of the medullary reticular formation. Intercollicular section of the brainstem produced no significant effect on this jerking, showing that it was independent of higher structures. Section of the upper cervical cord, on the other hand, depressed the reticular paroxysmal activity, as did curare paralysis. It seems therefore that a spino-reticular-spinal loop is involved in this paroxysmal activity. The myoclonic state is reversible, subsiding after the intravenous infusion of urea has been stopped.

They recorded from chronically implanted electrodes in the cortex, thalamus, caudate nucleus, lenticular nucleus, hypothalamus, cerebellum, sub-thalamus, hippocampus, amygdala, tectal area, mesencephalic reticular formation, pontine reticular formation and bulbar reticular formation. There were no signs of abnormal discharges above the level of the mesencephalon, except in the terminal stage when a generalised tonic-clonic fit developed. In sharp contrast to this, the reticular formation of the brainstem displayed a high degree of irritative paroxysmal activity which began after the first 60 to 70 minutes of the perfusion, before myoclonic jerks were seen either clinically or electromyographically. Irregular spikes and sharp waves occurred in these brainstem areas and this activity gradually increased. It was more in evidence in the bulbar region than elsewhere in the reticular formation, and was especially characteristic of the nucleus gigantocellularis and nucleus reticularis caudalis. During the terminal period when myoclonic seizures were replaced by generalised tonic-clonic seizures, the location of the epileptic activity shifted towards neo-cortical and palaeo-cortical structures. The myoclonic period, however, was characterised by the more localised spike activity in the lower brainstem.

Clinically, after 90 to 120 minutes of the infusion, small asynchronous twitches appeared at different levels, first of all in the facial muscles. These twitches gradually increased in magnitude, tended to become synchronised and merged into clear-cut localised myoclonic jerks. During this period loud noises and proprioceptive stimulation induced generalised jerks and startle responses. These involuntary movements progressively increased in amplitude and incidence over the next 15 to 20 minutes, and were then followed by more generalised myoclonic jerks occurring either spontaneously, or induced by voluntary movements or stimulation. The myoclonic jerks became continuous and were later interspersed with generalised myoclonic convulsions. Finally, about an hour later, pro-gressively longer-lasting generalised tonic-clonic convulsions supervened and the animal died in status epilepticus. If the infusion was arrested at the beginning of these paroxysmal changes, a milder syndrome developed without the tonic-clonic seizure, and this gradually subsided over a period of 1 to 3 hours.

Recording of single units in the medullary reticular formation showed that there was a significant increase in the number of spontaneously active units during urea infusion and the firing rate of individual units increased significantly. This increase began before there was any clinical evidence of a change in the muscles. Once the myoclonic syndrome was established, however, reticular and muscular activity closely paralleled each other. The discharge of the cells grad-ually changed their pattern, so that the EPSPs were of longer duration and each unit fired 2 to 5 spikes during each EPSP, whereas before the infusion most spikes were generated by independent EPSPs. At the medullary level only, another discharge was typically associated with a spontaneous or stimulus-induced myoclonic jerk. A large depolarisation wave of 30 to 160 msec occurred with a high frequency burst of 700 to 900/sec spikes superimposed on its rising phase. Usually a silence of 50 to 200 msec occurred after the burst of spikes, and the cell then started firing again at a slower rate of 30 to 150/sec. In summary, the animals underwent a gradual transition from small muscular twitches to synchronous myoclonic jerks and myoclonic convulsions. This was anticipated and accom-panied by typical epileptiform discharges at the level of the inferior reticular formation of the brainstem. This reticular discharge can be maintained following collicular section in the absence of the higher levels of the nervous system. The fact that it was greatly reduced by section of the upper cervical cord or by curare paralysis suggests, however, that the afferent inflow from the spinal cord is a critical factor. The authors conclude that the evidence points to the spino-bulbar-spinal loop to the nucleus gigantocellularis as the pathway involved.

THE ESSENTIAL MECHANISM OF MYOCLONIC JERKING

There is thus a great deal of evidence that the essential abnormality accompanying, and responsible for, both the generalised irregular myoclonic jerking of the skeletal musculature and the associated spikes and polyspike-slow-wave complexes in the EEG is a type of epileptiform activity arising in the reticular formation of the lower brainstem, and in particular in the nucleus gigantocellularis of the medulla. Superimposed upon this brainstem mechanism is a cortical loop, which depends on impulses travelling up the lemniscal pathway, relaying in the thalamus and in the sensorimotor cortex and travelling down from the cortex to the reticular formation.

There are two efferent pathways from the sensorimotor cortex to the moto-neurones, one via the reticular system leading to a generalised type of motor response with no somatotopic organisation, and the other travelling down by the pyramidal pathway to the spinal cord, in which the strictly localised somatotopic arrangement is maintained. Corresponding to these two alternative efferent pathways, there are two types of jerking encountered in association with enlarged cortical evoked responses. The first is represented by the generalised, irregular jerking of the skeletal musculature which is seen typically in progressive myoclonic epilepsy (Halliday, 1967b,c)[43,44] or following cerebral anoxia (Lance and Adams, 1963).[51] In this type of myoclonus the somatosensory potentials are greatly enlarged at the time that the patients are jerking, but not otherwise (Halliday, 1967a, b).[42,43] The second type of jerking is focal and reflects the strict somatotopic organisation of the direct cortico-spinal connections. It is illustrated by epilepsia partialis continuans of the type described by Kojevnikov (1895)[49], in which focal jerking of a single group of muscles in the limbs or face may occur in association with spiking in the contralateral Rolandic area. This jerking may remain limited for many years with only an occasional Jacksonian march ending in a grand mal attack. Such cases have been described by Dawson (1947b),[23] Kugelberg and Widén (1954),[50] Halliday (1967b),[43] Juul-Jensen and Denny-Brown (1966),[47] Naghiu and Bogdan (1969)[64] and Buser et al. (1971)[15] among others. Some of these patients show large somatosensory responses (Dawson, 1947b;[23] Kugelberg and Widén, 1954;[50] Lance and Adams, 1963;[51] Buser et al., 1971)[15] although this is not invariably the case (Halliday, 1967b).[43] A focal fast sinusoidal discharge at about 30/sec may accompany the jerking (Dawson, 1947b; Halliday, 1967b).[23,43]

In benign essential myoclonus (Daube and Peters, 1966; Halliday, 1967c; Mahloudji and Pikielny, 1967)[20,44,61] there is irregular myoclonic jerking of the skeletal musculature, which may be indistinguishable electromyographically from that occurring in progressive myoclonic epilepsy (Halliday and Halliday, 1970).[45] Apart from some atypical EEG abnormalities seen in a minority of cases (Littlejohn, 1949),[56] the jerking is usually associated with a normal EEG. Moreover, as the somatosensory response is within the normal range of amplitudes in the majority of cases, even while the patients are jerking, the cortical loop is presumably not involved in the abnormal activity (Halliday and Halliday, 1970).[45] If the mechanism of the myoclonic jerking is the same, and has its origin in the reticular formation of the lower brainstem, one has to explain the absence of the abnormal ascending discharge which produces the EEG disturbance in progressive myoclonic epilepsy, which there accompanies the abnormal descending discharge responsible for the myoclonus. One possibility is that this disorder may involve only those most caudal parts of the medullary reticular formation, whose neurones send fibres downwards to the spinal cord and have no corresponding ascending projection to the thalamus (Brodal, 1969).[14] In favour of such a view might be cited the evidence that there are a minority of recorded cases of essential myoclonus who show some spikes in the EEG (Littlejohn, 1949)[56] or exhibit a slightly enlarged somatosensory response (Halliday and Halliday, 1970).[45] It might be supposed that these were transitional cases. However, it should be remembered that the clinical picture is against the idea that benign essential myoclonus and progressive myoclonic epilepsy are merely two ends of a continuum. The former shows a clearly autosomal dominant pattern of inheritance, while by far the majority of the latter cases, where the condition is familial, show an autosomal recessive pattern. Moreover, there are other distinct clinical syndromes in which brief, irregular, generalised myoclonus is associated with a normal EEG, such as the myoclonic encephalopathy of infancy originally described by Kinsbourne (1962).[48]

The essential lesion leading to the abnormal epileptiform discharge in the reticular formation of the lower brainstem is as yet unknown, although an inherited metabolic disorder is clearly at the basis of many of the cases of progressive myoclonic epilepsy (Halliday, 1967c).[44] It appears that this type of abnormal activity, accompanied by myoclonus, can be 'released' in the experimental animal by lesions of the cortex (especially the sensorimotor area) or medial thalamic structures. Both these areas have important connections with the reticular formation in the pons and the medulla. Since another important afferent supply to the medial reticular formation of the lower brainstem is from the cerebellum via the fastigial nucleus (Sprague and Chambers, 1953; Brodal, 1969)[73,14] the myoclonus clinically associated with cerebellar lesions, or with lesions of the dentato-olivary system, may prove to be a release phenomenon of the same kind. But this remains to be demonstrated.

RHYTHMICAL MYOCLONUS

Quite distinct from the brief, irregular, shock-like contractions of myoclonic epilepsy is the variety of jerking labelled 'segmental myoclonus' by Halliday (1967b, c).[43,44] This is characterised by synchronous rhythmical jerks with a fairly constant frequency somewhere within the range of 20 to 180 per minute, localised to a group of muscles supplied by either one segment or several contiguous segments of the brainstem or spinal cord. In contrast to epileptiform myoclonus it is unaffected by sleep and may persist during anaesthesia or deep coma. It is often totally insensitive to sensory stimulation, and is usually uninfluenced by voluntary activity or the level of arousal.

This type of jerking is well illustrated by a 23-year-old girl, seen by the author, who had developed rhythmical myoclonus in the right lower limb following an operation for a congenital developmental deformity of the spine 3 years previously. The jerking involved the proximal muscles of the right leg supplied by the second and third lumbar segments and would continue for many hours at a time with a frequency of between 32 and 37 beats per minute (Fig. 6) Each jerk was associated with a burst of muscle action potentials lasting for 1 to 1.5 seconds, and the bursts were synchronous in both hamstrings and quadriceps. There was thus a breakdown of the normal reciprocal innervation. Neither the rate nor the strength of these contractions could be influenced by local stimulation of the leg, by passive movement or by a loud handclap. There was some sensory loss in both lower extremities, which was more marked in the right leg than in the left. The EEG was entirely normal, and the somatosensory evoked responses to electrical stimulation of the anterior tibial nerve at the ankle were small and asymmetrical, paralleling the sensory loss. There was no enhancement of the response, and no exaggeration of the surface negative component, of the type associated with progressive myoclonic epilepsy.

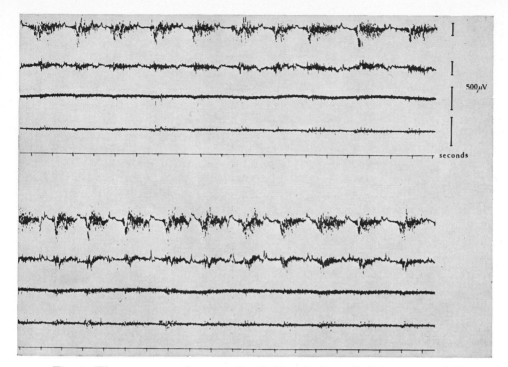

Fig. 6. Electromyograms from muscles of the right lower limb in a 23-year-old girl operated on 3 years previously for a spinal deformity. Synchronous burst discharges can be seen in the EMG of quadriceps femoris (1st channel) and biceps femoris (2nd channel) with a duration of 1–1.5 sec and a frequency between 32 and 37 per minute. The surface electrodes placed over tibialis anterior (3rd channel) and gastrocnemius (4th channel) show the same bursts at very much smaller amplitude, but this is almost certainly due to passive spread of the thigh muscle discharge to these electrodes. Time trace in seconds. Calibration 500 μV.

Garcin et al. (1968)[34] have described rhythmical jerking of the same type, occurring in the right arm of a 63-year-old lady with an astrocytoma involving the third, fourth and fifth cervical segments of the cord. Bursts of action potential occurred synchronously in the deltoid, biceps, supinator longus and triceps, and the frequency was unaffected by voluntary activity or sleep. After surgical removal of the tumour the rhythmic myoclonus disappeared and was replaced by irregular asynchronous contractions of biceps and supinator longus. Pre-operatively, the myoclonus was extremely regular with a frequency of 40 to 45 per minute. The length of the action potential bursts in the muscle was influenced however by mental arithmetic and by associated movements. Passive shortening of the biceps or deltoid increased their length (although stretching had no effect), while mental arithmetic tended to shorten the duration of bursts and sometimes to increase their amplitude. Voluntary contraction of the left arm increased the amplitude of the myoclonic bursts in the right. These authors draw attention to the patient described by Lhermitte (1919, Case 5, p. 36 and pp. 110-111).[55] This was a man who suffered a complete transection of the cord at the T6-T7 level, later verified at autopsy, and 7 months afterwards developed rhythmic contractions of the lower abdominal wall at a rate of 32 per minute. Patrikios (1938)[66] describes rhythmic rotatory movements of the scapula at between 10 and 12 per minute developing 3 months after a bullet wound to the cord at C4. He stresses the regularity, uniformity and rhythmicity of the movement which involved the inferior part of the trapezius, levator scapulae, the rhomboids and serratus anterior, supplied by C3 to C6. There was also an irregular jerking and hypertonus affecting the right hand. Avanzini et al. (1968)[13] have described rhythmical skeletal myoclonus involving the sternomastoid, trapezius, deltoid, biceps and triceps muscles of the right side in a 26-year-old woman with an acoustic neuroma of the cerebello-pontine angle, who presented with obvious brainstem involvement, including a right spastic hemiparesis and cerebellar syndrome. The myoclonus had a frequency of 4 to 5 per second. After operative removal of the tumour, she developed a complete facial paralysis on the right and a spino-facial anastomosis was carried out. Following re-innervation the rhythmical myoclonus spread to involve the right facial muscles. The rhythm was unaffected by mental calculation, or by the level of vigilance. Eadie (1969)[30] studied a 77-year-old woman with continuous rhythmical jerking in the left quadriceps. He found that the discharges could be inhibited by voluntary contraction of the antagonist hamstrings or by passive stretching of the muscle. Procaine 0.2 per cent infiltrated into the motor point of the muscles decreased the amplitude of the myoclonus, but an intrathecal infusion of procaine was ineffective. The author concluded that the abnormal movements depend on the gamma (fusimotor) innervation of the muscle, but the evidence seems somewhat tenuous.

The same type of rhythmical jerking occurs clinically in association with viral infections of the nervous system. This literature has been reviewed elsewhere by the author (Halliday, 1967b, c).[43,44] It is interesting and perhaps somewhat surprising to find that many of the same characteristics are shown by palatal myoclonus. Nathanson (1956)[65] has drawn attention to the unusual characteristics of this involuntary movement. All 12 patients studied by him showed synchronous, rhythmic contractions at a steady rate within the frequency range 100 to 180 per minute. The movements were unaffected in either rate or amplitude by any voluntary activity and persisted unchanged in natural sleep or under barbiturate anaesthesia. In 2 cases the myoclonus was still present and unaltered in deep coma, persisting until death. The myoclonus involved only the palate and posterior pharyngeal wall in some cases, but spread in others to involve the larynx, diaphragm, facial muscles and, rarely, even the eyes and upper limb musculature. In all cases the jerking was synchronous in all the affected muscles. Barbiturate anaesthesia, which left the palatal myoclonus unaffected, sometimes temporarily abolished the jerking elsewhere. Three of these cases came to autopsy, all neoplastic, and all showed a lesion involving the dentate nucleus, with hypertrophy and demyelination of the contralateral olive. Rhythmic tremor with a frequency of 120 per second in the muscles of the right shoulder girdle and upper limb, but unaccompanied by palatal myoclonus, was associated with a softening of the greater part of the left dentate nucleus with secondary changes in the right olive, in the case described by Garcin et al. (1963).[33] However, these movements ceased completely during sleep.

The mechanism of palatal myoclonus is obscure, and is discussed at length, on the basis of the published cases, by Rondot and Ben Hamida (1968)[67] and by Alajouanine and Hornet (1968).[2] Since Guillain and Mollaret (1931)[40] it has been widely believed that a lesion anywhere in the 'triangle' of the fibres connecting the dentate nucleus with the contralateral red nucleus via the central tegmental tract to the olive, will produce the syndrome. However, lesions of the red nucleus or the superior cerebellar peduncle are not followed by palatal myoclonus (Rondot and Ben Hamida, 1968; Alajouanine and Hornet, 1968).[67,2] Alajouanine and Hornet (1968)[2] regard the essential lesion as an olivary hypertrophy with a characteristic proliferation of the dendrites and *boutons terminaux*, and think that this follows either a lesion of the central tegmental tract interrupting the reticulo-olivary afferents, or a lesion of the hilum of the contralateral dentate nucleus interrupting dentato-olivary fibres travelling via the inferior cerebellar peduncle. Rondot and Ben Hamida (1968)[67] accept that hypertrophy of the olive is a very frequent concomitant of myoclonus of the palate or its associated musculature, or of the facial or skeletal muscles, but point out that there are a few cases in the literature, and an additional one of their own, not showing such olivary hypertrophy (Guillain et al., 1934; Döring, 1938; Van Bogaert, 1947).[39,29,77] Van Bogaert's case had a localised demyelination of the hilum of the dentate nucleus with pallor and gliosis of the olive, but no hypertrophy. Their own case had no lesions in the dentate nuclei, central tegmental tracts or the olives. These 4 exceptional cases have to be set against 54 cases in the literature collected by these authors, as well as 10 of their 11 personal observations, in the rest of which olivary hypertrophy was a constant accompaniment of the syndrome.

EXPERIMENTAL RHYTHMICAL MYOCLONUS IN ANIMALS

Rhythmical jerking showing the same characteristics as those exhibited in the clinical examples already quoted has been produced experimentally following the injection of Newcastle disease virus in cats (Luttrell and Bang, 1956, 1957; Luttrell et al., 1959; Feldberg and Luttrell, 1958).[58,59,60,31] Local infection of the cord or brainstem is followed by rhythmical, bilaterally synchronous jerking in the affected segments at a rate of 40 to 130 per minute. The myoclonus is not accompanied by any abnormality in the EEG and is unaffected by transection of the spinal cord. It remains confined to the affected segments or spreads gradually by contiguity to involve neighbouring segments. It therefore appears to be due to a direct, local effect on the motoneurones or interneurones of the cord. The jerks are predominantly flexor, but both agonist and antagonist are discharged synchronously. If the injection of virus was made into the cervical cord the myoclonus developed in the forelimb muscles, while an injection into the lower thoracic cord produced myoclonus of the hindlimbs. The jerks were associated with bursts of action potentials in the EMG. They were unaffected by

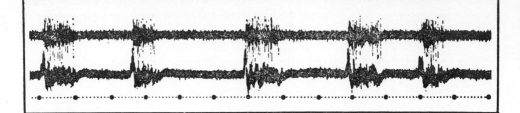

Fig. 7. Spontaneous burst discharges recorded from a rat sympathetic ganglia infected with pseudorabies virus. The upper channel is recorded from the preganglionic fibres and the lower channel from the postganglionic fibres. Time trace in 0.1 sec and 1 sec intervals. From Dempsher et al. (1955).[26] Courtesy of the editors of J. Amer. Physiol.

light ether anaesthesia, but, unlike some of the clinical cases, could be reversibly abolished by deep ether anaesthesia or anoxia. The rhythm could also be modified by low frequency auditory stimulation, such as handclapping.

An interesting light is thrown on the possible mechanism of the abnormal discharge responsible for the myoclonus by the experiments of Dempsher et al. (1955).[26] They recorded rhythmical burst discharges in the sympathetic ganglion of the rat infected with pseudo-rabies virus (Fig. 7). The recordings were made both in vivo and in vitro. The interest of the occurrence of rhythmical burst discharges in the isolated ganglion is that no internuncial neurones are involved, so that there is no question of a neuronal loop being responsible. The rhythmic discharge developed from 2 to 4 days after infection, parallel with the histological changes in the ganglionic cells. Repetitive bursts of impulses, each lasting about a second, recurred at a rate of about 20 per minute, and could be recorded from both pre-ganglionic and post-ganglionic nerves, even in the isolated ganglion. The pre-ganglionic discharge was therefore conducted antidromically. A great number of the fibres present participated in the bursts which were separated by periods of electrical silence. In the development of this spontaneous discharge, the post-ganglionic fibres began firing earlier than the pre-ganglionic fibres, but eventually failed to fire at the same time that synaptic transmission appeared to fail, and the pre-ganglionic fibres were then left discharging similar bursts on their own. It was also noted that *d*-tubocurarine, which blocks synaptic transmission in sympathetic ganglia, abolished the spontaneous discharge over the post-ganglionic nerves without affecting the pre-ganglionic discharge.

There are a number of important features in this experiment, to which the authors draw attention. The fact that the impulses in presynaptic and post-synaptic neurones fired in synchronous bursts demonstrates that there is an abnormal lateral spread of activity within the ganglion. This lateral spread of excitation must be either in the presynaptic fibres themselves or retrograde, since it involves the presynaptic fibres. The organisation into bursts may reflect either the periodicity of an underlying triggering process, or the temporal spacing produced by a period of refractoriness following firing. The authors suggest that the essential change may be a hyperexcitability of the presynaptic terminals. This would explain how the pre-ganglionic bursts can continue independently of the post-ganglionic discharge either after d-tubocurarine or in the late stage when synaptic transmission fails. It does not explain why the abnormal discharge first appears in the post-ganglionic fibres. The authors suggest that the presynaptic hyperexcitability may at first only be sufficient to activate the ganglionic cells transynaptically and that only later is the build-up of presynaptic excitability great enough to bring about antidromic activation of the pre-ganglionic fibres.

The interest of these results as a possible model for the abnormal electrical discharge responsible for rhythmical myoclonus is obvious. The rhythmical type of myoclonic jerking is already known to occur in local viral infections. It also occurs in neoplastic or traumatic lesions of the cord. In both it is typically limited to the segments involved. It remains to be shown whether lesions other than viral infection can produce comparable rhythmic discharges in the experimental preparation, but it is not inconceivable that a similar abnormal dendritic excitability change may accompany the localised pathology associated with segmental myoclonus and perhaps even also the abnormal dendritic proliferation of olivary hypertrophy, characteristic of many cases of palatal myoclonus

SUMMARY

There is now much evidence from the study of experimental myoclonus in animals that the irregular, brief, shock-like jerking of the type seen in myoclonic epilepsy and essential myoclonus, is associated with a characteristic epileptiform discharge in the reticular formation of the lower brainstem, particularly involving the nucleus gigantocellularis of the medulla. This nucleus forms part of a generalised non-somatotopic system, subserving the startle response, and controlling the 'arousal' of the motoneurones at all spinal levels. It is closely integrated with a 'higher level' cortical reflex loop, involving the medial lemniscus, sensorimotor cortex, and the cortico-reticular fibres. The enhanced somatosensory responses seen in progressive myoclonic epilepsy, reflect a facilitation of impulses in the cortical loop, under the influence of non-specific, convergent afferents acting via the medial thalamic structures.

The focal jerking of epilepsia partialis continuans represents abnormal impulses travelling down from the sensorimotor cortex via the somatotopically-organised cortico-spinal projections. The generalised, irregular jerking of myoclonus represents abnormal discharges travelling down from the medullary or pontine reticular formation via the non-somatotopically organised reticulo-spinal projections. It may or may not be accompanied by involvement of the cortical loop in the abnormal activity. In progressive myoclonic epilepsy, which is associated with a characteristic pattern of spike discharges in the EEG, the epileptiform discharge involves both the brainstem and cortex. In benign essential myoclonus, the same type of generalised, irregular jerking is associated with an undisturbed EEG, and the cortex is not involved in the abnormal discharges.

Rhythmical myoclonic jerking, unaffected by sleep, occurs in viral infections of the nervous system, and in local lesions of the cord or brainstem. A possible model for the mechanism has been provided by the rhythmical burst discharges recorded in isolated sympathetic ganglia infected with pseudorabies virus. The mechanism of this discharge may be a pathological hyperexcitability of the presynaptic terminals.

REFERENCES

1. ADRIAN, E. D. and MORUZZI, G. (1939): Impulses in the pyramidal tract. *J. Physiol.*, 97, 153.
2. ALAJOUANINE, T. and HORNET, T. (1968): Myoclonies de désafférentation olivaire. In: *Les Myoclonies*, pp. 143-146. Editors: M. Bonduelle and H. Gastaut. Masson et Cie., Paris.
3. ALBE-FESSARD, D. and BOWSHER, D. (1965): Responses of monkey thalamus to somatic stimuli under chloralose anaesthesia. *Electroenceph. clin. Neurophysiol.*, 19, 1.
4. ALVORD, E. C. and FUORTES, M. G. F. (1954): A comparison of generalized reflex myoclonic reactions elicitable in cats under chloralose anaesthesia and under strychnine. *Amer. J. Physiol.*, 176, 253.
5. ALVORD, E. C. and WHITLOCK, D. G. (1954): Role of brainstem in generalized reflex myoclonic reactions in cats under chloralose anaesthesia. *Fed. Proc.*, 13, 2.
6. ANGEL, A. (1964): The effect of peripheral stimulation on units located in the thalamic reticular nuclei. *J. Physiol.*, 171, 42.
7. ANGEL, A. (1969): An analysis of the effect of 1,2-dihydroxybenzene on transmission through the dorsal column sensory pathway. *Electroenceph. clin. Neurophysiol.*, 27, 392.
8. ANGEL, A. and DAWSON, G. D. (1961): Modification of thalamic transmission by sensory stimulation. *J. Physiol.*, 156, 23P.
9. ANGEL, A. and DAWSON, G. D. (1963): The facilitation of thalamic and cortical responses in the dorsal column sensory pathway by strong peripheral stimulation. *J. Physiol.*, 166, 587.
10. ANGEL, A. and DAWSON, G. D. (1964): The effect of 1,2-dihydroxybenzene on transmission in the sensory pathway of the rat. *Electroenceph. clin. Neurophysiol.*, 16, 312.
11. ASCHER, P. (1966): Lemniscal influences on motor responses of extralemniscal origin. *Brain Res.*, 2, 233.
12. ASCHER, P., JASSIK-GERSCHENFELD, D. and BUSER, P. (1963): Participation des aires corticales sensorielles à l'élaboration de réponses motrices extrapyramidales. *Electroenceph. clin. Neurophysiol.*, 15, 246.
13. AVANZINI, G., BELUFFI, M., CARACENI, T. and LEONE, B. (1968): Mioclonie ritmiche scheletriche in corso di neurinoma dell'acustico. *Riv. Neurobiol.*, 14, 644.
14. BRODAL, A. (1969): *Neurological Anatomy in Relation to Clinical Medicine*. Oxford University Press, New York.
15. BUSER, P., BANCAUD, J., BONIS, A. and TALAIRACH, J. (1971): Étude électrophysiologique d'un syndrome de Kojewnikow. *Rev. EEG Neurophysiol.*, 1, 369.
16. BUSER, P., ST LAURENT, J. and MENINI, C. (1966): Intervention du colliculus inférieur dans l'élaboration et le contrôle cortical spécifique des décharges cloniques au son chez le chat sous chloralose. *Exp. Brain Res.*, 1, 102.
17. CARMICHAEL, E. A., FELDBERG, W. and FLEISCHHAUER, K. (1962): The relation between seizure discharge and myoclonus during perfusion of the cerebral ventricles with tubocurarine. *J. Physiol.*, 164, 301.

18. CASEY, K. L. (1969): Somatic stimuli, spinal pathways, and size of cutaneous fibres influencing unit activity in the medial medullary reticular formation. *Exp. Neurol.*, *25*, 35.

19. CESA-BIANCHI, M. G., MANCIA, M. and MUTANI, R. (1967): Experimental epilepsy induced by cobalt powder in lower brain-stem and thalamic structures. *Electroenceph. clin. Neurophysiol.*, *22*, 525.

20. DAUBE, J. and PETERS, H. A. (1966): Hereditary essential myoclonus. *Arch. Neurol. (Chic.)*, *15*, 587.

21. DAWSON, G. D. (1946): The relation between the electroencephalogram and muscle action potentials in certain convulsive states. *J. Neurol. Neurosurg. Psychiat.*, *9*, 5.

22. DAWSON, G. D. (1947a): Cerebral response to electrical stimulation of peripheral nerve in man. *J. Neurol. Neurosurg. Psychiat.*, *10*, 134.

23. DAWSON, G. D. (1947b): Investigations on a patient subject to myoclonic seizures after sensory stimulation. *J. Neurol. Neurosurg. Psychiat.*, *10*, 141.

24. DAWSON, G. D., PODACHIN, V. P. and SCHATZ, S. W. (1959): Facilitation of cortical responses by competing stimuli. *J. Physiol.*, *148*, 24P.

25. DAWSON, G. D., PODACHIN, V. P. and SCHATZ, S. W. (1963): Facilitation of cortical responses by competing stimuli. *J. Physiol.*, *166*, 363.

26. DEMPSHER, J., LARRABEE, M. G., BANG, F. B. and BODIAN, F. (1955): Physiological changes in sympathetic ganglia infected with pseudorabies virus. *Amer. J. Physiol.*, *182*, 203.

27. DENNY-BROWN, D. (1968): Quelques aspects physiologiques des myoclonies. In: *Les Myoclonies*, pp. 121-129. Editors: M. Bonduelle and H. Gastaut. Masson et Cie., Paris.

28. DOMINO, E. F., MATSUOKA, S., WALTZ, J. and COOPER, I. S. (1965): Effects of cryogenic thalamic lesions on the somesthetic evoked response in man. *Electroenceph. clin. Neurophysiol.*, *19*, 127.

29. DÖRING, G. (1938): Myoklonussyndrom bei amyotrophischer Lateralsklerose. *Dtsch. Z. Nervenheilk.*, *147*, 26.

30. EADIE, M. J. (1969): Electrophysiological observations in a patient with segmental myoclonus. *Proc. Austr. Ass. Neurol.*, *6*, 65.

31. FELDBERG, W. and LUTTRELL, C. N. (1958): Observations on myoclonus in cats with Newcastle disease virus. *J. Physiol.*, *143*, 68.

32. FRIEDREICH, N. (1881): Paramyoklonus multiplex. *Virchows Arch. path. Anat.*, *86*, 421.

33. GARCIN, R., LAPRESLE, J. and FARDEAU, M. (1963): Myoclonies squelettiques rythmées sans nystagmus du voile. Étude anatomo-clinique avec présentation d'un film cinématographique. *Rev. neurol.*, *109*, 105.

34. GARCIN, R., RONDOT, P. and GUIOT, G. (1968): Rhythmic myoclonus of the right arm as the presenting symptom of a cervical cord tumour. *Brain*, *91*, 75.

35. GIBLIN, D. R. (1964): Somatosensory evoked potentials in healthy subjects and in patients with lesions of the nervous system. *Ann. N.Y. Acad. Sci.*, *112*, 93.

36. GOFF, W. R., BOBOWICK, A. R., ALLISON, T. and LEVY, L. (1971): K complexes evoked by somatic stimulation in patients with unilateral cerebral lesions. *Electroenceph. clin. Neurophysiol.*, *31*, 289.

37. GOLDRING, S., ARAS, E. and WEBER, P. C. (1969): Sensory input to motor cortex in man. In: *Abstracts, IX World Congress of Neurology and IV International Congress of Neurological Surgery, New York, 1969*, no. 37. Editors: C. G. Drake and R. Duvoisin. Excerpta Medica, Amsterdam.

38. GRINKER, R. R., SEROTA, H. and STEIN, S. I. (1938): Myoclonic epilepsy. *Arch. Neurol. Psychiat.* (*Chic.*), *40*, 968.

39. GUILLAIN, G., BERTRAND, I. and LEREBOULLET, J. (1934): Myoclonies arythmiques unilatérales des membres par lésion du noyau dentelé du cervelet. *Rev. neurol.*, *2*, 73.

40. GUILLAIN, G. and MOLLARET, P. (1931): Deux cas de myoclonies synchrones et rythmées vélo-pharyngo-laryngo-oculo-diaphragmatiques. Le problème anatomique et physiologique. *Rev. neurol.*, *11*, 545.

41. HALLIDAY, A. M. (1965): The incidence of large cerebral evoked responses in myoclonic epilepsy. *Electroenceph. clin. Neurophysiol.*, *19*, 102.

42. HALLIDAY, A. M. (1967a): Cerebral evoked potentials in familial progressive myoclonic epilepsy. *J. roy. Coll. Phycns Lond.*, *1*, 123.

43. HALLIDAY, A. M. (1967b): The electrophysiological study of myoclonus in man. *Brain*, *90*, 241.

44. HALLIDAY, A. M. (1967c): The clinical incidence of myoclonus. In: *Modern Trends in Neurology*, *Vol. 4*, pp. 69-105. Editor: D. Williams. Butterworth, London.

45. HALLIDAY, A. M. and HALLIDAY, E. (1970): Cortical evoked potentials in patients with benign essential myoclonus and progressive myoclonic epilepsy. *Electroenceph. clin. Neurophysiol.*, *29*, 106.

46. HALLIDAY, A. M. and WAKEFIELD, G. S. (1963): Cerebral evoked potentials in patients with dissociated sensory loss. *J. Neurol. Neurosurg. Psychiat.*, *26*, 211.

47. JUUL-JENSEN, P. and DENNY-BROWN, D. (1966): Epilepsia partialis continua. *Arch. Neurol.* (*Chic.*), *15*, 563.

48. KINSBOURNE, M. (1962): Myoclonic encephalopathy of infants. *J. Neurol. Neurosurg. Psychiat.*, *25*, 271.

49. KOJEVNIKOV, A. Y. (1895): Eine besondere Form von corticaler Epilepsie. *Neurol. Zentbl.*, *14*, 47.

50. KUGELBERG, E. and WIDÉN, L. (1954): Epilepsia partialis continuans. *Electroenceph. clin. Neurophysiol.*, *6*, 503.

51. LANCE, J. W. and ADAMS, R. D. (1963): The syndrome of intention or action myoclonus as a sequel to hypoxic encephalopathy. *Brain*, *86*, 111.

52. LANDIS, C. and HUNT, W. A. (1939): *The Startle Pattern*. Farrar and Rinehart, New York.

53. LARSON, S. J., SANCES, A. and CHRISTENSON, P. C. (1966): Evoked somatosensory potentials in man. *Arch. Neurol.* (*Chic.*), *15*, 88.

54. LENNOX, W. G. (1945): The petit mal epilepsies. *J. Amer. med. Ass.*, *129*, 1069.

55. LHERMITTE, J. (1919): *La section totale de la moelle dorsale*. Cited by Garcin, Rondot and Guiot (ref. 34).

56. LITTLEJOHN, W. S. (1949): Familial myoclonus: report of four cases with electroencephalograms. *Sth. med. J.*, *42*, 404.

57. LOCKE, S. MERRILL, J. P. and TYLER, H. R. (1961): Neurologic complications of uremia. *Arch. intern. Med.*, *108*, 519.

58. LUTTRELL, C. N. and BANG, F. B. (1956): Myoclonus in cats with Newcastle disease virus encephalitis. *Trans. Amer. neurol. Ass.*, *81*, 59.

59. LUTTRELL, C. N. and BANG, F. B. (1957): Pathophysiology of rhythmic myoclonus in cats subject to acute transections of central nervous system. *Trans. Amer. neurol. Ass.*, *82*, 86.

60. LUTTRELL, C. N., BANG, F. B. and LUXENBERG, K. (1959): Newcastle disease encephalomyelitis in cats. II. Physiological studies on rhythmic myoclonus. *Arch. Neurol. Psychiat.* (*Chic.*), *81*, 285.

61. MAHLOUDJI, M. and PIKIELNY, R. T. (1967): Hereditary essential myoclonus. *Brain, 90,* 669.

62. MILHORAT, T. H. (1967): Experimental myoclonus of thalamic origin. *Arch. Neurol. (Chic.), 17,* 365.

63. MUSKENS, L. J. J. (1928): *Epilepsy. Comparative Pathogenesis, Symptoms, Treatment.* Baillère, Tindall & Cox, London.

64. NAGHIU, A. and BOGDAN, F. (1969): A case of epilepsia partialis continua. *Electroenceph. clin. Neurophysiol., 27,* 629.

65. NATHANSON, M. (1956): Palatal myoclonus: further clinical and pathophysiological observations. *Arch. Neurol. Psychiat. (Chic.), 75,* 285.

66. PATRIKIOS, M. J. (1938): Sur un cas d'automatisme moteur particulier des membres supérieurs après traumatisme de la moelle cervicale. *Rev. neurol., 69,* 179.

67. RONDOT, P. and BEN HAMIDA, M. (1968): Myoclonies du voile et myoclonies squelettiques. Étude clinique et anatomique. In: *Les Myoclonies,* pp. 59-83. Editors: M. Bonduelle and H. Gastaut. Masson et Cie., Paris.

68. RUSSELL REYNOLDS, J. (1861): In: *Epilepsy,* pp. 63-66. Churchill, London.

69. SCHERRER, J. (1968): Les myoclonies physiologiques de la phase paradoxale du sommeil. In: *Les Myoclonies,* pp. 131-133. Editors: M. Bonduelle and H. Gastaut. Masson et Cie., Paris.

70. SEELIGMÜLLER, A. (1886): Ein Fall von Paramyoclonus multiplex (Myoclonia congenita). *Dtsch. med. Wschr., 12,* 405.

71. SHIMAMURA, M. and AOKI, M. (1969): Effects of spino-bulbo-spinal reflex volleys on flexor motoneurones of hindlimb in the cat. *Brain Res., 16,* 333.

72. SHIMAMURA, M. and LIVINGSTON, R. B. (1963): Longitudinal conduction systems serving spinal and brain-stem co-ordination. *J. Neurophysiol., 26,* 258.

73. SPRAGUE, J. M. and CHAMBERS, W. W. (1953): Regulation of posture in intact and decerebrate cat. I. Cerebellum, reticular formation, vestibular nuclei. *J. Neurophysiol., 16,* 451.

74. STOHR, P. E. and GOLDRING, S. (1969): Origin of somatosensory evoked scalp responses in man. *J. Neurosurg., 31,* 117.

75. TAMURA, K. (1972): Ipsilateral somatosensory evoked responses in man. *Folia psychiat. neurol. jap., 26,* 83.

76. TYLER, H. R. (1968): Neurologic disorders in renal failure. *Amer. J. Med., 44,* 734.

77. VAN BOGAERT, L. (1947): Paralysie bulbaire pure de Duchenne avec Paget localisé et syndrome myoclonique rhythmique du voile apparu peu de temps avant la mort. *Mschr. Psychiat. Neurol., 113,* 65.

78. VAN BOGAERT, L., RADERMECKER, J. and TITECA, J. (1950): Les syndromes myocloniques. *Folia psychiat. neerl., 53,* 650.

79. WATSON, C. W. and DENNY-BROWN, D. (1955): Studies of the mechanism of stimulus-sensitive myoclonus in man. *Electroenceph. clin. Neurophysiol., 7,* 341.

80. WILLIAMSON, P. D., GOFF. W. R. and ALLISON, T. (1970): Somato-sensory evoked responses in patients with unilateral cerebral lesions. *Electroenceph. clin. Neurophysiol., 28,* 566.

81. WOOLSEY, C. N. (1958): Organisation of somatic sensory and motor areas of the cerebral cortex. In: *Biological and Biochemical Bases of Behaviour,* pp. 63-82. Editors: H. F. Harlow and C. N. Woolsey. University of Wisconsin Press, Madison.

82. ZUCKERMANN, E. G. and GLASER, G. H. (1972): Urea-induced myoclonic seizures. *Arch. Neurol. (Chic.), 27,* 14.

Nonprogressive myoclonus

MARCEL KINSBOURNE and DAVID B. ROSENFIELD

Department of Pediatrics and Division of Neurology,
Duke University Medical Center, Durham, N.C., U.S.A.

Myoclonus is a brief, shock-like, involuntary muscular contraction which may involve a small number of muscle fibers, an entire muscle, or groups of muscles. The muscle groups may be simultaneously or successively involved. The involvement may be symmetrically synchronous or asymmetric. It seldom involves only one limb or one side of the body. The contraction may or may not cause movement of a limb segment. It seldom involves mutually antagonistic muscles. Bradshaw (1954)[7] restricts the term to arrhythmic movements; thus, he does not consider palatal myoclonus a true myoclonus. Others disagree with this approach (Aigner and Mulder, 1960; Yakovlev, 1957).[2,108] Denny-Brown believes that the movements may at times be almost rhythmical, especially the upper flexors (Juul-Jensen and Denny-Brown, 1966).[47]

The average myoclonic jerk lasts less than 0.5 seconds. When diffuse and of small amplitude, the myoclonic jerk may resemble fasciculation. However, a local anesthetic injection into the final common pathway stops myoclonus but not fasciculation (Bradshaw, 1954).[7] The latter, unlike myoclonus, is often associated with segmental muscle weakness and atrophy. Uncomplicated myoclonus, unlike fasciculation, is not associated with electromyographic evidence of lower motor neuron damage.

Myoclonic contractions may be generalized, scurrying from one muscle to another, or may be repeatedly focal. They often increase with emotional stress, fatigue, premenstrually, and after alcohol ingestion. The movements often occur in the early hours after awakening. Various types of stimulation accentuate myoclonus in some patients: light touch (often on hypersensitive zones), sudden noises, and flickering lights. Sudden changes in stimulus intensity are most effective (Aigner and Mulder, 1960).[2]

Myoclonic jerks, while not necessarily associated with an altered level of consciousness, may be associated with visible electroencephalographic discharges. They may precede a seizure by minutes, hours, or days. During this period of time they may occur as status myoclonicus. They occur less frequently for a variable period after an epileptic seizure (Aigner and Mulder, 1960).[2] More will be said later regarding myoclonus and epilepsy.

There are many valid ways of classifying myoclonus. Some approach it pathologically. Some employ clinical criteria of categorization. Denny-Brown

(1956)[18] proposes four major categories of myoclonic symptoms. The first, and most common, is 'spontaneous epileptic myoclonus'. This is characterized by occasional twitches of isolated muscles that occur in a patient liable to idiopathic epilepsy. Some call this 'epileptic myoclonus' or 'myoclonus of epilepsy'. The attack is frequently preceded by isolated limb twitchings which gradually increase in number and area until many muscles are involved and an epileptic attack begins. Again, more will be said about this later in the chapter.

'Stimulus-sensitive myoclonus' is characteristically seen in the familial myoclonic epilepsy of Lundborg and Unverricht. These patients have muscle twitchings in response to visual, auditory, proprioceptive, or tactile stimuli. The stimulus may lead to a seizure. Non-familial stimulus-sensitive myoclonus epilepsy is often more specialized in terms of stimulus (acoustic, photogenic, rarely proprioceptive — Denny-Brown, 1956).[18]

Palatal myoclonus, a spontaneous rhythmical palatal movement sometimes associated with other abnormal movements, is the third heading. The final type is 'bulbar myoclonus'. This may be rhythmical, symmetrical, and, at times, reduced to isolated twitchings. It consists of rhythmical upper limb flexions that are associated with protrusion of the lips and tongue and with dysarthria. The twitchings may be reduced to isolated contractions of one group of limb flexors or to movements solely of the tongue and lips. This type of myoclonus is associated with Creutzfeldt-Jakob disease (Denny-Brown, 1956).[18]

Yakovlev divides myoclonus into two broad categories: random and rhythmic. Random contractions are intermittent, asymmetric, and random. They are often symptoms of widespread degenerative brain disease that involves the cerebrum and brainstem. "Such a random myoclonus is frequently observed in a great variety of heterogeneous encephalopathies such as, for example, in advanced stage of general paresis, in tubercular meningitis, and in a variety of metabolic diseases of the nervous system such as Niemann-Pick's, Wilson's, Hallervorden-Spatz's diseases and particularly in viral encephalitides, notably in the epidemic encephalitis of 1918-21. Although, generally, the cerebral process is a widespread one, the cerebello-dentato-rubro-pallidal and thalamic relays seem to be rather consistently involved when random myoclonus occurs." (Yakovlev, 1957).[108]

Yakovlev considers 'rhythmic myoclonus' a more clear-cut and consistent clinical-anatomical syndrome. It frequently affects the branchial, palatal, laryngeal, pharyngeal, and facial jaw musculature. Occasionally the rhythmic branchial contractions spread to involve the somatic musculature of the shoulders, arms, diaphragm, abdominal wall, pelvic muscles, and leg muscles. The rate often ranges from 20 to 60 contractions per minute. The synergic contractions of the branchial muscles persist unaltered in sleep. The responsible lesions are usually in the hindbrain tegmentum, especially the bulbar tegmentum, and involve the bulbar reticular formation and the central tegmental tract (Yakovlev, 1957).[108]

Aigner and Mulder (1960)[2] classify 94 myoclonus patients as follows: (1) myoclonus, seizures, and objective evidence of neurologic or mental deficits or both (26 patients); (2) myoclonus and seizures without objective evidence of neurologic or mental deficits or both (45 patients); (3) myoclonus alone, without evidence of seizures and neurologic or mental deficits or both (19 patients); and

(4) myoclonus and a neurologic or mental deficit but no seizures (4 patients). Certain stimuli increased the myoclonus in all 4 groups: movement, fatigue, mental agitation, relaxation, and bright lights. The first two were the most potent. One patient had an exacerbation after he had received sodium thiopental for a minor surgical procedure. Two patients had increased difficulty after a minor bout of 'flu.' Myoclonus terminated in 1 patient after he had been treated with chlortetracycline, while in another it stopped spontaneously after 4 years without any apparent cause.

Krebs (1952)[52] employed a purely semeiological division. His categories were: (1) asynchronous, arrhythmical, asymmetrical, and asynergic myoclonus (paramyoclonus multiplex); (2) rhythmical or arrhythmical clonus in which movements are coordinate, as in degenerative epilepsy, essential epilepsy, and epilepsia partialis continua; and (3) rhythmical clonus (epidemic encephalitis and velar-palato-laryngeal clonic jerks).

Halliday (1967a)[34] considers 'myoclonus' an omnibus term applied indiscriminately to a number of involuntary regular or irregular muscle jerkings. He recognizes three subvarieties: (1) brief, irregular, shock-like contractions which appear to depend upon abnormal cortical spike discharges; (2) slower jerks which have a character similar to the intermittent beats of extrapyramidal tremor on fragments of athetoid movements or Parkinsonian posture; and (3) bilaterally synchronous rhythmical jerks at 20-100 per minute, unaccompanied by electroencephalographic discharges, persisting during sleep, which may be localized to a particular segment and perhaps produced by local irritations of motor neurons or interneurons of the affected segments. These three types are, respectively, Pyramidal, Extrapyramidal, and Segmental.

The electrophysiological aspects of myoclonus are more fully covered in other chapters. However, we shall briefly mention some abnormal electroencephalographic patterns and their relationship to classifications of myoclonus. One particular type of myoclonic jerking is characterized by brief, hypersynchronized electromyographic discharge which closely follows spike discharges in the contralateral cortex and depends on impulses traveling down the pyramidal tract. Four distinct electroencephalographic patterns are described: (1) focal Rolandic spiking; (2) diffuse spiking; (3) bilateral polyspike-slow wave complexes; and (4) fast sinusoidal after-discharge in Rolandic areas. There is another type of myoclonus that is characterized by prolonged bursts of motor unit discharges that probably depends upon the extrapyramidal pathways and is not associated with a particular electroencephalographic pattern. An exception is the contraction accompanying each slow-wave complex of subacute sclerosing panencephalitis. A 3 per second spike and wave rhythm can occur in association with either the 'pyramidal' or 'extrapyramidal' types of myoclonus. Evidence exists that a third type of myoclonus may be produced by spinal cord or brainstem lesions. When a segment of the cord is affected, the jerking does not depend on supraspinal influences and can be maintained in a spinal preparation (Halliday, 1967b).[35]

The above classifications are all valid. There are also many other approaches. The field of study of myoclonus has become so muddled with different definitions, approaches, and concepts that the authors of this chapter hesitate to inject an additional approach. We have modified the classification advocated by Swanson et al. (1962)[93] and make comments where they appear appropriate.

Swanson et al. note that myoclonic jerks of varying degrees of complexity may be confused with other involuntary movements arising within different integrative levels of the central nervous system. They suggest that all these forms of sudden, unwilled movements, although assigned different clinical nomenclatures, represent instances within a wide spectrum of altered excitability at different levels of neuraxial organization. Thus, when the alteration occurs predominantly at a cerebral level, one has seizures. When the defect is interneuronal in the brainstem or the spinal cord, one has myoclonus. They present experimental, clinical, and anatomical data to justify this approach. They offer an etiologic classification which takes cognizance of the fact that local or generalized myoclonus may accompany a wide variety of acute and chronic central nervous system afflictions.

Classification of myoclonus (Swanson et al., modified)[93]

I. Segmental
A. Type
    1. Brainstem
        a. Eye
        b. Palate
        c. Jaw
        d. Face
        e. Neck and tongue
    2. Spinal cord
        a. Limb
        b. Trunk
        c. Diaphragm
B. Etiology
    1. Vascular
    2. Infectious
    3. Demyelinating
    4. Neoplastic
    5. Traumatic
    6. Unknown

II. Generalized myoclonus (subcortical, brainstem, or spinal cord involvement)
A. Acute and subacute
    1. Encephalomyelitic (including poliomyelitis)
    2. Toxic
        a. Other infections
            (1) Tetanus
            (2) Nonspecific
        b. Strychnine
        c. Other (including drugs)
    3. Anoxic

4. Metabolic (uremia, hepatic insufficiency, other)
5. Degenerative (including inclusion body encephalitis)
B. Chronic
  1. Progressive myoclonus epilepsy (Lafora-body group, lipidosis, system degeneration — Ramsay Hunt)
  2. Non-progressive intermittent myoclonus with epilepsy
  3. Essential myoclonus (paramyoclonus multiplex)
  4. Nocturnal myoclonus

Epilepsia partialis continua with appropriate electroencephalographic changes is omitted because it is difficult to distinguish clinically from segmental myoclonus. Massive myoclonic seizures of infancy with changes in consciousness have also been excluded because they, too, are usually grouped with the epilepsies. The separation of segmental from generalized myoclonus may in some instances be difficult, since segmental myoclonus may become widespread. Swanson et al. believe that this distinction is justified since there is much prominence of segmental involvement in certain cases. We shall discuss epilepsia partialis continua when we discuss myoclonus and seizures.

SEGMENTAL MYOCLONUS

Brainstem

Singultus is a myoclonic movement that involves several parts of the body. Perhaps it should not be considered under segmental brainstem myoclonus. However, since brainstem lesions are known to cause hiccups, it seems appropriate to discuss it here.

Singultus probably involves the vagus and thoracic nerves, respiratory centers, vestibulospinal fibers, the fasciculus gracilis and cuneatus, and the nucleus ambiguus. It used to be thought that singultus was the result of diaphragmatic spasms that cause sudden inspiratory movements, audibly terminated by glottic closure. However, hiccups persist after bilateral section of the phrenic nerves (Haymaker and Kuhlenbeck, 1971).[39]

Hiccups can be associated with: diaphragmatic hernia, gastrointestinal disturbances, cerebrovascular insufficiency, sulphonamides, uremia, aortic aneurism involving the phrenic nerve, peritonitis, mediastinitis, pericarditis, pleurisy, tumors of the fourth ventricle, basilar artery insufficiency, non-tumor cervical cord lesions, increased intracranial pressure, and encephalitis lethargica (Haymaker, 1969; Souadjian and Cain, 1968).[38,90]

'Opsoclonus' was introduced by Orzechowski in 1913 to describe conjugate, unequal, continuous, rapid eye movements associated with somatic myoclonus and ataxia in non-epidemic encephalitis (Smith and Walsh, 1960).[88] In 1947, Walsh described 3 children with 'ataxic conjugate movements of the eyes' that began as a sudden onset of non-rhythmical, wide amplitude movements followed by recovery in 6 to 8 weeks. He called this opsoclonus, a state in which the eyes were continually moving, usually in the horizontal plane. Cogan (1968)[12] defined the entity as ataxic, conjugate, irregular jerkings of the eyes in all planes. Walsh stated that during remissions, the difficulties appeared mainly when the eyes changed their position, whether intentionally or involuntarily. Between the horizontal shakings which always predominated, there were sudden jerks which occurred in other directions. Walsh's patients had rates of movement from 15 to 40 per minute. They initially experienced the sudden onset of malaise, fatiguability, and unsteadiness followed by vomiting with at times a low fever. One week later, these constant, chaotic eye movements appeared. They were gross in amplitude, conjugate, and not associated with diplopia. Closing one eye decreased the amplitude of the movements. The movements occurred during sleep, but the amplitude and rate were decreased. Aigner and Mulder (1960)[2] and Herrmann and Brown (1967)[42] believe that they can stop during sleep. Vision was slightly blurred and improved upon covering one eye. There were no complaints of diplopia; red lens test was not commented upon. Myoclonic jerks were often present in the neck, face, and extremities. The sensorium was clear and, except for slight cerebellar disturbances, no other major neurological abnormalities were present. Despite normal otologic findings, cold caloric testing produced no ocular movements. One patient had bilateral normal optokinetic nystagmus; another case had depressed testing on one side only. Walsh thought that the efferent optomotor neurons were intact and that the central vestibular pathways were affected. Full recovery occurred in 4 months (Smith and Walsh, 1960).[88]

Opsoclonus may be observed in brainstem or cerebellar outflow (dentato-thalamo-cortical connections) dysfunction or both in association with benign encephalitis (Cogan, 1968).[12] It has also been reported in adults with pathologically demonstrated cerebellar disease in association with carcinoma of the uterus, breast (Ellenberger et al., 1968),[22] and lung (Ross and Zeman, 1967).[85] One should distinguish opsoclonus from ocular bobbing, which may sometimes be seen in palatal myoclonus (Haymaker and Kuhlenbeck, 1971).[39]

Opsoclonus may have been what Cushing and Wolbach (1927)[14] described when they reported 3 cases of eye fluttering in patients with neuroblastoma and acute cerebellar encephalitis. Kinsbourne (1962)[49] described 6 previously normal infants who had an acute onset between the ninth and twentieth month of incoordination secondary to frequent widespread and irregular isolated myoclonic intrusions. The jerking reached its maximal severity within a week and involved the limbs, trunk, and head in rapid, irregular, shock-like contractions. These varied in strength and distribution. There was an associated 'ocular dance' which was rapid, irregular, chaotic, conjugate, and in all planes. The ocular dancing occurred at a frequency of approximately 8 per second (Ford, 1966,[23] has called this opsoclonus). This spectrum of dancing eyes and flickering muscle contractions produced a characteristic and unmistakable appearance. The myoclonus stopped only in deep sleep and was increased by startle or voluntary movement. The electromyogram revealed that the jerks were associated with short bursts of action potentials. The illness was non-febrile and there was no clouding of consciousness. The electroencephalogram was normal. None of the patients had any epileptic seizures. Neurological examination was otherwise normal. The cerebrospinal fluid was normal in content and in pressure. Some cases had pneumoencephalography and cortical biopsies; they were normal. The course of the illness in the untreated case was prolonged and fluctuated; however, it was non-progressive and eventually self-limiting. In the treated cases, the symptoms disappeared within a few days after the administration of adreno-corticotrophin. Others have not had the same good results with steroids (Dyken and Kolar, 1968).[20] The etiology of this syndrome is not known, but it may be due to a viral affliction involving the brainstem, an allergic condition, or perhaps a disturbance of IgG immunoglobulins.

The chaotic irregularity of the involuntary eye movements distinguished them from the phasic nystagmus of some cases of acute cerebellar ataxia (which can also be associated with myoclonus — Klingman and Hodges, 1944),[50] the opso-clonia found on occasion in non-epidemic encephalitis (Orzechowski, 1927),[77] polioencephalitis (Marmion and Sandilands, 1947),[67] and the 'cog-wheel' rotatory nystagmus of the Pelizaeus-Merzbacher syndrome. The irregularity and dis-tribution of the involuntary movements, which affected the limbs, eyes, and axial musculature, differentiated the condition from spasmus nutans (Osterberg, 1937).[78]

Myoclonus may simulate an action tremor since both are accentuated during active movement. This occurred in Kinsbourne's cases. However, the persistence of a less marked degree of irregular jerking at rest and during sleep is clinical evidence of myoclonus.

Dyken and Kolar (1968)[20] expanded upon Kinsbourne's 'myoclonic encephalo-pathy of infancy'. They called it 'infantile polymyoclonia'. Again, the main clinical features were dancing eye movements, somatic myoclonic ataxia, and marked irritability. The onset was acute and occurred during infancy. The course was non-progressive but protracted with recurrences and remissions. Laboratory and electroencephalographic studies were normal.

Dyken and Kolar observed some of their patients for several years. They noted no ocular dysmetria but observed that the eye movements resembling ocular flutter and opsoclonus existed in both of their patients at different stages of this disorder, suggesting a spectrum of involvement. Perhaps opsoclonus, ocular flutter, and ocular dysmetria differ only in that the first represents a more severe and extensive disturbance. Perhaps the myoclonus represents the clinical ex-pression of an irritative disturbance of the dentato-rubro-thalamic network. They review the clinical-pathological correlates in their paper.

The association of an acute myoclonic encephalopathy and neuroblastoma in infants has been described by several authors. In several cases, the opsoclonus disappeared after removal of the tumor (Brissaud and Becuvais, 1969; Davidson et al., 1968; Moe and Nellhaus, 1970; Solomon and Chutoria, 1968).[9,16,72,89] Neuroblastoma and other tumors should be considered in cases that do not respond to adrenocorticotrophin (Martin and Griffith, 1971).[68]

Palate

Palatal myoclonus, called rhythmic myoclonus by some, is localized to the oral-branchial-respiratory muscles, with occasional extension beyond these boundaries.

It has two outstanding characteristics, regular rhythm and persistence during sleep. The latter is antithetical to all other forms of myoclonus except that of epidemic encephalitis. The rhythmic movements may be classified by some as tremor instead of myoclonus, as mentioned in the beginning of this chapter. We believe that it should be considered with the myoclonias because of previous custom and the fact that the anatomical-clinical correlations provided by this syndrome form one of the focal points of our knowledge of the physiological disturbances of many myoclonic syndromes (Bonduelle, 1968; Dobson and Riley, 1941; Riley and Brock, 1933).[5,19,83]

The first clinical descriptions of palatal myoclonus were by Politzer (1862)[80] and Spencer (1886).[91] They employed the terms pharyngeal and laryngeal 'nystagmus'. The classical descriptions are by Guillain and Mollaret (1931).[32] The rate of movement may vary from 60-180 per minute (Herrmann and Brown, 1967).[42] It may be higher. In the least developed forms, the soft palate alone is involved in regular successive movements of elevation and descent. Each phase is of roughly equal duration. Initial affection of the palate is the most common but not the only avenue of onset. Unilateral movements may later involve the other side. The myoclonus may spread in a characteristically progressive manner to involve, in decreasing order of frequency, the pharyngeal muscles, including the levator of the mouth and the Eustachian tube, the intrinsic and extrinsic muscles of the larynx, the muscles of the floor of the mouth, the lower part of the face, the ocular muscles, the diaphragm, and the intercostals. Although these approximate to the muscles of the oro-brancho-respiratory axis, there is no systematic distribution on an embryological or functional basis. The electroencephalogram is usually normal (Bonduelle, 1968).[5]

An analysis of 43 cases of palatal myoclonus (Riley and Brock, 1933)[83] revealed that 70 percent occurred between the ages 41 to 70, with highest frequency occurring in the 50 to 60 age range. Symptoms varied. Forty percent complained of dizziness and symptoms referable to cerebellar dysfunction; 25 percent complained of difficulty in speaking and/or swallowing. Two-thirds had hemiplegia or pyramidal tract disease. Five of the reported cases had unilateral palatal myoclonus. The rate ranged from 50 to 240 per minute, usually in the 140 to 180 range. Several patients had involuntary, synchronous eye movements, often with different directions for each eye. Seven of the patients had involvement of the diaphragm. The abnormal movements usually persisted during sleep.

Dobson and Riley (1941)[19] reported 6 patients with palatal myoclonus, all of whom had disturbances in ocular control, loss of conjugate eye gaze, weak external recti, facial palsy, or bilateral laryngeal involvement. The latter disappeared on attempted speaking.

The ocular movements often consist of rotatory oscillations with alternating and regular equal jerking movements, synchronous with the movements of the other muscles that are involved. The resulting movement of the eyes is not influenced by labyrinthine stimulation. However, the characteristics may be changed if a true nystagmus is also present, i.e., as a result of a vestibular pathway lesion (Bonduelle, 1968).[5]

Tahmoush et al. (1972)[96] recorded electromyograms, electro-oculograms, and electroencephalograms during wakefulness and sleep. These patients had eye 'myoclonus' and palatal myoclonus. Branchial myoclonus was persistently present and irregularly varied (65-75 per minute in one patient; 130-150 in the other). The amplitude varied directly with electromyographic background activity during sleep and wakefulness. The complex abnormal ocular movements occurred at the same frequency as did the branchial myoclonus. These eye movements disappeared during sleep and returned during desynchronized sleep following REM activity. Voluntary extremity movements provoked in these patients a rhythmical myoclonus of identical frequency to the simultaneously recorded branchial myoclonus.

Subjective symptoms of palatal myoclonus may be limited to mild dysarthria and the awareness of a rhythmic sound that apparently is the result of the undulating opening and closing of the Eustachian tube. The sound is occasionally audible to others. The patients may be completely unaware of any abnormality (Bonduelle, 1968).[5] Swanson et al. (1962)[93] had a patient with palatal myoclonus who complained of a clicking in his ears; this was unrelieved by sectioning the levator palati muscle. One of the authors observed a man who developed marked unilateral palatal and facial myoclonus following subacute bacterial endocarditis but was subjectively unaware of any abnormality, even after observing the contractions.

The rate of palatal contraction may be decreased by voluntary or reflex muscle contraction (e.g., speaking, deglutition); sometimes it may even be transiently obliterated by these maneuvers (Herrmann and Brown, 1967).[42] Franck et al. (1965)[24] observed that the rhythm varied from day to day and even moment to moment. They further observed that the synchronicity might be disrupted and that the rhythm might vary among muscles, especially between those of the oro-branchio-respiratory and the oculo-facio-cervical groups. Rondot et al. (1965)[84] described palatal myoclonus with an irregular frequency between 150 and 180 per minute and myoclonus of the face at 300-600 per minute, also combined with an irregular upper limb myoclonus.

Autopsy findings on 10 patients with palatal myoclonus revealed that the main causative factor was probably an acute brainstem infarction. Most of the patients had pontine or cerebellar vascular softening. The condition has been reported in multiple sclerosis, trauma, tumor, brainstem angioma, progressive bulbar palsy, encephalitis, and syringobulbia (Swanson et al., 1962).[93]

Jaw, face, and neck

As stated above, myoclonus of the facial muscles may be seen in the associated spectrum of palatal myoclonus. They rarely precede the palatal component; when they do, they are soon joined by it. Some authors might consider facial myokymia a type of myoclonus. The decision is arbitrary. Most employ the term to describe a form of abnormal movement confined to one side of the face. The movements involve all the muscles supplied by the facial nerve and are rapid, rhythmic, regular, and disappear during sleep. They are asynchronous from one muscle group to another. They are constantly present during the course of the condition which persists for several weeks to several months. Bonduelle (1968)[5] observed 145 patients with multiple sclerosis who had this finding. He believes that it is symptomatic of a pontine lesion.

Spinal cord

The patients included in this category have myoclonic movements that are limited to muscles supplied from one or more spinal cord segments and not associated with any neurologic abnormality at a higher level. Swanson et al. (1962)[93] describe a young adult with myoclonus of the left deltoid, forearm flexor, and abdominal muscles which had been present during the patient's entire life. The electroencephalogram was normal. Electromyography suggested that the site of origin was the spinal cord.

GENERALIZED MYOCLONUS

The remaining types of myoclonus are included in this category. The etiologies vary widely, but the category can be considered in terms of acute, subacute, and chronic. However, one must realize that occasionally a patient may have an acute illness that causes myoclonus to persist for an extended time period.

1. Acute and subacute

Encephalomyelitis may cause generalized myoclonus. In septicemia or other generalized severe infections, myoclonus may be observed as a non-specific effect. We shall not consider the relationship between infections and myoclonus in this chapter.

Toxins, such as mercury (McAlpine and Araki, 1959),[69] strychnine, and tetanus toxin can produce myoclonus. Strychnine and tetanus toxin rapidly and specifically depress inhibitory synaptic activity on motor neurons. This suggests that the associated myoclonus results from a removal of inhibition at the level of the spinal cord. Strychnine poisoning is characterized by sudden contractions and tonic spasms which are aggravated by external stimuli (Bradley et al., 1953; Brooks et al., 1957; Wilson, 1940).[6,10,105]

Excessive administration of penicillin has also been associated with myoclonus. A series of 9 patients, aged 60 to 80 years except for one, was reported. They developed myoclonic jerks after having received 25 million units of intravenous penicillin a day. All had renal insufficiency (editorial in *Brit. med. J.*, 1967).[21]

A case has been reported of myoclonus following methyl bromide ingestion. The patient had an 'action myoclonus', myoclonic activity upon attempting coordinated movements (Lance, 1968).[54] Major motor seizures and myoclonic jerks may follow exposure to C_4, a plastic explosive (Ketel and Hughes, 1972).[48]

Myoclonus may also follow hypoxic damage (Swanson et al., 1962).[93] Lance (1968)[54] reported 6 patients in whom there had been a definite history of difficult labor, fetal distress, and hypoxia after birth. He also reported 3 cases in which the birth appeared normal but the history and physical signs suggested cerebral disturbance from birth trauma. Six of the 9 patients had abnormal physical signs, mainly upper motor neuron in type. Seven were retarded. Eight were subject to major motor seizures, and 3 also had focal seizures.

Lance (1968)[54] discusses 4 patients who became hypoxic from airway obstruction or from cardiac arrest. All had physical signs, mainly cerebellar, of disease. Action myoclonus and falling attacks were a constant problem in many of his patients. All except 1 had normal mental ability.

Courville (1939)[13] stated that 'muscular twitchings of the extremities ... at times assumed the proportions of true convulsive movements' in patients who survived anoxia for more than a few hours. He went on to describe athetosis and choreiform movements in some patients who had made a partial recovery. Gastaut and Remond (1952)[28] list anoxia as a cause of myoclonus. Aigner and Mulder (1960)[2] noted that 2 of their 94 patients from the Mayo Clinic dated the onset of their myoclonus from the time of surgery.

Lance and Adams (1963)[55] reported 4 patients who developed severe, persistent myoclonus after periods of hypoxia. Each of them also had cerebellar abnormalities. Walking without assistance was impossible. All 4 were dysarthric. Generalized myoclonus became a feature of the early stages of the illness soon after the hypoxic episode. Consciousness was regained within a few days. When the patients' condition stabilized, the movements became restricted in site and all rhythmicity was lost. Two of the patients primarily had involvement of the arms, the other 2 of the legs. The myoclonus had certain uniform characteristics in all 4 of the patients. Each jerk lasted less than 0.2 seconds and was associated with a variable degree of muscle locomotion. The contraction was sometimes single but usually comprised a series of contractions of variable amplitude; these were mostly confined to the active limb but occasionally spread to an adjacent group of muscles or to those on the opposite side of the body. Although voluntary movement could be normally initiated, it was interrupted by sudden jerks and pauses, resulting in chaotic fragmentation of contraction. The patients' failure to sustain muscular contraction was even more apparent when they attempted to walk. Their tendency to fall appeared due to a lapse in antigravity muscle contraction which might or might not be associated with visible myoclonic jerks.

Each of the 4 patients could be cajoled into relaxing sufficiently to obliterate all traces of myoclonus. It was possible to manipulate a limb slowly without evoking any involuntary movement during this relaxed state. On the other hand, one or several myoclonic jerks might immediately result if the patient tensed a muscle or made a slight muscular adjustment to correct posture. The overall picture was that of an arrhythmic fine or coarse jerking of a muscle or a group of muscles in a non-orderly fashion. This was excited mainly by muscular activity, especially when a conscious attempt at precision was required. It was worsened by emotional arousal, suppressed by barbiturates, and superimposed upon a mild cerebellar ataxia.

Abnormalities in the electroencephalogram were recorded in 3 of the 4 patients: positive-negative spike discharges arising from the sensorimotor cortical region. The spikes often occurred in brief bursts and increased in amplitude in a manner similar to the 'augmenting response' recorded from experimental animals' sensorimotor cortex after repetitive stimulation of the specific thalamic relay nuclei. Each separate spike or burst of spikes was followed by a diphasic slow wave. During this the normal cortical rhythm was suppressed. The latent interval from the initial positive deflection of the cortical spike to the myoclonic jerk was approximately 7 msec for occipital muscles, 12 msec for biceps, 16 msec for wrist extensors, and 32 msec for quadriceps.

Periods of inhibition of muscular activity, lasting up to 340 msec, were recorded in all muscle groups tested in the limb(s) affected by the myoclonic jerks. These 'silent periods' commonly followed myoclonic jerks but occasionally occurred as isolated phenomena. H reflexes could be elicited during the silent periods, and the periods were unaltered by a procaine blockade of the gamma efferent system. This periodic inhibition of volitional activity resulted in lapses of postural control. Lance and Adams considered that such lapses were sufficient to explain the falling attacks of myoclonus. They postulated that the basic disturbance in their patients, and perhaps in all patients with action myoclonus, was the synchronous and repetitive firing of the ventrolateral thalamic nucleus in response to afferent impulses from the cerebellum, and that the thalamocortical volley that resulted was relayed down the corticospinal tract as a myoclonic impulse.

In most of the reported cases of myoclonus secondary to hypoxia (Lance and Adams, 1963; Swanson et al., 1962),[55,93] a generalized, rhythmical jerking occurred once per second during the comatose state. Otherwise, the myoclonus was irregular, asynchronous, and shock-like. The jerking of these patients was made much worse by voluntary movement or emotional arousal. It frequently improved markedly during the first weeks after the anoxic insult but persisted thereafter without change, extending for 8 years in one particular case.

Cases of myoclonic epilepsy have also been reported following carotid thrombosis (Nevin et al., 1960)[76] and angiography (1950). In Guillain et al.'s (1934)[31] patient, vascular encephalopathy, a pseudo-bulbar syndrome, right hemiplegia, and unilateral myoclonus were associated with an area of softening in the ipsilateral dentate nucleus.

Various metabolic disturbances may be associated with involuntary muscle jerks which have all the characteristics of segmental or generalized myoclonus. Adams and Foley (1953)[1] emphasized that they are best demonstrated by holding the arms outstretched. They noted rapid contractions at irregular intervals consisting of two phases: rapid flexion and slower extension of the outstretched fingers and wrist. These tended to occur in bursts. The legs, lips, and tongue manifested similar movements. Electromyography demonstrated gross lapses in posture which corresponded to a silent interval followed by brief beats of rhythmic discharge with a frequency of 8 to 10 per second.

Myoclonus may also be seen in the terminal stages of uremia. These patients have a myoclonus which is usually generalized and stimulus-sensitive. Hypocalcemia, hyperkalemia, and acidosis may be contributory metabolic derangements.

Locke et al. (1961)[60] studied 13 cases of acute anuria; myoclonus was a common phenomenon. It was minimal when the patients were alert, absent when comatose. Rapid restoration of blood chemistries to normal often increased the myoclonic movements or revealed them when heretofore they had been absent. The quantity of the myoclonic jerks was proportional to the rate of change of the abnormal chemistries, not the absolute values.

Acute and subacute degenerative diseases may be associated with myoclonus. These forms of progressive myoclonus will be covered more extensively in other chapters.

2. Chronic

Progressive myoclonic epilepsy may be difficult to differentiate from Wilson's disease. Absence of seizures, the presence of the Kayser-Fleischer corneal ring, and disturbed copper and amino acid metabolism aid in the diagnosis of the latter (Wohlfahrt and Hook, 1951).[106]

A familial disorder which is characterized by dementia, generalized myoclonus, and seizures was first described by Unverricht (1891, 1895).[98,99] He reported 8 cases in 2 families. All had a similar course. Seizures began at ages 6 to 13 years. After several months, the patients noted irregular jerks of their tongue, trunk, extremities, and occasionally the orbicularis oculi. The contractions increased with emotional stress and decreased or disappeared with sleep. Voluntary movements aggravated them. They were more severe prior to a major motor seizure. Unverricht's patients appeared to be intellectually intact, but Lundborg (1903, 1904, 1912)[61,62,63] believed that these patients frequently had intellectual deficiencies. He attributed the condition to central nervous system degeneration and claimed that progression was slow with a duration ranging from 10 to 60 years. Terminally, the patients became rigid and demented.

Harriman and Millar (1955)[37] divided their reported cases of progressive familial myoclonic epilepsy into three groups: (1) Lafora-body group; (2) lipoid inclusion group; and (3) degenerative group. The latter included several heterogeneous cases.

The most widely promulgated were Hunt's (1921)[44] cases; he called these 'dyssynergia cerebellaris myoclonica'. The syndrome consists of hereditary spinocerebellar degeneration, myoclonus, and, less constantly, major or myoclonic epilepsy. The clinical features resemble Friedreich's ataxia but may be confined to the cerebellum. The myoclonic epilepsy, when present, is usually violent and accompanied by spike and slow wave EEG discharges, especially in the drowsy state or upon waking; it is also sensitive to photic stimulation. The spasms may be so violent that they fling the patient from a chair to the ground. This epileptic myoclonus is accompanied by non-epileptic myoclonus which, when it occurs alone, is not associated with any change in the electroencephalogram. Various forms are seen, from complex myoclonus with violent segmental involvement to asynchronous and irregular fasciculations with asynergistic elementary myoclonus. Proximal limb muscles are primarily affected, but the entire musculature may be involved. Most observers maintain that the myoclonus is precipitated or augmented by movement or by the maintenance of posture. It sometimes takes the form of moving the extremity in the direction opposite to that intended ('myoclonies oppositionistes'). This postural or intention myoclonus, combined with the cerebellar syndrome, causes a severe dyskinesia seen in hepatolenticular degeneration. It also resembles that of the myoclonic epilepsy of Unverricht-Lundborg but is seldom accompanied by dementia (Bonduelle, 1968).[5] In some cases (Gilbert et al., 1963),[30] the disease progresses minimally and the symptoms of myoclonus and the cerebellar syndrome remain discrete.

Hunt (1921)[44] tried to demonstrate that the association of diffuse myoclonus and cerebellar dysfunction, especially intention tremor, signified the existence of a dentate lesion. His first 4 cases had epilepsy, myoclonus, and an intention tremor. Two later cases, twins who had developed myoclonus in their third decade and who had an intention tremor, had a sensory deficit consistent with Friedreich's ataxia. One of these patients died 10 years later; he had dentate atrophy and rarefaction of the myelin in the superior peduncles and degeneration of the spinocerebellar tracts. Hunt maintained that the myoclonus was associated with a lesion of the dentate nucleus. He was describing a syndrome, as is evident from the diversity of his patient population. Epilepsy was absent in 2 of the original patients labeled as having this syndrome (Gilbert et al., 1963).[30] However, many later physicians used the appellation 'dyssynergia cerebellaris myoclonica' for a disease combining epilepsy, myoclonus, and aberrancies of cerebellar function (Kreindler et al., 1959).[53] The term has come to refer to cases of myoclonic epilepsy in which signs of cerebellar dysfunction are prevalent, a most confusing usage.

Gilbert et al. (1963)[30] described a family in which myoclonus and cerebellar dysfunction, particularly intention ataxia and tremor, constituted the main combination of symptoms in a slowly progressive disease. Perhaps this family exemplifies an almost pure form of the association described by Hunt. The course of the illness was prolonged and without excessive disability. The myoclonus and cerebellar disorder occurred together with unilateral preponderance, right-sided in 3, left-sided in 1. There were no seizures or mental deterioration. The myoclonus was asymmetrical and asynchronous. The onset was in childhood. The uric acid in the cerebrospinal fluid was elevated in 2 patients; the reason for this is uncertain. The disease may be inherited as an autosomal dominant.

Perhaps the myoclonus and cerebellar dysfunction are related through a common dentate lesion. The myoclonus may be secondary to an irritative dentate lesion which eventually produces discrete paroxysmal discharges through the corticospinal system. It may appear as a discrete syndrome (good prognosis) or be associated with major motor seizures and mental deterioration as part of a diffuse neuronal process.

There are several ways of approaching myoclonus and its relationship to seizures. As noted above, some types may be chronic and progressive; these are more fully covered in other chapters. However, a few words might well be in order. Obviously, the association of numerous variable forms of epilepsy and myoclonus is a clinical feature common to the progressive myoclonic epilepsy of Unverricht-Lundborg and to the lipidoses. Diffuse lesions are present in all of these complex syndromes and, indeed, Watson and Denny-Brown (1953)[104] regard myoclonic epilepsy as a symptom of diffuse neuronal disease. Under this label, they gathered all the conditions where the two symptoms coexisted, including the lipidoses, acute inclusion body encephalitis, and myoclonic epilepsy. They believe that both myoclonus and epilepsy are symptomatic and related only to the presence of a diffuse intracellular process, regardless of its nature. They observed that the significance of myoclonus in these disorders ('myoclonic epilepsy') has been considerably confused by the prominence of myoclonus associated with olivary and dentate degeneration in conditions such as palatal myoclonus and dyssynergia cerebellaris myoclonica. This illustrates the ambiguity of the term myoclonus and the pandemonium resulting from the use of the same word to describe, not only a form of epilepsy, but also a non-convulsive phenomenon that may occur in association with epilepsy.

Bonduelle (1968)[5] distinguishes two categories. The first is myoclonic epilepsy, which may present either as a pure myoclonic petit mal or associated with other manifestations of petit mal or major motor seizures, but without other neurological or psychiatric signs or symptoms. These segmental or massive bilateral myoclonic discharges, frequently flicker sensitive, are accompanied by multiple electroencephalographic spike complexes, although the two phenomena are not necessarily synchronous (Gastaut and Remond, 1952).[28] More will be said later.

The second category of Bonduelle may be considered 'extrapyramidal myoclonus'. The electroencephalogram is normal. This form is variable, synchronous or asynchronous, synergistic or asynergistic, partial, massive, or global, frequently arrhythmic, and often catalyzed by movement or sensory stimuli. This type of myoclonus may well develop without evidence of epilepsy. However, it may also be associated with any type of epilepsy, including myoclonic epilepsy. In the latter cases, myoclonus coexists with epilepsy. The Ramsay Hunt syndrome illustrates that such a combination may occur.

One should note that it is virtually impossible to make a true distinction between epileptic and non-epileptic myoclonus solely on the existence of a correspondence between the discharges in the electroencephalogram and muscular contractions. Some epileptic patients who have no other clinical abnormality may have partial, asynchronous, asymmetrical myoclonus which is not accompanied by any electroencephalographic change (Bonduelle, 1968).[5]

Nonprogressive myoclonus with epilepsy was early differentiated by Lundborg (1903)[61] because of lack of underlying progressive disease. He attributed the first description to Rabot (1899),[81] who followed a patient for over 15 years in whom mild myoclonic jerks over a period of several days adumbrated seizures. Lundborg observed that in some cases the myoclonus might dominate the clinical picture and that there were intermediate cases between seizures with a few myoclonic jerks and progressive myoclonic epilepsy. In 1861, Reynolds had noted that 57 percent of 56 patients showed this phenomenon. Muskens (1928)[74] estimated that over 60 percent of epileptics may have a myoclonic jerk soon after awakening.

Hodskins and Yakovlev (1930)[43] studied 300 epileptics and found that 10 to 15 percent of them had myoclonus. They employed more stringent criteria than others, including only jerking which they themselves had observed. The family history was frequently positive. Pyramidal tract symptoms were more frequently seen than they were in non-selected instances of epilepsy, whereas extrapyramidal symptoms were noted less frequently. One-third of the myoclonic patients had cerebellar symptoms, compared to a 10 percent incidence in the entire group of epileptics. These authors believed that myoclonus was an amyostatic syndrome, a disturbance of the realm of static and postural neuromuscular function. They autopsied 18 myoclonic patients over a period of 17 years and found three types of lesions: (1) primary atrophic lesions; (2) degenerative cellular changes, sometimes identical with those found in amaurotic familial idiocy; and (3) abnormal inclusions, extracellular and intracellular, amyloid bodies, lipoid inclusions, and fatty degeneration. Based on clinical and pathological criteria, they divided their cases into two major types: myoclonus epilepsy and myoclonus without epilepsy. The former demonstrated deterioration in the dentate system and basal ganglia, diffuse lesions in the central nervous system, and extrapyramidal symptoms. The latter category manifested no deterioration or changes in the central nervous system. Both categories had cerebellar symptoms.

Aigner and Mulder (1960)[2] reported that 45 of 94 patients with myoclonus had seizures that were not associated with other neurological or mental defects. These patients had a good prognosis. Symonds (1953)[94] noted that some epileptics have myoclonus provoked by sensory stimuli such as flicker and that the contractions may occur for several mornings before leading to a generalized convulsion.

Swanson et al. (1962)[93] observed that myoclonus is seldom a prominent complaint in non-institutionalized epileptics. They noted, however, that some patients with seizures may be partially disabled because of myoclonic jerks. Rarely, a seizure may be brought under control only to be replaced with myoclonic movements.

In 1881, Gowers noted that many epileptics occasionally have myoclonic jerks. The incidence may range from 15 to 70 percent (Hodskins and Yakovlev, 1930; Reynolds, 1861).[43,82] Bradshaw (1954)[7] stated that probably 60 percent of all epileptics have occasional myoclonus.

Denny-Brown (1956)[18] noted that stimulus-sensitive myoclonus leading to epilepsy is related most frequently to lipidosis or other inclusion body diseases, i.e., Lafora's. It also occurs in inclusion body encephalitis. He maintained that it may be useful in differentiating such diffuse neuronal disease from white matter disease. In its relation to a progressive illness, it serves as a distinction between, for example, inclusion body encephalitis, where it is almost invariable, as opposed to Schilder's disease, where it is usually absent.

In recent years, discussion of myoclonic epilepsy has become confused by the augmenting tendency to attach the term 'myoclonic' to the syndrome of infantile spasms with hypsarrhythmia. This syndrome is discussed in another chapter. It should be noted, however, that true myoclonic epilepsy differs in many respects from the infantile spasms syndrome. Harper (1968)[36] described 14 cases of true myoclonic epilepsy in children. The seizures consisted of a sudden violent contraction of the neck and trunk muscles associated with jerkings of the arms; this was often followed by a violent fall. The attacks frequently occurred in the morning or when the child was tired late in the day. Sometimes they occurred at night. The attack lasted a fraction of a second with only a slight post-ictal period. Loss of consciousness was absent or minimal. Injuries were common. Only 1 child had a strong family history of epilepsy. These patients had a later onset of symptoms than the patients with infantile spasms, at an average age of $3\frac{1}{2}$ years. In 9 of the children, the myoclonic attacks were preceded by other forms of epilepsy, usually major motor, for a period ranging from 3 months to 2 years. Most of the children had normal physical examinations. None of them had abnormal cerebellar signs. The prognosis was good. There was a tendency toward improvement with advancing age. Eight of the children had no intellectual deficits, and the remainder were benefiting from special education. Drug control was difficult and frequently required many different medications.

True myoclonic epilepsy in children is uncommon. However, it is probably more common than is currently appreciated, owing to the confusion with cases in the infantile spasm group (Harper, 1968; Jeavons and Bower, 1964; Wright, 1969).[36,45,107] Confusion with 'akinetic attacks' may also account for the failure to recognize some cases of true myoclonic epilepsy. The reported incidence varies widely. Muskens (1909)[73] and Hodskins and Yakovlev (1930)[43] found myoclonic episodes in between 10 to 15 percent of all cases of epilepsy. They were describing all the patients in whom myoclonic attacks occurred in association with major motor seizures. Aigner and Mulder (1960)[2] also considered the incidence of myoclonus in association with major epilepsy to be approximately 10 percent of all cases. Gastaut (1954)[26] stated that the incidence of myoclonic epilepsy was 0.3 percent of all forms of epilepsy including all ages. Bridge (1949)[8] stated that 1 to 2 percent of his children with epilepsy had the myoclonic form of attack. In Harper's series, 14 children out of 376 (3.8 percent) new cases of epilepsy admitted to the hospital over a 10-year period had this form of epilepsy. Whereas the sex incidence of infantile spasms is 2 males per female, there was an equal sex incidence in Harper's cases; this approximated the overall incidence of childhood epilepsy (excluding infantile spasms) of 1.2 males per female. The mortality for infantile spasms is approximately 13 percent, whereas none of Harper's cases had died.

The electroencephalogram of Harper's patients did not manifest hypsarrhythmia. Serial readings showed atypical spike and wave discharges, often with polyspikes. Three children showed photic sensitivity. All of the children showed abnormal electroencephalograms at some time.

Gibbs and Gibbs (1952)[29] analyzed myoclonic seizures. They consider the seizures to be characterized clinically by a sudden single jerk of the head, limbs, or trunk and usually associated with multiple high voltage spikes, often mixed with slow waves so as to form a disorganized pattern of the petit mal type. In mild cases, only the head or arms may be involved, but in more severe cases the entire body is affected. The jerk is violent, and the patient may be thrown to the ground, even if initially sitting. In their experience, a single seizure lasts from 1 to 2 seconds, and consciousness is essentially unimpaired. The contractions usually occur in clusters of 4 or 5 with an interval of 3 to 6 seconds. They are especially prone to occur upon waking or going to sleep. Some patients are so severely affected that they are almost incapable of getting dressed in the morning.

As can be gleaned from Table 2, 64 percent of patients with myoclonic epilepsy have major convulsions. At that point in time, the myoclonic seizures usually increase in frequency and severity to the point where they are almost continuous; then a generalized seizure occurs. Twenty-one percent of patients with myoclonic epilepsy have clinical petit mal seizures, and only 1.5 percent have psychomotor seizures. Of the 133 patients with myoclonic seizures, 113 (85 percent) had unknown etiologies (Harper, 1968).[36]

Gibbs and Gibbs (1952)[29] and Gastaut and Fischer-Williams (1959)[27] describe a petit mal variant of myoclonus. The petit mal of the myoclonus type occurs before the convulsive seizure when widespread interference with cerebral function acts in a slow and progressive manner (i.e., anoxia, oxygen intoxication, hypoglycemia, pentylenetetrazole injection, picrotoxin, chloralose, bromide of camphor). Focal lesions cause bilateral myoclonic jerks of the petit mal type only if they are near the midline or a widespread activator is given (i.e., pentylene-tetrazole). The myoclonus may be provoked by sound (santonin), touch and sound (bromide of camphor), or with photic stimulation and pentylenetetrazole.

TABLE I

Incidence of myoclonic seizures (based on analysis of 11,612 cases of clinical seizures)

Type	Number	Percentage
Grand mal	5598	48
Infantile spasm	132	1
Grand mal and myoclonic	67	<1
Myoclonic	37	<1
Petit mal, grand mal, and myoclonic	17	<1
Petit mal and myoclonic	10	<1
Psychomotor, myoclonic, grand mal, and petit mal	1	<1
Myoclonic and psychomotor	1	<1
Psychomotor	678	5.8
Petit mal	335	2.9

(Adapted from Gibbs and Gibbs, 1952)[29]

TABLE 2

Analysis of 133 cases with myoclonic epilepsy

Type	Number	Percentage
Myoclonus	37	27.8
Myoclonus and grand mal	67	50.5
Myoclonus and petit mal	10	7.5
Myoclonus, petit mal, and grand mal	17	12.8
Myoclonus and psychomotor	1	0.7
Myoclonus, petit mal, grand mal, and psychomotor	1	0.7

(Adapted from Harper, 1968)[36]

TABLE 3

Neurologic signs and symptoms of 133 patients with myoclonic seizures

Finding	Number	Percentage
Hemiplegia	4	8.0
Athetosis	1	0.7
Rigidity	1	0.7
Blindness with optic atrophy	1	0.7
Strabismus	6	4.5
Nystagmus	2	1.5
Speech impairment	2	1.5
Aphasia	1	0.7
No significant neurological findings	117	88.0

(Adapted from Harper, 1968)[36]

TABLE 4

Psychiatric symptoms in 133 patients with myoclonic seizures

Symptom	Number	Percentage
Neurosis	1	0.7
Behavioral problem	1	0.7
Irritability	1	0.7
Temper tantrums	1	0.7
Hyperactivity	1	0.7
Total	5	3.5
Mental deficiencies	22	16.5

(Adapted from Harper, 1968)[36]

The petit mal variant is a spike and wave pattern that is slower than the 3 per second pattern but which in many other ways resembles it. A large percentage of these patients are subject to massive myoclonic jerks or to brief, severe, lightning-like seizures. These generalized jerks occur in children not yet walking. Another form is a sudden loss of posture ('akinetic seizures') with head nodding or body collapse with a forward or backward plunge, often resulting in head trauma. Astatic might be a better term for this type of seizure. They may occur several hundred times a day (Gibbs and Gibbs, 1952).[29]

The electroencephalogram in adult myoclonic epilepsy is well recognized. Bilateral, synchronous, and symmetrical 'polyspike' discharges appear (Gastaut, 1954).[26] Forty-two patients with myoclonus had electroencephalograms (Aigner and Mulder, 1960).[2] Of these, 27 showed diffuse atypical spike and wave activity varying from 1 to 4 cycles per second. Of these 27 patients (age unstated but mainly adults), 13 demonstrated sensitivity to photic stimulation. Their evaluation is more thoroughly and critically discussed later in this chapter.

At this point, we shall briefly discuss epilepsia partialis continua (Kojevnikov's syndrome). Kojevnikov (1895)[51] described 4 patients with continuous interictal focal jerking attacks without loss of consciousness and limited to one limb or part of the body. The jerking remained localized to the initially affected part of the body. If it did spread, it did so by a typical Jacksonian march. There was none of the fragmentary contraction of muscle parts or the seemingly haphazard flitting of contractions from place to place of true myoclonus.

Epilepsia partialis continua may be defined as clonic muscular twitchings repeated at rather short but regular intervals in one part of the body for a period of days or weeks. Each jerk lasts approximately one-fourth to one second and usually continually involves the same muscle group. Occasionally, other related muscles in the same limb or same side are also involved. Consciousness is not lost. The condition differs from focal epilepsy in the absence of progression from a tonic phase to a clonic phase and in the 'march' of the tonic phase from one muscle group to another as the focus of activity becomes more extensive (Juul-Jensen and Denny-Brown, 1966).[47]

As stated earlier, some do and others do not wish to include epilepsia partialis continua in the category of myoclonus. Perhaps the arguments that it is not a variety of myoclonus are valid. The twitch of myoclonus is more rapid, usually lasts less than half a second, and involves a variable number of muscles and is repeated in different groups of muscles at irregular (according to some) intervals. It is seldom limited to one limb or to one side. In some conditions, myoclonus may become almost rhythmically repeated in some muscle groups, especially the upper limb flexors; and each myoclonic twitch may become prolonged or multiple. Myoclonus may also make a transition to a generalized seizure at some point in increasing severity. In such a case, myoclonus may have no feature that completely differentiates it from epilepsia partialis continua except the absence of a consistent unilateral focus. From this point of view, the syndrome may well have some features in common with myoclonus (Lennox and Lennox, 1954).[57] When limited to the face, it may be differentiated from facial spasm by its regularity and by the absence of contraction in the intervals between twitches (Juul-Jensen and Denny-Brown, 1966).[47]

Juul-Jenson and Denny-Brown reported 9 cases with pathological findings. The electroencephalogram revealed a large blunt wave, frequently polyphasic, with its highest voltage over the opposite hemisphere's central region. There was no discrete focus. It was at times generalized through both hemispheres, although always larger in the hemisphere opposite the clinically observed movements. Unlike petit mal, consciousness was not necessarily disturbed. The rhythm of contractions and electroencephalographic abnormality, usually 60 to 120 beats per minute, was slower than the 3 per second spike of petit mal, although Lennox and Lennox (1954)[57] mention cases of transition from one rhythm to another. Common to all the cases was a cortical or subcortical lesion contralateral to the involved muscles. Multiple bilateral lesions and dystonia were frequent, perhaps indicating that a diffuse impairment of extrapyramidal function is a necessary background for the occurrence of this condition.

The close relationship between cortical and electromyographic discharges in many cases resembles that of pyramidal myoclonus. This jerking can be eliminated by local cortical excision. However, the excised tissue may fail to show any definite pathology; the nature and site of the underlying lesion is frequently obscure (Dawson, 1947; Gastaut and Remond, 1952; Van Bogaert et al., 1950).[17,28,101] As the jerking attacks may show the tonic and clonic phases of a small abortive convulsive 'fit', the condition seems well named.

Many 'normal' people frequently experience sudden, involuntary jerks of the limbs upon just dropping off to sleep. These are frequently accompanied by a vivid dream experience or hallucination. The subject wakes with a startle and then drops off to sleep. The jerk may recur. It never occurs under other circumstances. Thus, it occurs at night in bed or, less frequently, upon napping during the day. The contractions do not appear to be precipitated by emotional distress or fatigue. Symonds (1953)[94] refers to this phenomenon as 'nocturnal jerks'. He attributes 'nocturnal myoclonus' to those patients who suffer involuntary clonic movements at night which are markedly in excess of those occurring in normal persons. Oswald (1959)[79] believes that many 'normals' can have several contractions per night. Thus he does not make this distinction. Symonds maintains that, on the whole, nocturnal myoclonus differs from the variety of myoclonic epilepsy in which the seizures may be provoked by external stimuli, visual, proprioceptive, auditory, or tactile.

Symonds maintains that a history of excessive nocturnal jerks is sometimes obtained from patients with idiopathic epilepsy of late onset, but that the question of a relationship between these jerks and nocturnal myoclonus and the possibility of a familial incidence has not been answered. Muskens (1928)[74] stated that cases occur where in a family there exists a more marked tendency than usual to myoclonic discharges, and epilepsy suddenly appears. This phenomenon is further discussed in Symonds' paper (1953).[94]

Symonds goes on to discuss 5 patients who complained of involuntary contractions of the body or limbs that occurred at the moment of falling asleep, during sleep, or in a state of mental and physical relaxation during the day. Each patient complained that the symptoms greatly interfered with their going to sleep. He presented evidence for supposing that this syndrome of nocturnal myoclonus is an epileptic variant which may be familial.

One should note that when normal persons are subjected to regularly recurring stimuli, to which they are required to make regular responses, they tend to drop into a light sleep in between those responses just as did Pavlov's dogs. Oswald (1959)[79] reviews this subject.

Oswald questioned 50 'normals' about these nocturnal contractions. All but 7 reported having had them. Half of them thought that they had occurred up to 3 times a year. Discussion with several of the subjects' wives revealed that the individuals had far more myoclonic contractions than they realized. Many who thought that they had had a few per year actually had, according to their wives, a few on most nights.

Oswald recorded electroencephalograms, electrocardiograms, respiratory patterns, and limb movements during a number of these contractions. The jerks only occurred during light sleep. Perhaps the dream events act as stimuli for some jerks; on the other hand, perhaps the jerk initiates the dream. They frequently occurred during poorly developed electroencephalographic K-complexes. However, K-complexes are common, and this finding proves nothing. A sudden, sharp expiratory movement sometimes immediately followed the myoclonic contraction. Alternatively, a more delayed deep inspiration sometimes occurred. Oswald, unlike Symonds, believed that anxiety could provoke the contraction.

Johnson et al. (1971)[16] reported a case of hereditary chin trembling with nocturnal myoclonus and tongue biting in one of a dizygous twin pair. The patient's chin trembling was considered a form of a benign and familial tremor. The other twin, the father, and several other male paternal relatives had a similar chin tremor, indicating an autosomal recessive inheritance pattern (Laurance et al., 1968)[56].

The initial concept of myoclonus probably originated in Friedreich's (1881)[25] description of paramyoclonus multiplex. This is the same as 'essential myoclonus'. Others would add to the latter category the phenomenon of 'familial myoclonus', the electric chorea of Henoch-Bergon and various myoclonic syndromes (Biemond, 1963; Bonduelle, 1968).[4,5] We shall briefly discuss some of these.

Friedreich's patient had suffered a frightening experience at the age of 45 years, followed by shakes and twitches during waking hours. There was no similar family history. He described sharp jerks that involved the entire muscle in strong contractions without displacing the limb except for a slight movement produced by the most powerful jerks. These contractions were bilateral and symmetrically distributed, perhaps a little more prominent on the right side. They were asynchronous. The proximal muscles of the upper and lower limbs were primarily affected. The muscles of the face, trunk, and distal appendages were frequently spared. In the forearm, only the supinator longus was involved. Since this muscle can only act in synergy with the biceps and brachialis, its isolated contraction had been regarded by Unverricht as indicative of organic disease as opposed to hysteria. The overall effect was continuous chaotic muscular twitching varying in intensity and frequency from 10 to 50 contractions per minute. Occasionally, they summated to cause a form of painful tetanus. The contractions were augmented by cutaneous stimulation, by cold, or by pressure applied to the muscles. They were also increased by emotional stress. They were maximal at rest and disappeared during voluntary movement. They ceased during sleep except for an occasional sudden thigh flexion which was followed by the reappearance of the myoclonus. There were no other signs of organic disease in this rare entity (Bonduelle, 1968; Friedreich, 1881).[5,25]

The original description was of a single case. But by 1891, Unverricht could critically review and evaluate approximately 40 cases of paramyoclonus multiplex; he rejected approximately 80 percent. He considered the symptom complex described by Friedreich to be essential for the diagnosis, especially the isolated asynergistic, asynchronous jerks which only occasionally resulted in slight movement. He did concur with others that the entire musculature, including the face and tongue, might be involved.

Mahloudji and Pikielny (1967)[65] evaluated 5 patients who had myoclonus commencing in the first decade of life and running a benign course, compatible with an active existence. The jerky contractions were only present during the waking hours and aggravated by emotional tension. Volitional movement had a variable effect on the contractions. There were no seizures, mental changes, or other neurological deficits. The electroencephalograms were normal. Inheritance was autosomal dominant. Fourteen patients in this category were followed by Aigner and Mulder up to 12 years. Three were improved, 13 were unchanged, and 1 died.

Because of great confusion over the actual meaning of the term paramyoclonus multiplex, Malhoudji and Pikielny (1967)[65] substituted the term 'hereditary essential myoclonus'. They considered this a benign syndrome with the following diagnostic criteria: onset of myoclonus in the first or second decade; equal affection of males and females; a benign course, often variable but compatible with an active life of a normal span; autosomal dominant inheritance with variable severity; absence of seizures, dementia, gross ataxia, and other neurological deficits; and a normal electroencephalogram. This type of myoclonus has a predilection for the face, trunk, and the proximal limb muscles. The involvement may be generalized, confined to one side, or even segmental. It is absent during sleep and is aggravated by emotional distress.

Malhoudji and Pikielny distinguish hereditary essential myoclonus from other familial neurological conditions showing myoclonus (i.e., syndrome of Unverricht and Lundborg) by their malignant course, seizures, mental deterioration, motor deficits, and recessive modes of inheritance (Harriman and Millar, 1955).[37] Ramsey Hunt's syndrome of dyssynergia cerebellaris myoclonica refers merely to the association of severe cerebellar dysfunction with myoclonus (Hunt, 1921).[44]

Halliday (1967a)[34] describes 2 patients with essential myoclonus whose myoclonic activity temporarily disappeared during periods of amenorrhea, due to pregnancy in 1 patient, anorexia nervosa in the other.

Aigner and Mulder (1960)[2] recently tried to assess the prognostic significance of myoclonus. In a follow-up study of 94 patients with myoclonus seen at the Mayo Clinic over a 12-year period, they observed that 71 also had seizures. The number of non-epileptic myoclonic patients may, however, be lower than expected in this series because among a further 50 patients who were eliminated from the study were some who had myoclonus only in the drowsy period preceding or following sleep. Of 23 patients without epilepsy included, 4 had other neurological signs, and 19 were typical cases of essential myoclonus. Only 14 of these patients had obtainable information: 1 had died from unknown causes at the age of 30, having had myoclonic jerks of the hand without progression since he was 11 years old; 10 other patients were unchanged, and 3 had improved. Myoclonus did not worsen in any of the patients in this group.

Halliday (1967a)[34] believes that many epileptics have myoclonus and that essential myoclonus exists as a truly benign phenomenon in a small number of individuals. In some of these the myoclonus is familial. This essential myoclonus shows no sign of progression and is probably carried by an autosomally dominant gene.

Daube and Peters (1966)[15] presented the laboratory and clinical findings of 12 patients in 2 families with hereditary essential myoclonus. They considered the syndrome to be one of multiple, generalized, irregular, involuntary jerks of variable severity, primarily affecting the proximal muscles. The onset was in childhood or adolescence and was at times associated with slowly progressive impaired cerebellar function. Routine laboratory investigations and electro-encephalography were normal.

Familial myoclonus, described by Unverricht in 1895, is closely related to paramyoclonus multiplex but has an epileptic component which precedes the myoclonus. In 1903, Lundborg included Unverricht's cases with his own in a category distinct from Friedreich's essential myoclonus. He underlined the syndrome's epileptic component and offered the name 'progressive myoclonic epilepsy'. He considered that the main features were the heredo-familial occurrence and the progressive course, a point of distinction from the myoclonic epilepsy of Rabot (1899).[81] He attached much less importance than Friedreich to the precise form taken by the myoclonus.

It is true that most reports of this entity have concerned themselves with patients having a familial incidence of the disorder. In some of these patients, the clinical details described by Friedreich were faithfully reproduced. In some there was marked limb movement, and in some the clinical picture of Henoch-Bergeron.

The electric chorea of Henoch-Bergeron (Henoch, 1892)[41] is a symptom complex, often in children, consisting primarily of synchronous or synergistic jerks producing sudden, irregular segmental movements. The movements, which have the appearance of resulting from an electric shock, affect mainly the shoulders and neck, producing displacement of the head in various directions, elevation of the shoulders, and adduction of the arms. It might also involve the 2 limbs on one side and sometimes all 4 limbs and the trunk. At times the tongue, face, glottis, and diaphragm might also be affected. The frequency is usually slower than that of the myoclonias, ranging from 1 to 6 per minute. Postural changes or volitional movements fail to alter the number or the intensity of the jerks. Emotions intensify the jerks; they disappear during sleep. The prognosis is good according to Berland and Guertin, less good according to Henoch (Bonduelle, 1968; Krebs, 1952).[5,52] One may certainly consider the electric chorea of Henoch-Bergeron as distinct from the paramyoclonia multiplex of Friedreich. These two forms, however, may well occur in combination. Neither entity carries with it any etiological implication and each solely contributes to a descriptive classification of the myoclonic syndromes.

Perhaps it is best to use the term 'essential myoclonus' when dealing with a myoclonic syndrome unassociated with any other neurological abnormalities, whether clinical or electroencephalographic. There is no doubt that this term is imprecise. One must remember that there are cases which appear to be transitional between the essential myoclonias and those diseases of which myoclonus is one of the main features. Littlejohn (1949)[59] reported the syndrome of familial myoclonus associated with a diffuse spike and wave abnormality in the electroencephalogram. Van Leeuwen and Lauwers (1947)[102] described a family where distinct varieties of the myoclonic syndrome appeared in 3 children. One child had progressive myoclonic epilepsy without mental deterioration; another child had irregular palatal, tongue, and facial myoclonus without mental aberrations; and the third child had dystrophia adiposogenitalis, epileptic fits and absences, and generalized myoclonus which sometimes affected the tongue, palate, face, and diaphragm. The authors contended that this family formed a connection between paramyoclonus multiplex and familial progressive myoclonic epilepsy.

Gilbert et al. (1963)[30] reported an instance in which the Ramsay Hunt syndrome without epilepsy followed an unusually benign course. A connection of essential myoclonus with dyssynergia cerebellaris myoclonica may be entertained.

Van Bogaert (1949)[100] described a patient whose complex myoclonus produced limb movements; this was associated with simple myoclonus and fasciculations induced by maintenance of posture.

Analysis of such cases of essential myoclonus, whether sporadic or familial, leads one to surmise that they are *formes frustes* of hereditary degenerative disorders. Bonduelle (1968)[5] believes that in the fully developed form the myoclonic syndrome is only one aspect of a diffuse neuronal disease which often includes epilepsy, dementia, and evidence of subthalamic or cerebellar lesions.

Myoclonus has represented many things to many people. It has been defined and redefined many times. It is extremely difficult to subcategorize, since the symptom can be seen in many diseases and in many 'normals'. In addition, it can also be seen in multiple sclerosis (Guillain and Mollaret, 1935),[33] acrodynia (Haymaker, 1969),[38] smallpox, Schilder's disease, syringomyelia, acute and chronic encephalitis lethargica, subacute inclusion encephalitis, infantile paralysis, bilateral symmetric degeneration of the thalamus (Schulman, 1957),[86] lead poisoning (Leubuscher, 1911),[58] myelitis associated with herpes zoster (Netter, 1920),[75] general paresis, malaria (Marinesco, 1921),[66] lipoidosis, tuberculous meningitis, diffuse progressive degeneration of the gray matter (Alpers, 1931),[3] meningeal gliomatosis (Castleman and Kibbe, 1958),[11] Hallervorden-Spatz syndrome, Wilson's disease, Huntington's chorea, Newcastle disease in cats (Luttrell and Bang, 1956),[64] epidemic neuromyasthenia (Henderson and Shelokov, 1959),[40] maple syrup urine disease (Menkes et al., 1954),[70] amino acid disturbances (Shih et al., 1969),[87] and a congenital disorder of baby pigs (Stromberg and Kitchell, 1958).[92] Fright, trauma, infectious diseases, intoxications, and abuse of tranquilizers have also produced myoclonus (Merlis, 1954).[71] Myoclonic contractions confined to a few muscle groups are allegedly endemic in Siberia (Aigner and Mulder, 1960).[2]

REFERENCES

1. ADAMS, R. D. and FOLEY, J. M. (1953): The neurological disorder associated with liver disease. *Res. Publ. Ass. nerv. ment. Dis.*, *32*, 198.
2. AIGNER, B. R. and MULDER, D. W. (1960): Myoclonus. Clinical significance and an approach to classification. *Arch. Neurol. (Chic.)*, *2*, 600.

3. ALPERS, B. J. (1931): Diffuse progressive degeneration of the gray matter of the cerebrum. *Arch. Neurol. Psychiat.*, *25*, 469.

4. BIEMOND, A. (1963): Paramyoclonus multiplex. *Psychiat. Neurol. Neurochir.*, *66*, 270.

5. BONDUELLE, M. (1968): The myoclonias. In: *Diseases of the Basal Ganglia*, p. 29. Editors: P. J. Vinken and G. W. Bruyn. North Holland Publ. Co., Amsterdam.

6. BRADLEY, K., EASTON, D. M. and ECCLES, J. C. (1953): An investigation of primary or direct inhibition. *J. Physiol. (Lond.)*, *122*, 474.

7. BRADSHAW, J. P. P. (1954): A study of myoclonus. *Brain*, *77*, 138.

8. BRIDGE, E. M. (1949): *Epilepsy and Convulsive Disorders in Children.* McGraw-Hill Co., New York.

9. BRISSAUD, H. E. and BECUVAIS, P. (1969): Opsoclonus and neuroblastoma. *New Engl. J. Med.*, *280*, 1242.

10. BROOKS, V. B., CURTIS, D. R. and ECCLES, J. C. (1957): The action of tetanus toxin on the inhibition of motor neurones. *J. Physiol. (Lond.)*, *135*, 655.

11. CASTLEMAN, B. and KIBBE, B. U. (1958): Case records of the Massachusetts General Hospital. *New Engl. J. Med.*, *259*, 688.

12. COGAN, D. (1968): Opsoclonus, body tremulousness, and benign encephalitis. *Arch. Ophthal.*, *79*, 545.

13. COURVILLE, C. B. (1939): Untoward effects of nitrous oxide anesthesia. Quoted in: The syndrome of intention or action myoclonus as a sequel to hypoxic encephalopathy. J. W. Lance and R. D. Adams (1963): *Brain*, *86*, 111. (Ref. 55)

14. CUSHING, H. and WOLBACH, S. B. (1927): The transformation of a malignant paravertebral sympathicoblastoma into a benign ganglioneuroma. *Amer. J. Path.*, *3*, 203.

15. DAUBE, J. R. and PETERS, H. A. (1966): Hereditary essential myoclonus. *Arch. Neurol. (Chic.)*, *15*, 587.

16. DAVIDSON, M., TOLENTINO, Y. and SAPIR, S. (1968): Opsoclonus and neuroblastoma. *New Engl. J. Med.*, *279*, 948.

17. DAWSON, G. D. (1947): Investigations of a patient subject to myoclonic seizures after sensory stimulation. *J. Neurol. Neurosurg. Psychiat.*, *10*, 141.

18. DENNY-BROWN, D. (1956): Discussion of paper by Luttrell, C. N. and Bang, F. *Trans. Amer. neurol. Ass.*, *81*, 62.

19. DOBSON, J. P. and RILEY, H. A. (1941): Rhythmic myoclonus. A clinical report of six cases. *Arch. Neurol. Psychiat. (Chic.)*, *45*, 145.

20. DYKEN, P. and KOLAR, O. (1968): Dancing eyes, dancing feet: infantile polymyoclonia. *Brain*, *91*, 305.

21. EDITORIAL (1967): Penicillin encephalopathy. *Brit. med. J.*, *3*, 384.

22. ELLENBERGER JR., C., CAMPA, J. F. and NETSKY, M. G. (1968): Opsoclonus and parenchymatous degeneration of the cerebellum. *Neurology (Minneap.)*, *18*, 1041.

23. FORD, F. R. (1966): *Diseases of the Nervous System in Infancy, Childhood and Adolescence.* Charles C. Thomas, Springfield, Ill.

24. FRANCK, G., CHANTRANE, A., MELON, J. and MOUCHETTE, R. (1965): Le syndrome clonique du voile du palais. Etude clinique, électromyographique et cinématographique. *Rev. neurol.*, *113*, 46.

25. FRIEDREICH, N. (1881): Neuropathologische Beobachtungen. I. Paramyoklonus multiplex. *Virchows Arch. path. Anat.*, *86*, 421.

26. GASTAUT, H. (1954): *The Epilepsies. Electro-clinical Correlations.* Charles C. Thomas, Springfield, Ill.

27. GASTAUT, H. and FISCHER-WILLIAMS, M. (1959): The physiopathology of epileptic seizures. In: *Handbook of Physiology, Section 1, Neurophysiology.* Editor: J. Field. Physiological Society, Washington, D. C.

28. GASTAUT, H. and REMOND, A. (1952): Etude électroencéphalographique des myoclonies. *Rev. neurol.*, *86*, 596.
29. GIBBS, F. A. and GIBBS, E. C. (1952): *Atlas of Electroencephalography*, *Vol. 2*.
Addison-Wesley Publishing Co., Boston, Mass.
30. GILBERT, G. J., McENTEE, W. J. and GLASER, G. H. (1963): Familial myoclonus
and ataxia. *Neurology (Minneap.)*, *13*, 365.
31. GUILLAIN, G., BERTRAND, I. and LEREBOULLET, J. (1934): Myoclonies arythmiques
unilatérales des membres par lésion du noyau dentelé du cervelet. *Rev. neurol.*, *2*, 73.
32. GUILLAIN, G. and MOLLARET, P. (1931): Deux cas de myoclonies synchrones et
rhythmées vélo-pharyngo-laryngo-oculo-diaphragmatiques. *Rev. neurol.*, *2*, 545.
33. GUILLAIN, G. and MOLLARET, P. (1935): Le syndrome myoclonique synchrone et
rythmé: Vélo-pharyngo-laryngo-oculo-diaphragmatique. *Presse méd.*, *1*, 57.
34. HALLIDAY, A. M. (1967a): The clinical evidence of myoclonus. In: *Modern Trends
in Neurology*, *Vol. 4*, p. 69. Editor: D. Williams. Butterworth, London.
35. HALLIDAY, A. M. (1967b): The electrophysiological study of myoclonus in man.
Brain, *90*, 241.
36. HARPER, J. R. (1968): True myoclonic epilepsy in childhood. *Arch. Dis. Childh.*,
43, 28.
37. HARRIMAN, D. G. F. and MILLAR, J. H. D. (1955): Progressive familial myoclonic
epilepsy in three families: Its clinical features and pathological basis. *Brain*, *78*, 325.
38. HAYMAKER, W. (1969): *Bing's Local Diagnosis in Neurological Diseases*. C. V. Mosby
Co., St. Louis, Mo.
39. HAYMAKER, W. and KUHLENBECK, H. (1971): Disorders of the brainstem and its
cranial nerves. In: *Clinical Neurology*, p. 16. Editors: A. B. Baker and L. H. Baker.
Harper and Row, New York.
40. HENDERSON, D. A. and SHELOKOV, A. (1959): Epidemic neuromyasthenia – clinical
syndrome? *New Engl. J. Med.*, *260*, 757.
41. HENOCH, E. (1892): *Vorlesungen über Kinderkrankheiten*, *6th ed.* Berlin.
42. HERRMANN C., JR. and BROWN, J. W. (1967): Palatal myoclonus: A reappraisal.
J. neurol. Sci., *5*, 473.
43. HODSKINS, M. B. and YAKOVLEV, P. I. (1930): Anatomico-clinical observations on
myoclonus in epileptics and on related symptom complexes. *Amer. J. Psychiat.*,
9, 827.
44. HUNT, J. R. (1921): Dyssynergia cerebellaris myoclonica – primary atrophy of the
dentate system: A contribution to the pathology and symptomatology of the
cerebellum. *Brain*, *44*, 490.
45. JEAVONS, P. M. and BOWER, B. D. (1964): Infantile spasms. In: *Clinics in Developmental Medicine*, *No. 15*. Spastics Society, London.
46. JOHNSON, L. F., KINSBOURNE, M. and RENUART, A. (1971): Hereditary chin
trembling with nocturnal myoclonus and tongue biting in dizygous twins. *Develop.
Med. Child Neurol.*, *13*, 726.
47. JUUL-JENSEN, P. and DENNY-BROWN, D. (1966): Epilepsia partialis continua.
Arch. Neurol. (Chic.), *15*, 563.
48. KETEL, W. B. and HUGHES, J. R. (1972): Toxic encephalopathy with seizures
secondary to ingestion of Composition C-4 – a clinical and electroencephalographic
study. *Neurology (Minneap.)*, *22*, 871.
49. KINSBOURNE, M. (1962): Myoclonic encephalopathy of infants. *J. Neurol. Neurosurg.
Psychiat.*, *25*, 271.
50. KLINGMAN, W. D. and HODGES, R. G. (1944): Acute ataxia of unknown origins in
children. *J. Pediat.*, *24*, 536.

51. KOJEVNIKOV, A. Y. (1895): Eine besondere Form von corticaler Epilepsie. *Neurol. Zbl.*, *14*, 47.
52. KREBS, E. (1952): Les myoclonies (étude séméiologique). *Rev. neurol.*, *86*, 549.
53. KREINDLER, A., CRIGHEL, E. and POILICI, I. (1959): Clinical and electroencephalographic investigations in myoclonic cerebellar dyssynergia. *J. Neurol. Neurosurg. Psychiat.*, *22*, 232.
54. LANCE, J. W. (1968): Myoclonic jerks and falls: aetiology, classification and treatment. *Med. J. Aust.*, *1*, 113.
55. LANCE, J. W. and ADAMS, R. D. (1963): The syndrome of intention or action myoclonus as a sequel to hypoxic encephalopathy. *Brain*, *86*, 111.
56. LAURANCE, B. M., MATTHEWS, W. B. and DIGGLE, J. H. (1968): Hereditary quivering of the chin. *Arch. Dis. Childh.*, *43*, 249.
57. LENNOX, W. G. and LENNOX, M. A. (1954): *Epilepsy and the Functional Anatomy of the Human Brain.* Little, Brown and Co., Boston, Mass.
58. LEUBUSCHER, quoted by Oppenheim, H. (1911): *Text-Book of Nervous Diseases for Physicians and Students.* Editor and Translator: A. Bruce. T. N. Foulis, London.
59. LITTLEJOHN, W. S. (1949): Familial myoclonus: report of four cases with electroencephalograms. *Sth. Med. J.*, *42*, 404.
60. LOCKE, S., MERRILL, J. P. and TYLER, H. R. (1961): Neurologic complications of uremia. *Arch. intern. Med.*, *108*, 519.
61. LUNDBORG, H. (1903): *Die progressive Myoklonus-Epilepsie.* Uppsala.
62. LUNDBORG, H. (1904): Ist Unverricht's sogenannte familiäre Myoklonie eine klinische Entität, welche in der Nosologie berechtigt ist? *Neurol. Zbl.*, *23*, 162.
63. LUNDBORG, H. (1912): Der Hergang der progressiven Myoklonus-Epilepsie. *Z. ges. Neurol. Psychiat.*, *9*, 353.
64. LUTTRELL, C. N. and BANG, F. B. (1956): Myoclonus in cats with Newcastle disease virus encephalitis. *Trans. Amer. neurol. Ass.*, *81*, 59.
65. MAHLOUDJI, M. and PIKIELNY, R. T. (1967): Hereditary essential myoclonus. *Brain*, *90*, 669.
66. MARINESCO, M. G. (1921): Report on a case of myoclonic encephalomyelitis of malarial origin. *Brain*, *44*, 223.
67. MARMION, D. E. and SANDILANDS, J. (1947): Opsoclonia — a rare ocular sign in polioencephalitis. *Lancet*, *2*, 508.
68. MARTIN, E. S. and GRIFFITH, J. F. (1971): Myoclonic encephalopathy and neuroblastoma. *Amer. J. Dis. Child.*, *122*, 257.
69. McALPINE, D. and ARAKI, S. (1959): Minamata disease: rate effects of an unusual neurological disorder caused by contaminated fish. *Arch. Neurol. (Chic.)*, *1*, 522.
70. MENKES, J. H., HURST, P. L. and CRAIG, J. M. (1954): New syndrome: progressive familial infantile cerebral dysfunction associated with unusual urinary substance. *Pediatrics*, *14*, 462.
71. MERLIS, S. (1954): Neurological concomitants of the tranquilizer therapies. *Arch. Neurol. (Chic.)*, *1*, 122.
72. MOE, P. G. and NELLHAUS, G. (1970): Infantile polymyoclonia: opsoclonus syndrome and neural crest tumors. *Neurology (Minneap.)*, *20*, 756.
73. MUSKENS, L. J. J. (1909): Regional and myoclonic convulsions. *Epilepsia*, *1*, 156.
74. MUSKENS, L. J. J. (1928): *Epilepsy: Comparative Pathogenesis, Symptoms, Treatment.* William Wood and Co., New York.
75. NETTER, M., quoted by Harvier, P. and Levaditi, C. (1920): Virulence des centres nerveux dans l'encéphalite, 6 mois après le début de la maladie: virus encéphalitiques atténués. *Bull. Soc. Méd. Hôp.*, *44*, 1487.

76. NEVIN, S., McMENEMEY, W. H., BEHRMAN, S. and JONES, D. P. (1960): Subacute spongioform encephalopathy — a subacute form of encephalopathy attributable to vascular dysfunction (spongioform cerebral atrophy). *Brain*, *83*, 519.

77. ORZECHOWSKI, C. (1927): De l'ataxie dysmétrique des yeux dite myoclonique (opsoclonie opsochorie). *J. Psychol. Neurol. (Lpz.)*, *35*, 1.

78. OSTERBERG, G. (1937): On spasmus nutans. *Acta ophthal.*, *15*, 457.

79. OSWALD, I. (1959): Sudden bodily jerks on falling asleep. *Brain*, *82*, 92.

80. POLITZER, H. (1862): Quoted by: Riley, H. A. and Brock, S. (1933). (ref. 83).

81. RABOT, L. (1899): *La Myoclonie Epileptique*. Thesis, University of Paris, France.

82. REYNOLDS, J. R. (1861): *Epilepsy: Its Symptoms, Treatment and Relation to Other Chronic Convulsive Diseases*. John Churchill, London.

83. RILEY, H. A. and BROCK, S. (1933): Rhythmic myoclonus of muscles of palate, pharynx, larynx, and other regions. *Arch. Neurol. Psychiat. (Chic.)*, *29*, 726.

84. RONDOT, P., GUIOT, G., ARFEL, G. and DEROME, P. (1965): Syndrome myoclonique complexe. Etude clinique et dérivation des activités thalamiques. *Sem. Hôp. Paris*, *41*, 457.

85. ROSS, A. T. and ZEMAN, W. (1967): Opsoclonus, occult carcinoma, and chemical pathology in dentate nuclei. *Arch. Neurol. (Chic.)*, *17*, 546.

86. SCHULMAN, S. (1957): Bilateral symmetrical degeneration of the thalamus: a clinico-pathological study. *J. Neuropath. exp. Neurol.*, *16*, 446.

87. SHIH, V. E., EFRON, M. C. and MOSER, H. W. (1969): Hyperornithinemia, hyper-ammonemia and homocitrullinuria: a new disorder of amino acid metabolism associated with myoclonic seizures and mental retardation. *Amer. J. Dis. Child.*, *117*, 83.

88. SMITH, J. L. and WALSH, F. B. (1960): Opsoclonus — ataxic conjugate movements of the eyes. *Arch. Ophthal.*, *64*, 244.

89. SOLOMON, G. E. and CHUTORIA, A. M. (1968): Opsoclonus and occult neuro-blastoma. *New Engl. J. Med.*, *279*, 475.

90. SOUADJIAN, J. V. and CAIN, J. C. (1968): Intractable hiccup: etiologic factors in 220 cases. *Postgrad. Med.*, *43*, 72.

91. SPENCER, H. R. (1886): Pharyngeal and laryngeal 'nystagmus'. *Lancet*, *2*, 702.

92. STROMBERG, M. W. and KITCHELL, R. L. (1958): Studies on myoclonia congenita. I. Review of literature and field investigations. *Amer. J. vet. Res.*, *19*, 377.

93. SWANSON, P. D., LUTTRELL, C. N. and MAGLADERY, J. W. (1962): Myoclonus — a report of 67 cases and review of the literature. *Medicine*, *41*, 339.

94. SYMONDS, C. P. (1953): Nocturnal myoclonus. *J. Neurol. Neurosurg. Psychiat.*, *16*, 166.

95. SYMONDS, C. P. (1954): Myoclonus. *Med. J. Aust.*, *1*, 765.

96. TAHMOUSH, A. J., BROOKS, J. E. and KELTNER, J. L. (1972): Palatal myoclonus associated with abnormal ocular and extremity movements. *Arch. Neurol. (Chic.)*, *27*, 431.

97. THIRY, S. (1950): Etude clinique et encéphalographique d'un cas d'épilepsie myoclonique apparu après artériographie cérébrale. *Rev. neurol.*, *83*, 585.

98. UNVERRICHT, H. (1891): *Die Myoclonie*. Franz Deuticke, Leipzig — Vienna.

99. UNVERRICHT, H. (1895): Über familiäre Myoclonie. *Dtsch. Z. Nervenheilk.*, *7*, 32.

100. VAN BOGAERT, L. (1949): Essai sur le paramyoclonus multiplex de Friedreich. *Encéphale*, *38*, 145.

101. VAN BOGAERT, L. RADERMECKER, J. and TITECA, J. (1950): Les syndromes myo-cloniques. *Folia psychiat. neerl.*, *53*, 650.

102. VAN LEEUWEN, A. M. and LAUWERS, H. (1947): A partial form of familial myoclonus. *Brain*, *70*, 479.

103. WALSH, F. B. (1947): *Clinical Neuro-ophthalmology*. Williams and Wilkins Co., Baltimore, Md.

104. WATSON, C. W. and DENNY-BROWN, D. (1953): Myoclonus epilepsy as a symptom of diffuse neuronal disease. *Arch. Neurol. Psychiat. (Chic.)*, *70*, 151.

105. WILSON, S. A. (1940): *Neurology*. Williams and Wilkins Co., Baltimore. Md.

106. WOHLFAHRT, G. and HOOK, O. (1951): A clinical analysis of myoclonus epilepsy (Unverricht-Lundborg), myoclonic cerebellar dyssynergy (Hunt) and hepato-lenticular degeneration (Wilson). *Acta psychiat. scand.*, *26*, 219.

107. WRIGHT, F. S. (1969): Myoclonic seizures in infancy and childhood. *Postgrad. Med.*, *46*, 100.

108. YAKOVLEV, P. I. (1957): Discussion of paper by Luttrell, C. N. and Bang, F. *Trans. Amer. neurol. Ass.*, *82*, 87.

Myoclonus epilepsy in progressive disease

DHRUVA G. SULIBHAVI and LARRY SCHNECK

Department of Neurology and Psychiatry,
Kingsbrook Jewish Medical Center,
Brooklyn, N.Y., U.S.A.

Myoclonus is defined as a disturbance of neuronal activity giving rise to sudden, sharp, involuntary jerking of a single muscle, part of a muscle, or a group of muscles. The movements range from fasciculations to massive generalized jerks. These may be synergistic or asynergistic, rhythmic or arrhythmic. Denny-Brown (1962)[1] used the term 'myoclonus' for synergistic muscular contractions giving rise to movement of the affected part. Myoclonus is associated with diseases and conditions of varying etiology and anatomico-physiological significance.

HISTORICAL REVIEW

Friedreich, in 1881[2] described with great precision, a sharp jerk involving the entire musculature in a strong contraction without, however, moving the affected limb. The jerk was provoked by touch and cold, and disappeared during sleep. Myoclonus of a mild degree was noted as a common phenomenon among epileptics by Muskens (1928)[3] and Hodskins and Yakovlev (1930).[4] Unverricht (1891),[5] in his original monograph, described one sibship of whom half were affected between the ages of 9 and 15 years. His cases, however, differed from Friedreich's case and he did not comment on the incidence of epilepsy in his cases. Lundborg (1903),[6] in his monograph, underlined the association of epilepsy, mental deterioration, and familial incidence. Lafora and Glueck (1911)[7] described a 17-year-old boy with progressive fatal myoclonus epilepsy of great severity and with specific intranuclear infusion bodies. Boschi (1913)[8] recorded myoclonus in cases of familial cerebellar degeneration. Ramsay Hunt (1921)[9] described in detail the association of hereditary spinocerebellar degeneration with myoclonus. Jones and Nevin (1954)[10] have described a syndrome frequently associated with myoclonus, characterized by progressive dementia, vague motor and sensory disturbances. Watson and Denny-Brown (1953)[11] have popularized the concept of diffuse neuronal disease as the basis for myoclonus epilepsy.

CLINICAL DEFINITION AND DESCRIPTION

While myoclonus may exist as a benign phenomenon occasionally transmitted by a dominant gene, it should be regarded as a pathologic condition until proven otherwise.[12] The term 'myoclonus' in the syndrome of myoclonus epilepsy implies 'myoclonic response' or 'myoclonic involvement'. Myoclonus epilepsy should not be confused with other types of seizures that have myoclonic-like movements. The term 'myoclonus epilepsy' is used in reference to a syndrome in which myoclonus is symptomatic of various diffuse neuronal diseases of neurodegenerative disorders,[11] characterized by the triad of epilepsy, myoclonus, and dementia. However, myoclonus may occur in the absence of seizures as in Friedreich's cases. It may constitute the predominant feature of the disease as in Lafora body disease or may be an exceptional feature as in Alzheimer's disease.[13] Little is known about the pathology of various types of myoclonus epilepsy; and whether it is due to a diffuse neuronal disease or nuclear or tract lesion remains controversial.[14] In this field, clinicians and pathologists have entered into a territory where anatomical charts are still to be drawn and where physiology has scarcely yet established a foothold.

Myoclonus is greatly variable in its synchronicity, rhythmicity, distribution and range of movements. Stimulus sensitivity of myoclonus was fully appreciated by Unverricht (1891)[5] and Lundborg (1903).[6] Myoclonus may be provoked by the beginning of a voluntary movement, by stretching of the muscle,[15] or by photic or auditory stimulus. Myoclonus may herald by several days, the onset of a fit.[16] All observers agree that myoclonus may be precipitated or increased by movement or maintenance of a posture. This intention element in Ramsay Hunt syndrome has all the characteristic features of intention myoclonus as emphasized by Lance and Adams (1963).[17] Sometimes, the myoclonus moves the limb in the direction opposite to that intended ('myoclonies oppositionistes'). Foley and Denny-Brown (1955)[18] described 'bulbar myoclonus'. Oculogyric spasm

TABLE 1

Diseases in which myoclonus epilepsy is a prominent clinical feature

1. Unverricht-Lundborg disease
2. Lafora body disease
3. Dyssynergia cerebellaris myoclonica and other heredofamilial ataxias
4. Ganglioside storage diseases
5. Ceroid-lipofuscinosis and other types of amaurotic idiocies
6. Leukodystrophies
7. Niemann-Pick disease
8. Diffuse progressive degeneration of gray matter in infancy
9. Presenile dementias
     a. Jakob-Creutzfeldt disease
     b. Subacute spongiform encephalopathy
     c. Alzheimer-Pick disease
10. Hepatolenticular degeneration
11. Hallervorden-Spatz disease
12. Tuberous sclerosis
13. Multiple sclerosis
14. Amyotrophic lateral sclerosis

has also been described. An interesting condition known as 'opsoclonus' consists of jerking of the eyes and is characterized by irregularity in timing and direction, by the absence of a fast and slow component, and by the overshooting on attempted fixation. They may occur spontaneously and continuously. These movements are usually conjugate and do not give rise to diplopia. Opsoclonus has been described in Lafora body disease,[19] lipidosis,[20] and in systemic degenerative diseases.[21] Segmental myoclonus of spinal etiology has been reported only in inflammatory and neoplastic conditions.[22]

The list of diseases in which myoclonus is a clinical feature is voluminous, including Hallervorden-Spatz disease,[21] hepatolenticular degeneration,[23,24] multiple sclerosis,[25] tuberous sclerosis,[26] leukodystrophies,[27] and in diffuse progressive degeneration of cerebral gray matter of infancy.[28,29,30,31] Myoclonus is said to be more common than epilepsy in Niemann-Pick disease,[32] particularly in the late onset type[33,34,35] (see Table 1).

NEUROPHYSIOLOGICAL BASIS OF MYOCLONUS AND CHANGES IN THE EEG

The electrophysiology of myoclonus is being reviewed elsewhere and only the relevant features will be summarized here. Muskens (1928)[3] considered myoclonus as a 'reflex phenomenon' to touch and acoustic stimuli. Watson and Denny-Brown (1955)[36] postulated that a breakdown in the polysynaptic resistance (particularly in the subcortical structure) was responsible for myoclonus. Myoclonus is considered to result from increased excitability and/or decreased inhibition at different levels of the nervous system.[22] A lesion at the cortical level leads to 'seizures',[37] whereas a lesion at the level of anterior horn cells leads to segmental myoclonus. Therefore, myoclonus per se may result from lesions anywhere between the cortex and anterior horn cells. Thus, opsoclonus and palatal myoclonus may represent lesions at the brainstem level. Gastaut[38,39,40] considered myoclonus as a positive excitatory phenomenon, involving the rostral reticular substance and spreading along the ascending and descending tracts to the cortex and spinal cord. In contrast, Milhorat (1967)[41] felt that it is a release phenomenon, resulting from loss of inhibition in the reticular formation.

Grinker et al. (1938)[37] first noted the temporal association of myoclonic twitches to spike activity of the electroencephalogram (EEG). In subacute sclerosing panencephalitis, the periodicity of the jerks and its temporal relationship to the cortical events have been well demonstrated.[42,43]

Watson and Denny-Brown (1953)[11] noted during repetitive stimulation, that the slow wave component appeared to facilitate the appearance of the cortical spikes which were directly related to the muscular contractions. It has been suggested that the spikes may be independent of the myoclonus. This subject has been complicated by the observation that the spikes may precisely coincide with, or may follow, the muscle action potential. The temporal relation of the cortical potentials and EMG bursts may depend upon the site of the evoked response. Dawson (1947)[15] observed that patients with myoclonus may have very abnormal cerebral evoked responses. Halliday (1967),[44] reviewing the studies on evoked response in myoclonus, suggests at least three types of myo-clonus on electrophysiological and clinical grounds:

1. The *pyramidal* type involves the pyramidal tracts and is closely associated with the spike potentials in the contralateral cortical area. There is a characteristic and fixed latency following the spike and this delay is proportional to the length of the pathway from the cortex to the muscle. Clinically this results in a brief shock-like contraction. In petit mal myoclonus, the jerk is similarly related to the initial surface positive phase of the spike and wave complex.

2. The *extrapyramidal* type of myoclonus is not necessarily accompanied by any cortical discharge. Where it is, there is loose correlation between the polyphasic slow wave complexes and the EMG bursts. This suggests that both the cortical and EMG discharges are secondary to discharges in the deep-lying structures.

3. The *segmental* type, according to Halliday (1967),[44] is associated with viral infections or vascular lesions of the cord. The first type may occur in patients with progressive myoclonus epilepsy.

Electroencephalographic studies have been reported in many of the diseases list-ed in Table 1.[19,36,37,42,45,46,47,48,49] Electroencephalographic changes in myoclonus epilepsy only indicate diffuse cerebral damage. The EEG in 'bulbar myoclonus' of Foley and Denny-Brown (1955)[18] showed a generalized frequency of 5-7 cycles per second and 2-4 cycles per second in the comatose patient. Katzman et al. (1961)[50] considered the EEG changes as constituting the diagnostic triad in presenile dementia along with akinetic mutism and myoclonus. In subacute sclerosing panencephalitis, and subacute spongiform encephalopathy, the electroencephalographic pattern is suggestive of the underlying disease.[51,52] The outstanding feature of the electroencephalogram recorded in these studies is complete or partial obliteration of the normal rhythm with widespread high volt-age slow wave activity, and generalized sharp monophasic, diphasic, or triphasic complexes occurring about once a second. These complexes are rather constant, synchronous, and appear in every lead. There may also be periodic intermissions of slow sharp wave activity and runs of low voltage slow activity. The myoclonus is synchronous with the sharp wave activity in the EEG.

DISEASES ASSOCIATED WITH PROGRESSIVE MYOCLONUS EPILEPSY

There is a great deal of confusion about the entities of Unverricht-Lundborg type and Lafora body disease. Some authors have considered them as one entity, and cases belonging to Lafora body disease have been reported as Unverricht-Lundborg type.[53] This confusion is partly due to the fact that the characteristic Lafora bodies of myoclonic inclusion bodies are not specific for the condition described by Lafora and have been found in other neurodegenerative conditions, including Unverricht-Lundborg disease.[54] A number of authors have distin-guished these clinical entities.[55,56] They have emphasized the uniformity of the clinical picture in Lafora body disease,[57,58,59] but unfortunately, this uniformity continues to be ignored because of the scarcity of cases and the continual emphasis on the presence of Lafora bodies in a variety of diseases. There is an obvious need for more critical correlation and evaluation of the clinical and pathological material.

In 1891, Unverricht[5] reported a detailed study of a familial degenerative disease with isolated, lightning-like contraction of individual muscles. His report described 5 cases of myoclonus occurring in this family of 15 children born to normal parents. The onset was between 6 and 15 years. The jerking, which initially occurred nocturnally, became frequent over a period of 2 years and eventually led to epileptic seizures. His patients attended school and had no disturbance in memory. He also reviewed 40 cases from the literature and excluded most cases by rigid criteria of defining myoclonus as being isolated, asynchronous, asynergic jerks, capable of moving the limb. His patients were disabled by the myoclonus and in the terminal stages displayed rigidity and dyskinetic movements.

Twelve years after Unverricht's[5] monograph, Lundborg,[6] in a report entitled 'Unverricht Myoklonie', reviewed the literature on myoclonus which occurred in Scandinavian families. He apparently considered all the cases to be essentially similar and constituting a distinct disease entity. The cases described by Lundborg belong to a heterogenous group,[59,60] and he commented on the marked variability of the disease in regard to its evolution and duration of symptoms. He emphasized that the onset and development of the disease was usually accompanied by intellectual changes resulting in dementia. However, some of his cases were border-line defectives. While Lundborg reviewed the pathological anatomy available to him at the time, no mention was made of the studies done on the patients under his personal observation. He brought out the association of epilepsy, the high incidence of consanguinity, and the incidence of the condition in 25 percent of the sibships. The Lundborg type differs from Unverricht type on the basis of the familial incidence, late onset, and protracted course. While there is no variability in certain clinical, metabolic, and pathological features of the Unverricht type vs Lundborg type,[60,61] both 'diseases' can be considered a single clinical entity. Dementia is universal and in some instances, patients have been described as mentally defective from an early age.[59] The disease is inexorably progressive and ends fatally in 2 to 10 years with an average of 6 years.[62] Lundborg was aware of the hereditary nature of the disease and remarked that it was common to see the disease in siblings, but was unusual to observe cases in successive generations within the same family. Unverricht-Lundborg disease is usually transmitted by autosomal recessive gene, but may on occasion show dominant inheritance.[37] Horenko and Toivakka (1961)[63] have calculated that the incidence of Unverricht-Lundborg disease is one in 30,000 births in the Finnish population.

Lafora and Glueck in 1911[7] described a 17-year-old boy, one of 15 brothers who, at 14 years, had his first epileptic seizure. He developed myoclonic jerking of the face, hands, body, and rapidly progressive dementia. The patient died 22 months later. They reported characteristic lesions described as spherical corpuscles in the neurons throughout the nervous system. Lafora considered it an amyloid substance. His case differed from the cases of Unverricht and Lundborg by nature of its rapid progression and prominent myoclonus. Since then, other cases have been reported by Seitelberger et al. (1964),[58] Von Heycop et al. (1963),[59] Janeway et al. (1967),[62] Barolin and Peteisky (1969),[53] and Noveletto (1958).[64] The disease is familial with no predilection for either sex. The disease becomes clinically manifest at the end of the first decade and the patient is often the product of a consanguineous marriage. Dementia is frequently the first sign of the disease. Many of these patients are committed to psychiatric wards. Epileptic seizures were noted in almost all patients. The seizures usually precede the myoclonus, which is present in 90 percent of the cases. In the original case reports of Lafora, other types of seizure disorder had been described in various members of the family. The cases of Von Heycop et al. (1963)[59] had associated visual aura, euphoria, and kyphoscoliosis. Many other associated clinical features have been described.[65,66,67] These include deaf mutism, akinetic attacks, ataxia, transient loss of consciousness, dysarthria, choreoathetosis, paralysis agitans, and endocrinopathies.

Dementia and myoclonus are the hallmark of the disease. Since Lafora bodies are found in other clinical conditions, their presence is not diagnostic of Lafora body disease, which is a distinct clinical entity.[60] Suzuki et al. (1971)[68] describe a 59-year-old man with dementia, motor neuron disease, and sensory neuropathy. They found intraneuronal inclusion bodies, histochemically and electron microscopically similar to Lafora bodies. Since their patient had no seizures and no myoclonus, their case should not be considered as Lafora body disease.

Myoclonic inclusion bodies (Lafora bodies) are spherical and may be homogeneous or may be of stratified type.[69] They were first thought to consist of amyloid material.[70] Lafora thought that the albuminoid material is deposited first and amylaceous substances are later added. Harriman and Miller (1955)[19] consider these bodies to consist of a mucopolysaccharide. Further support of deranged carbohydrate metabolism is provided by the observations of Edger (1963),[61] Janeway et al. (1967),[62] Yokoi (1968),[71] Kraus-Rupport et al. (1970),[60] Gambetti et al. (1971),[72] and Seitelberger (1968).[73] Recent ultrastructural biochemical and histochemical studies have further elucidated the nature of these inclusions. The bodies are now believed to be composed of a protein core, surrounded by branched polyglucosan. Miller and Neill (1959)[74] noted low serum mucopolysaccharide in both affected and unaffected members of families of Lafora body disease. However, this has not been consistently demonstrated.[75]

Additional observations on brain tissue have revealed a non-specific increase in GM_3.[76] Taurine level in 24-hour urine is said to be low in patients with Lafora body disease as well as in mongoloids.[62] This finding is intriguing and may be helpful as a screening procedure in the future. Lowenthal (1965)[77] has found increased alpha-2 globulin in the affected and unaffected members of the family. This however, needs further evaluation.

DYSSYNERGIA CEREBELLARIS MYOCLONICA OR RAMSAY HUNT SYNDROME

Boschi, in 1913,[8] first reported myoclonus in a case of Marie's hereditary cerebellar ataxia. He also noted Friedreich's and Marie's ataxia associated with epilepsy in other members of the family. Hunt, in 1921,[9] reported 6 patients with spino-cerebellar degeneration associated with myoclonus and less frequently with epilepsy. Hunt did not comment on the familial aggregation of the cases, although 2 of his 6 cases were twins. The familial incidence has been stressed by Jacobs (1965),[78] Gilbert et al. (1963),[79] and May and White (1968).[80] The suggested mode of transmission for this condition is autosomal dominant with incomplete penetrance.[79]

The disease usually starts early in life with dysarthria, intention tremor, and dyssynergia. Some cases have been described in the second decade, but, because the disease is slowly progressive, the diagnosis is often not established prior to the fourth decade.[81] Nystagmus may be absent; dementia and epilepsy are usually absent. Myoclonus is a late finding in over 50 percent of the reported cases. Its quality, severity, and distribution is variable. It can be extremely violent and cause considerable functional disability.[78] The myoclonus may vary from irregular fasciculations and asynergic, isolated muscle myoclonus to general-ized jerks, severe enough to cause the patient to fall from the chair or bed. Myoclonus sometimes may cause the limb to move in the direction opposite of the intended action. It may be readily exacerbated by stimuli such as emotional excitement, concentration, and by efforts to move or even speak. This latter aspect, an intention or action myoclonus, was first described by Lance and Adams (1963).[17] On EMG, there is often electrical silence of muscle that lasts from 50 to 120 milliseconds and rarely up to 300 milliseconds.[82] Some clinicians have ques-tioned the existence of myoclonus in Ramsay Hunt syndrome where severe cere-bellar dysfunction is present and may clinically mimic the myoclonic move-ments.[24]

Noveletto (1958)[64] stated that drop attacks are common in Ramsay Hunt syndrome. This observation has not been substantiated in the other reported cases. Some affected cases had deafness and polyneuropathy. Similar lesions have been noted in other unaffected members of the family.[46,80] Associated skeletal abnormalities, common in spinocerebellar degeneration, are also reported in Ramsay Hunt syndrome.[83] The presence of pes cavus in a case of myoclonus should suggest the possibility of a degenerative lesion.[84] Ramsay Hunt syndrome, in our opinion, is not a unique clinical entity. There is nothing very distinctive about this syndrome that distinguishes it from the other spinocerebellar ataxias except for the additional feature of myoclonus.

Pathological changes are usually found in the rubro-dentato-olivary circuit.[85] Hodskins and Yakovlev (1930),[4] Wohlfart and Hook (1951),[24] Watson and Denny-Brown (1953),[11] and Harriman and Miller (1955)[19] have found lesions involving the dentato-rubral pathways. Hunt (1921)[9] found lesions in the dentate nucleus, superior cerebellar peduncles, spinocerebellar tracts, and Clark's column, but did not describe any lesions in the red nucleus, cerebellum, olives, or in the thalamus. Not all cases of Ramsay Hunt syndrome have lesions in the dentate nucleus,[14,16,86] and conversely, involvement of the dentate nucleus may be found without myoclonus.[87] For example, in 20 percent of the cases of hereditary spinocerebellar ataxia with dentate nucleus involvement, myoclonus is absent. Serum mucoprotein studies were done in cases of Ramsay Hunt syndrome, but the reports are conflicting. In some cases, autopsy specimens have shown large extracellular deposits of amyloid staining material in the central nervous system.

PRESENILE DEMENTIAS

In its classical form, Jakob-Creutzfeldt disease is characterized by progressive dementia in the presenium, associated with pyramidal and extrapyramidal signs, and subjective and objective twitchings. Pathologically, there is neuronal degeneration and glioses in the cortex, basal ganglion, cerebellum, brainstem, and spinal cord. Clinically, the disease occurs in the presenium and is characterized by paresis, hyperkinesia, ataxia, and abnormalities in muscle tone. Myoclonus consists of twitchings of facial muscles and may involve the entire musculature. These asynchronous, arrhythmic movements may be superimposed on the rhythmic dyskinesia, leading to violent movements. Since the clinical picture is variable, attempts at classification have given rise to at least five subgroups, depending upon the presence or absence of a clinical sign or a pathological feature.[88] For example, subacute spongiform encephalopathy of Jones and Nevin was considered as a subgroup of Jakob-Creutzfeldt disease where myoclonus dominated the clinical picture and where pathologically, there was marked spongiosis of the cortex, especially in the occipital lobe.[89,90] Similar cases were reported by a number of authors.[18,91,92,93,94] The disease usually becomes manifest between 50 and 70 years. Prodromal symptoms like headache, giddiness, and weakness precede focal cerebral lesions.[95] Epileptic fits occur in a few cases. Myoclonus is the outstanding feature. It involves the face and upper extremities. These movements are easily provoked by touch, movement, and noise. In our opinion, there is sufficient evidence to justify a separate classification of cases resembling Jones' and Nevin's description. This should be considered as a clinical variant of Jakob-Creutzfeldt disease.[96,97,81] The variability of the clinical picture can be explained by the diversity in the site of the maximum pathology.[98]

Recent studies have suggested the possibility that the Jakob-Creutzfeldt disease may be caused by a slow virus,[99,100,101] which may be activated by nonspecific insults to the central nervous system, e.g. head injury, stroke, hypoglycemia.[102] Similar clinical symptoms and pathological changes were reproduced in chimpanzees injected with brain material from the patients.[98,103] Amantadine, an anti-viral drug, has been found to halt the progress and partially reverse the clinical symptoms.[104] Until the viral transmission of this disease has been definitely established, the unitary theory for this group of disorders awaits final proof.[105]

Among the presenile dementias,[106] myoclonus is most common in Jakob-Creutzfeldt disease and its clinico-pathological variants. The myoclonus, which is stimulus-sensitive, is consistent with basal ganglia involvement.[107] In Alzheimer's disease, myoclonus is rare,[13] but when it does occur, it often indicates the onset of a rapidly fulminating course. Muscular activity may increase the frequency and amplitude of the myoclonic movements. There are no specific changes in the EEG.

LIPIDOSIS AND RELATED DISORDERS

It is remarkable that most of the reported cases of myoclonus in lipidosis belong to the group of amaurotic family idiocy.[108,109,110,111,112] The previous clinical classification of this group of diseases into early, late infantile, juvenile, and adult forms is now being replaced by definitive chemical and enzymatic criteria[113,114,115,116,117,118,119,120,121] (see Table 2).

TABLE 2

Disease	Sphingolipid	Enzyme deficiency	Clinical features
1. Generalized gangliosidosis	GM_1-ganglioside	B-Galactosidase	Psychomotor retardation, cherry-red spot, hepatomegaly, bone marrow involvement
2. Tay-Sachs disease	GM_2-ganglioside	Hexosaminidase A	Psychomotor retardation, cherry-red spot, 'startle reaction'
3. Sandhoff's disease	GM_2-ganglioside	Hexosaminidase A+B	Similar to Tay-Sachs disease
4. Gaucher's disease (infantile)	Ceramide glucoside	B-Glucosidase	Psychomotor retardation (infantile form), hepatosplenomegaly, bone involvement, 'Gaucher cells'
5. Krabbe's disease	Ceramide galactoside	B-Galactosidase	Early and severe psychomotor arrest, generalized spasticity, neurogenic fever
6. Fabry's disease	Ceramide trihexoside	A-Galactosidase	Reddish-purple maculopapular rash, renal and cardiac involvement, cornea opacities, peripheral neuralgia
7. Metachromatic leukodystrophy	Sulfatide	Sulfatidase	Mental retardation, psychiatric disturbances (adult), ataxia, prolonged nerve conduction time
8. Ceramide lactosidosis	Ceramide lactoside	B-Galactosidase	Psychomotor deterioration, organomegaly, macrocyte anemia, leukopenia, thrombocytopenia
9. Niemann-Pick disease — Type A	Sphingomyelin	Sphingomyelinase	Psychomotor arrest, cherry-red spot, hepatosplenomegaly, 'NPD' cells

Ganglioside storage diseases are characterized by the ubiquitous accumulations of gangliosides throughout the central nervous system. This accumulation is due to the deficiency of a specific lysosomal enzyme which is required for the sequential degradation of the ganglioside.[122,123,124,125,126] It is observed that myoclonus is common in lipidosis involving the cerebellum, but is rare in primary cerebellar degenerations.[127] Therefore, it is unlikely that the lesions in the cerebellum per se are responsible for the myoclonic movements. Clinically, ganglioside storage diseases are characterized by progressive mental and motor deterioration appearing in early childhood. Retinal changes are common;[128] visceral and skeletal changes are variable.[129,130,131]

In Tay-Sachs disease, a GM_2-gangliosidosis, myoclonus is seen early in the disease. It involves the isolated muscles in rapid contraction, provoked by various stimuli, notably touch and auditory stimuli. Myoclonus, which may be synchronous, involves the muscles of the face, neck and limbs. There is a characteristic early motor response to sound,[132,133] consisting of an initial upward extension of the arms with flexion and/or extension of the lower extremities and a startled expression. This has been referred to as hyperacusis or auditory myoclonus.[36] However, operationally this cannot be considered as myoclonus since it shows negative adaptation to stimuli.

The pathogenesis of the late infantile, juvenile, and adult forms remains controversial.[134,135] There has been an attempt to reclassify some of these clinical entities into a new category called neuronal ceroid lipofuscinosis.[136,137,138] Pathologically, there is accumulation of autofluorescent 'wear and tear' pigment.[139,140] The late infantile, juvenile, and adult types are differentiated on clinical and morbid anatomical basis.[141] Myoclonus, in many of the cases, was an early and prominent clinical feature. These diseases are inherited through autosomal recessive gene. Clinically, these disorders present with failure of psychomotor development, seizures, extrapyramidal and cerebellar signs. Myoclonus is common but usually mild in the juvenile type. Visual failure is associated with optic atrophy, more frequently with retinitis pigmentosa, and exceptionally with cherry-red spot.[142]

The adult type of amaurotic family idiocy of Kuf's disease is rare. The disease usually begins insidiously during the second or third decade and the clinical picture is a combination of progressive dementia, epilepsy, and myoclonus. Dementia is often minimal. There may be amaurosis associated with the retinitis pigmentosa, but in some cases, vision was said to be normal. The disease gradually progresses to muscular rigidity, incoordination, and bulbar paralysis. This disease is usually transmitted by autosomal recessive gene, but it can be transmitted by a dominant gene.[143] The dominant transmitted type is remarkably homochronical and homotypical. The clinical picture develops sequentially with major fits, progressive cerebellar ataxia, myoclonic jerks, massive myoclonus, progressive dementia, and moderate hypertension. Vacuolated lymphocytes and hypergranulated neutrophilic leukocytes are often seen. There is extensive accumulation of autofluorescent lipopigment in the neurons and astrocytes. Myoclonus bodies of the 'protein' type are found in the neurons of the substantia nigra. Since the clinical features are by no means specific, the pre-morbid diagnosis must depend upon the electroencephalogram and other electrophysiological changes,[144] on the morphology of the white blood cells,[138] and the biopsy appearances of rectum, brain, and other tissues.[145]

The nature and cause of myoclonus remains shrouded in mystery. The myth about myoclonus is inseparably linked with the underlying disease. There is great confusion about Unverricht-Lundborg disease and Lafora body disease.

In our opinion, each deserves to be recognized as a distinct clinical entity. The relation between Lafora bodies and myoclonus remains in doubt. There is need for critical evaluation of cases of myoclonus epilepsy in which Lafora bodies exist in the presence of myoclonus and vice versa. In order to justify the Ramsay Hunt syndrome as a distinct clinical entity, more rigid criteria are required to distinguish between cerebellar dyskinesias and myoclonus. Until more detailed clinical, pathological, physiological, and biochemical correlative studies are performed, myoclonus will continue to remain a symptom in search of a disease.

REFERENCES

1. DENNY-BROWN, D. (1962): *The Basal Ganglia and their Relation to Disorders of Movement*, p. 81. Oxford University Press, London.
2. FRIEDREICH, N. (1881): Neuropathologische Beobachtung beim Paramyoclonus multiplex. *Virchows Arch. Path. Anat., 86,* 421.
3. MUSKENS, L. J. J. (1928): *Epilepsy. Comparative Pathogenesis, Symptoms and Treatment.* William Wood and Co., New York, N.Y.
4. HODSKINS, M. B. and YAKOVLEV, P. I. (1930): Anatomico-clinical observations on myoclonus in epilepsies and in related symptom complexes. *Amer. J. Psychiat., 9,* 827.
5. UNVERRICHT, H. (1891): *Die Myoklonie,* p. 128. Franz Deuticke, Leipzig-Vienna.
6. LUNDBORG, H. (1903): *Die progressive Myoclonus-Epilepsie (Unverricht Myoklonie),* p. 207. Almqvist and Wiskell, Uppsala.
7. LAFORA, G. and GLUECK, B. (1911): Beitrag zur Histopathologie der Myoklonischen Epilepsie. *Z. ges. Neurol. Psychiat., 6,* 1.
8. BOSCHI, G. (1913): Atassia ereditaria con paramioclono molteplice lipo Unverricht. *J. Neurol. (Brux.), 18,* 141.
9. HUNT, J. R. (1921): Dyssynergia cerebellaris myoclonica: primary atrophy of the dentate system, a contribution to the pathology and symptomatology of the cerebellum. *Brain, 44,* 490.
10. JONES, D. P. and NEVIN, S. (1954): Rapidly progressive cerebral degeneration with mental disorder, focal disturbances and myoclonic epilepsy. *J. Neurol. Neurosurg. Psychiat., 17,* 148.
11. WATSON, C. W. and DENNY-BROWN, D. (1953): Myoclonus epilepsy as a symptom of diffuse neuronal disease. *Arch. Neurol. Psychiat. (Chic.), 70,* 151.
12. DAWSON, G. D. (1946): The relation between electroencephalogram and muscle action potentials in certain convulsive states. *J. Neurol. Neurosurg. Psychiat., 9,* 5.
13. LETEMENDIA, F. and PAMPIGLIONE, G. (1958): Clinical and EEG observations in Alzheimer's disease. *J. Neurol. Neurosurg. Psychiat., 21,* 167.
14. GREENFIELD, J. A. (1955): Pathology of involuntary movements. *Excerpta Med. (Amst.), Sect. VIII,* 767.
15. DAWSON, G. D. (1947): Investigations on a patient subject to myoclonic seizures after sensory stimulation. *J. Neurol. Neurosurg. Psychiat., 10,* 141.
16. SYMMONDS, C. (1954): Myoclonus. *Med. J. Aust., 41,* 765.
17. LANCE, J. W. and ADAMS, R. D. (1963): The syndrome of intention or action myoclonus as a sequel to hypoxic encephalopathy. *Brain, 86,* 111.
18. FOLEY, J. M. and DENNY-BROWN, D. (1955): Subacute progressive encephalopathy with bulbar myoclonus. *Excerpta Med. (Amst.), Sect. VIII,* 782.
19. HARRIMAN, D. G. F. and MILLER, J. H. D. (1955): Progressive myoclonus epilepsy

in three families and its clinical features and pathological basis. *Brain, 78,* 325.

20. BIRD, A. (1948): The lipidosis and the central nervous system. *Brain, 71,* 434.

21. YAKOVLEV, P. I. (1942): Myoclonus epilepsy: report of a case with presentation of a moving picture and anatomic slides. *Arch. Neurol. Psychiat. (Chic.), 48,* 1025.

22. SWANSON, P. D., LUTTRELL, C. M. and MAGLADERY, J. W. (1962): Myoclonus, a report of 67 cases and review of the literature. *Medicine (Baltimore), 41,* 339.

23. DENNY-BROWN, D. (1968): Clinical symptomatology of disease of basal ganglia. In: *Handbook of Clinical Neurology, Vol. 6,* pp. 133-172. Editors: P. J. Vinken and G. W. Bruyn. North Holland Publ. Co., Amsterdam.

24. WOHLFART, G. and HOOK, O. (1951): A clinical analysis of myoclonus epilepsy (Unverricht-Lundborg type), myoclonic cerebellar dyssynergia (Hunt) and hepatolenticular degeneration (Wilson). *Acta psychiat. scand., 26,* 219.

25. AIGNER, R. B. and MILDER, D. W. (1960): Myoclonus, clinical significance and an approach to classification. *Arch. Neurol. (Chic.), 2,* 600.

26. ROTH, J. S. and EPSTEIN, C. J. (1971): Infantile spasm and hypopigmented early manifestations of tuberous sclerosis. *Arch. Neurol. (Chic.), 25,* 547.

27. CUMMINGS, J. N. (1970): The lipidoses. In: *Handbook of Clinical Neurology, Vol. 10,* p. 330. Editors: P. J. Vinken and G. W. Bruyn. North Holland Publ. Co., Amsterdam.

28. ALPERS, B. (1931): Diffuse progressive degenerations of the grey matter of the cerebrum. *Arch. Neurol. Psychiat. (Chic.), 25,* 469.

29. CHRISTENSEN, E. and KRABBE, K. H. (1949): Poliodystrophia cerebri, progressive infantalis. *Arch. Neurol. Psychiat. (Chic.), 61,* 28.

30. FORD, F. R., LIVINGSTON, S. and SPRYLES, C. V. (1957): Familial degeneration of cerebral grey matter in children. *J. Pediat., 39,* 33.

31. PALINSKY, M., KOZINN, P. J., ZAHTZ, H. et al. (1954): Acute familial infantile heredodegenerative disorder of the central nervous system. *J. Pediat., 65,* 538.

32. FORD, F. R. (Ed.) (1960): *Disease of the Nervous System in Infancy, Childhood and Adolescence, 4th ed.,* p. 823. Charles C. Thomas, Springfield, Ill.

33. CROCKER, A. C. and FARBER, S. (1958): Niemann-Pick disease: a review of 18 cases. *Medicine (Baltimore), 37,* 1.

34. FORSYTHE, W. I., McKEOWN, E. F. and NEILL, D. W. (1959): Three cases of Niemann-Pick disease in children. *Arch. Dis. Childh., 34,* 406.

35. SCHNECK, L. and VOLK, B. W. (1967): Clinical manifestations of tsd in Niemann-Pick disease. In: *Inborn Errors of Sphingolipid Metabolism,* p. 403. Editors: S. Arson and B. W. Volk. Pergamon Press, New York.

36. WATSON, C. W. and DENNY-BROWN, D. (1955): Studies of the mechanism of stimulus sensitive myoclonus in man. *Electroenceph. clin. Neurophysiol., 7,* 341.

37. GRINKER, R. R., SEROTA, H. and STEIN, S. I. (1938): Myoclonic epilepsy. *Arch. Neurol. Psychiat. (Chic.), 40,* 968.

38. GASTAUT, H. and REMOND, A. (1952): Etude électroencéphalographique des myoclonies. *Rev. neurol., 86,* 596.

39. GASTAUT, H. and HUNTER, I. (1950): An experimental study of the mechanism of photic activation in idiopathic epilepsy. *Electroenceph. clin. Neurophysiol., 2,* 263.

40. GASTAUT, H. (1958): The physiopathology of grand mal seizures generalized from the start. *J. nerv. ment. Dis., 127,* 21.

41. MILHORAT, T. H. (1967): Experimental myoclonus of thalamic origin. *Arch. Neurol. (Chic.), 17,* 365.

42. COBB, W. and HILL, D. (1950): Electroencephalogram in subacute progressive encephalitis. *Brain, 73,* 392.

43. COBB, W. (1966): Periodic events of SSPE. *Electroenceph. clin. Neurophysiol.*, *21*, 278.

44. HALLIDAY, A. M. (1967): Cerebral evoked potentials in familial progressive myoclonus epilepsy. *J. roy. Coll. Phycns (Lond.)*, *1/2*, 123.

45. HALLIDAY, A. M. (1967): Electrophysiological study of myoclonus in man. *Brain*, *90*, 241.

46. HALLIDAY, A. M. (1965): The incidence of large cerebral evoked responses in myoclonic epilepsy. *Electroenceph. clin. Neurophysiol.*, *19*, 101.

47. ROSENBAUM, H. E. and STEIN, J. M. (1953): EEG findings in infantile tsd. *Electroenceph. clin. Neurophysiol.*, *5*, 603.

48. SCHNECK, L. (1965): Early electroencephalographic and seizure characteristics of Tay-Sachs disease. *Acta neurol. scand.*, *41*, 163.

49. WILLIAMS, J. D. and GIBBS, F. A. (1939): Electroencephalography in clinical neurology: its value in routine diagnosis. *Arch. Neurol. Psychiat. (Chic.)*, *41*, 519.

50. KATZMAN, R., KAGAN, E. H. and ZIMMERMAN, H. M. (1961): A case of Jakob-Creutzfeldt disease (1) clinicopathological analysis. *J. Neuropath. exp. Neurol.*, *20*, 78.

51. COBB, W., MARTIN, F. and PAMPIGLIONE, G. (1952): Cerebral lipidosis: electroencephalographic study. *Brain*, *75*, 343.

52. PAMPIGLIONE, G. and HARDEN, A. (1964): Polygraphic studies of some involuntary movements in SSPE. *Arch. Dis. Childh.*, *39*, 558.

53. BAROLIN, G. S. and PETEISKY, K. (1969): Siblings with Unverricht-Lundborg myoclonus epilepsy: a familial and longitudinal investigation. *Electroenceph. clin. Neurophysiol.*, *27*, 211.

54. HALTIA, M., KRISTEINSE, K. and SOURENDER, R. (1969): Neuropathological studies in 3 Scandinavian cases of progressive myoclonus epilepsy. *Acta neurol. scand.*, *45*, 63.

55. DIEBOLD, K., HAFNER, H. and VOGEL, F. (1967): Zur Klinik der progressive Myoklonusepilepsien. *Dtsch. Z. Nervenheilk.*, *190*, 199.

56. VOGEL, F., HAFNER, H. and DIEBOLD, K. (1965): Zur Genetik der progressiven Myoklonusepilepsien (Unverricht-Lundborg). *Humangenetik*, *1*, 437.

57. SCHWARZ, G. A. and VANOFF, M. (1965): Lafora body disease: a distinct, genetically determined form of Unverricht-Lundborg syndrome. *Arch. Neurol. (Chic.)*, *12*, 172.

58. SEITELBERGER, F., JACOB, H., PEIFFER, J. and COLMANT, H. J. (1964): Die Myoklonuskorperkrankheit. *Fortschr. Neurol. Psychiat.*, *32*, 305.

59. VON HEYCOP, T., HAM, M. W. and DE JAGER, H. (1963): Progressive myoclonus epilepsy with Lafora bodies: clinical and pathological features. *Epilepsia (Amst.)*, *4*, 95.

60. KRAUS-RUPPORT, R., OSTERLAG, B. and HAFNER, H. (1970): A study of late form (type Lundborg) of progressive myoclonus epilepsy. *J. neurol. Sci.*, *11*, 1.

61. EDGER, G. W. F. (1963): Progressive myoclonus epilepsy as an inborn error of metabolism. *Epilepsia (Amst.)*, *4*, 120.

62. JANEWAY, R., RAVENS, J. R., PEARCE, L. A. et al. (1967): Progressive myoclonus epilepsy with Lafora bodies: clinical, genetic, histopathological and biochemical study. *Arch. Neurol. (Chic.)*, *16*, 565.

63. HORENKO, A. and TOIVAKKA, E. I. (1961): Myoclonus epilepsy in Finland. *Acta neurol. scand.*, *37*, 282.

64. NOVELETTO, A. (1958): Problèmes actuels de la myoclonie-épilepsie progressive de Unverricht-Lundborg. Revue bibliographique et critique. *Encéphale*, *47*, 223.

65. VAN LEEUWEN, A. and LAUWERS, H. (1947): A partial form of familial myoclonus (the family Gl...). *Brain*, *70*, 479.

66. SCHULMAN, S. (1957): Bilateral symmetrical degeneration of the thalamus: a clinicopathological study. *J. Neuropath. exp. Neurol.*, *16*, 446.

67. HAMBERT, O. and PETERSON, I. (1970): EEG and neurophysiological studies in the syndrome of progressive myoclonus epilepsy. *Acta neurol. scand.*, *46*, 149.

68. SUZUKI, K., DAVID, E. and KUTSCHMAN, B. (1971): Presenile dementia with Lafora-like intraneuronal inclusions. *Arch. Neurol. (Chic.)*, *25*, 69.

69. ROIZIN, L. and FERRARO, J. (1942): Myoclonus epilepsy. *J. Neuropath. exp. Neurol.*, *1*, 297.

70. LAFORA, G. (1955): Myoclonus, physiological and pathological considerations. *Excerpta Med. (Amst.)*, *Sect. VIII*, 769.

71. YOKOI, S., AUSTIN, J., WHITMAN, F. and SAKAI, M. (1968): Studies in myoclonus epilepsy (Lafora body form): isolation and preliminary characterization of Lafora bodies in 2 cases. *Arch. Neurol. (Chic.)*, *19*, 15.

72. GAMBETTI, P., DiMAURO, S., HUNT, L. and BLUME, R. P. (1971): Myoclonus with Lafora bodies. *Arch. Neurol. (Chic.)*, *25*, 483.

73. SEITELBERGER, F. (1968): Myoclonus body disease. In: *Pathology of the Nervous System*, *Vol. 1*, p. 1121. Editor: J. Minckler. McGraw-Hill, New York.

74. MILLER, J. H. D. and NEILL, D. W. (1959): Serum mucoprotein in progressive myoclonus epilepsy (a preliminary report). *Epilepsia (Amst.)*, *1*, 115.

75. MATTHEWS, W. B., HOWELL, D. A. and STEVENS, D. L. (1969): Progressive myoclonus epilepsy without Lafora bodies. *J. Neurol. Neurosurg. Psychiat.*, *32*, 116.

76. PEARCE, L. A., JANEWAY, R., RAVENS, J. R., ODOR, D. L. and SUZUKI, K. (1965): Lafora's disease. *Trans. Amer. neurol. Ass.*, *90*, 102.

77. LOWENTHAL, A. (1965): Clinical and biochemical study of epilepsy. *Epilepsia (Amst.)*, *6*, 198.

78. JACOBS, J. (1965): Myoclonus and ataxia occurring in a family *J. Neurol. Neurosurg. Psychiat.*, *28*, 272.

79. GILBERT, A. J., McENTEE, W. J. and GLASSER, G. M. (1963): Familial myoclonus and ataxia: pathophysiologic implications. *Neurology (Minneap.)*, *13*, 365.

80. MAY, D. L. and WHITE, H. H. (1968): Familial myoclonus cerebellar ataxia and deafness. *Arch. Neurol. (Chic.)*, *19*, 331.

81. SIEDLER, H. and MALAMUD, H. (1963): Creutzfeldt-Jakob disease: clinicopathologic report of 15 cases and review of the literature (with special reference to a related disorder designated as subacute spongiform encephalopathy). *J. Neuropath. exp. Neurol.*, *22*, 381.

82. TASSINARI, C. A., ROGERS, J., REGIS, H., SEDAN, R. et al. (1971): The action of myoclonus in dyssynergia cerebellaris myoclonica of Ramsay-Hunt syndrome and in Lance-Adams syndrome. *Electroenceph. clin. Neurophysiol.*, *31*, 410.

83. SKREE, H. and LOOKEN, A. C. (1970): Myoclonus epilepsy and subacute presenile dementia in heredoataxia. *Acta neurol. scand.*, *46*, 18.

84. NOAD, K. B. and LANCE, W. J. (1960): Familial myoclonic epilepsy and its association with cerebellar disturbance. *Brain*, *83*, 618.

85. GREENFIELD, J. A. (1954): *The Spinocerebellar Degenerations*, p. 79. Blackwell, Oxford.

86. BRADSHAW, J. (1954): A study of myoclonus. *Brain*, *77*, 138.

87. BONDUELLE, M. (1968): The myoclonus. In: *Handbook of Clinical Neurology*, *Vol. 6*. Editors: P. J. Vinken and G. W. Bruyn. North Holland Publishing Co., Amsterdam.

88. GOLDHAMMER, V., BUBIS, J. J., SAROVA-PINHAS, I. and BRAHAM, J. (1972): Subacute spongiform encephalopathy and its relation to Jakob-Creutzfeldt disease. *J. Neurol. Neurosurg. Psychiat.*, *35*, 1.

89. NEVIN, S., McMENEMY, W. H., BEHRMAN, S. and JONES, D. P. (1960): Subacute spongiform – a subacute form of encephalopathy attributed to vascular dysfunction

(spongiform cerebral atrophy). *Brain, 83,* 519.

90. VAN ROSSUM, O. (1968): Creutzfeldt-Jakob disease. In: *Handbook of Clinical Neurology, Vol. 6,* p. 726. Editors: P. J. Vinken and G. W. Bruyn. North Holland Publ. Co., Amsterdam.

91. FISCHER, C. M. (1960): The clinical picture in Creutzfeldt-Jakob disease. *Trans. Amer. neurol. Ass., 85,* 147.

92. FOLEY, J. M. and DENNY-BROWN, D. (1957): Subacute progressive encephalopathy with bulbar myoclonus. *J. Neuropath. exp. Neurol.,* 16, 133.

93. MCMENEMY, W. H. and NEVIN, S. (1955): Subacute cerebral degeneration in myoclonus epilepsy. *Excerpta Med. (Amst.), Sect. VIII,* 780.

94. PALLIS, L. A. and SPILLANE, J. D. (1957): A subacute progressive encephalopathy mutism hyperkinesia, rigidity, and myoclonus. *Quart. J. Med., 26,* 349.

95. BIGNAME, A. and FORNO, L. S. (1970): Electron microscopic study of cortical biopsy. *Brain, 9,* 89.

96. KIRSCHBAUM, W. R. (1968): *Creutzfeldt-Jakob Disease.* Elsevier Publ. Co., New York.

97. KIRSCHBAUM, W. R. (1968): *Creutzfeldt-Jakob Disease in Pathology of the Nervous System,* pp. 1410-1419. Editor: J. Minckler. McGraw-Hill, New York.

98. LAMPERT, P. W., GAJDUSEK, D. C. and GIBBS, C. J. (1972): Subacute spongiform virus encephalopathy. *Amer. J. Path., 68,* 627.

99. GAJDUSEK, D. C., GIBBS, C. J. and ALPERS, M. (1968): Experimental transmission of kuru-like syndrome to chimpanzee. *Nature (Lond.), 209,* 794.

100. GIBBS, C. J., JR. and GAJDUSEK, D. C. (1969): Infection as aetiology of spongiform encephalopathy of Jakob-Creutzfeldt disease. *Science, 165,* 1023.

101. GIBBS, C. J., JR., ASHER, D. M., ALPERS, W. D., BECK, E., DANIEL, P. H. and MATTHEWS, W. D. (1968): Creutzfeldt-Jakob disease (spongiform encephalopathy). Transmission to the chimpanzee. *Science, 161,* 388.

102. NEVIN, S. (1967): On some aspects of cerebral degeneration in late life. *Proc. roy. Soc. Med., 60,* 516.

103. BECK, E., DANIEL, P. M., MATTHEWS, W. D., STEVENS, D. L., ALPER, M. P., ASHER, D. M., GAJDUSEK, D. C. and GIBBS, C. J. (1969): Creutzfeldt-Jakob disease: the neuropathy of a transmissible experiment. *Brain, 92,* 699.

104. ABRAHAM, J. (1971): Jakob-Creutzfeldt disease: treatment by amantadine. *Brit. med. J., 1,* 212.

105. VERNON, M. L., HORTA-BARBOSA, L., FUCILLO, D. A., SEVER, J. L., BARINGER, J. R. and BIRNBAUM, G. (1970): Virus-like particles and nucleoprotein type filament in brain tissue from two patients with Creutzfeldt-Jakob disease. *Lancet, 1,* 964.

106. MAY, W. W. (1968): Creutzfeldt-Jakob disease. *Acta psychiat. scand., 44,* 1.

107. DENNY-BROWN, D. (1968): Clinical symptomatology of disease of basal ganglia. In: *Handbook of Clinical Neurology, Vol. 6,* p. 165. Editors: P. J. Vinken and G. W. Bruyn. North Holland Publ. Co., Amsterdam.

108. RAPIN, I. and SCHEINBERG, L. (1968): Neuronal storage disorder starting in childhood. *Trans. Amer. neurol. Ass., 93,* 145.

109. SEITELBERGER, F. (1961): Sonderformen zerebraler Lipidosen, histochemische und histologische Befunden. In: *Proceedings, IV International Congress of Neuropathology, München, Vol. I,* p. 3. Editor: H. Jacob. Georg Thieme, Stuttgart.

110. SJODGREN, J. (1931): Die juvenile amaurotische Idiotie. Klinische und erblich-keitsmedizinische Untersuchungen. *Hereditas (Lund), 14,* 197.

111. WESTPHAL, A. and SIOLI, F. (1925): Einschlusse in den Ganglienzellen (Corpora amylacea) ausgezeichneten Fall von Myoclonus-Epilepsie. *Arch. Psychiat. Nervenkr., 73,* 145.

112. EDGER, G. W. F. and POST, P. J. (1963): Amaurotic idiocy and epilepsy. *Epilepsia (Amst.)*, 4, 241.

113. GONATAS, N. K., TERRY, R. D. and WINKLER, R. (1963): A case of juvenile lipidosis, significance of electron microscopic and biochemical observations of a cerebral biopsy. *J. Neuropath. exp. Neurol.*, 22, 557.

114. O'BRIEN, J. S., STERN, M. B., LANDING, B. H., O'BRIEN, J. K. and DONELL, G. (1965): Generalized gangliosidosis, another inborn error of metabolism. *Amer. J. Dis. Child.*, 109., 338.

115. O'BRIEN, J. S. (1969): Five gangliosidoses. *Lancet*, 1, 805.

116. O'BRIEN, J. S. (1969): Generalized gangliosidosis. *J. Pediat.*, 75, 167.

117. MENKES, J., O'BRIEN, J. S., OKADA, S., GRIPPO, G., ANDRES, J. M. and CINCILLA, P. A. (1971): Juvenile GM_2-gangliosidosis: biochemical and ultrastructural studies on a new variety of tsd. *Arch. Neurol. (Chic.)*, 25, 14.

118. SUZUKI, K., SUZUKI, K., RAPIN, SUZUKI, Y. and ISHI, N. (1970): Juvenile GM_2-gangliosidosis. *Neurology (Minneap.)*, 20, 190.

119. DERRY, D. M., FAWCETT, J., ANDERMANN, F. and WOLFE, L. S. (1968): Late infantile systemic lipidosis. *Neurology (Minneap.)*, 18, 340.

120. SUZUKI, Y. and SUZUKI, K. (1970): Partial deficiency of hexosaminidase A in juvenile GM_2-gangliosidosis. *Neurology (Minneap.)*, 20, 848.

121. SCHNECK, L., FRIEDLAND, J., POURFAR, M., SAIFER, A. and VOLK, B. W. (1970): Hexosaminidase activities in a case of systemic GM_2-gangliosidosis of late infantile type (34613). *Proc. Soc. exp. Biol. N.Y.*, 133, 997.

122. OKADA, S. and O'BRIEN, J. S. (1968): Generalized gangliosidosis b-galactosidase deficiency. *Science*, 160, 1002.

123. OKADA, S. and O'BRIEN, J. S. (1969): Tay-Sachs disease: generalized absence of a b-d-n-acetyl hexosaminidase component. *Science*, 165, 698.

124. OKADA, S., VEATH, M. L. and O'BRIEN, J. S. (1970): Juvenile GM_2-gangliosidosis, partial deficiency of hexosaminidase A. *Pediatrics*, 77, 1063.

125. PITZ, H., SANDHOFF, K. and JATZKEWITZ, G. (1966): A disorder of ganglioside metabolism with storage of ceramide lactoside, monosialoceramide lactoside and and tsd ganglioside in brain. *J. Neurochem.*, 13, 1273.

126. SANDHOFF, K., ANDREAE, U. and JATZKEWITZ, G. (1968): Deficient hexosaminidase activity in an exceptional case of Tay-Sachs disease with additional storage of kidney globoside in visceral organ. *Life Sci.*, 7, 283.

127. DAM, M. and MOLLER. E. (1968): Myoclonus epilepsy. *Acta neurol. scand.*, 44, 596.

128. HALLIDAY, A. M. (1969): The clinical incidence of myoclonus. In: *Modern Trends in Neurology*, Vol. 4, p. 69. Editor: D. Williams. Appleton-Century-Crofts, New York.

129. CRAIG, J. M., CLARA, J. J. and BANKER, B. A. (1959): Metabolic neuro-visceral disorder with accumulation of unidentified substance, a variant of Hurler's syndrome. *Amer. J. Dis. Child.*, 98, 577.

130. LANDING, B. H., SILVERMAN, F. N. and CREIG, J. M. (1964): Familial neurovisceral lipidosis. *Amer. J. Dis. Child.*, 108, 503.

131. NORMAN, R. M., URICH, H., TINGLEY, A. H. and GOODBODY, R. A. (1959): Tay-Sachs disease with visceral involvement and its relationship to Niemann-Pick disease. *J. Path. Bact.*, 78, 409.

132. BUXTON, P., CUMMINGS, J. N., ELLIS, R. B., LAKE, B. D., MAIR, G. P., ROBERTS, J. R. and YOUNG, E. P. (1972): A case of GM_2-gangliosidosis of late onset. *J. Neurol. Neurosurg. Psychiat.*, 35, 685.

133. SCHNECK, L. (1964): Clinical manifestations of Tay-Sachs disease. In: *Tay-Sachs Disease*, p. 16. Editor: B. W. Volk. Grune and Stratton, New York-London.

134. JERVIS, G. A. (1969): Juvenile amaurotic idiocy. *Amer. J. Dis. Child.*, *97*, 663.

135. VOLK, B. W., WALLACE, B. J., SCHNECK, L. and SAIFER, A. (1964): Late infantile amaurotic family idiocy. *Arch. Path.*, *78*, 488.

136. ZEMAN, W. and DYKEN, P. (1969): Neuronal ceroid lipofuscinosis (Batten's disease) relationship to amaurotic idiocy. *Pediatrics*, *44*, 570.

137. ZEMAN, W. (1970): Historical development of the nosological entity of amaurotic family idiocy. In: *Handbook of Clinical Neurology*, *Vol. 10*, p. 212. Editors: P. J. Vinken and G. W. Bruyn. North Holland Publ. Co., Amsterdam.

138. ZEMAN, W.., DONAHUE, S., DYKEN, P. and GREEN, J. (1970): The neuronal ceroid lipofuscinosis (Batten-Vogt syndrome). In: *Handbook of Clinical Neurology*, *Vol. 10*, p. 588. Editors: P. J. Vinken and G. W. Bruyn. North Holland Publ. Co., Amsterdam.

139. RYAN, G. B., ANDERSON, R. M., MENKES, J. A. et al. (1970): Lipofuscin (ceroid) storage disease of the brain. Neuropathological and neurochemical studies. *Brain*, *93*, 617.

140. GONATES, N. K., KOREY, S. R. and TERRY, R. D. (1964): A case of juvenile lipidosis, electron microscopic and biochemical observations of cerebral biopsy. *J. Neuropath. exp. Neurol.*, *23*, 185.

141. Editorial (1973): Amaurotic family idiocy. *Lancet*, *1*, 469.

142. TITTRELLI, R. and SPADETTA, V. (1966): Typical ophthalmological picture of cherry red spot in an adult with myoclonus epilepsy. *Brit. J. Ophthal.*, *50*, 414.

143. BOEHME, D. H., COTTRELL, J. C., LEONBERG, S. C. and ZEMAN, W. (1971): A dominant form of neuronal ceroid lipofuscinosis. *Brain*, *94*, 745.

144. PAMPIGLIONE, G. and HARDEN, A. (1973): Neurophysiological identification of a late infantile form of neuronal lipidosis. *J. Neurol. Neurosurg. Psychiat.*, *36*, 68.

145. CARPENTER, S., KARPATI, G. and ANDERMAN, F. (1972): Specific involvement of muscle, nerve and skin in late infantile and juvenile amaurotic idiocy. *Neurology (Minneap.)*, *22*, 170.

146. KELLY, R. E. and LAURENCE, D. R. (1955): Treatment of progressive myoclonic epilepsy with mephenesin. *Brit. med. J.*, *1*, 456.

147. SCHMIDT, R. P. and WILDER, B. T. (1968): *Epilepsy*. Contemporary Neurology Series, F. A. Davis Co., Philadelphia.

Infectious diseases associated with myoclonus

DONALD F. FARRELL and PHILLIP D. SWANSON

Division of Neurology,
University of Washington School of Medicine,
Seattle, Wash., U.S.A.

Myoclonic movements may appear as prominent symptoms of certain infectious diseases of the central nervous system. It is clear that myoclonus is a non-specific occurrence, having many non-infectious causes including hypoxia, uremia, and degenerative diseases.[1]

Nevertheless, when an otherwise healthy person develops myoclonic jerks without known precipitating factors, an infectious cause is very likely. In this chapter we will discuss acute infectious diseases associated with myoclonus, and two chronic disorders which are very likely to be due to 'slow virus' infections of the nervous system and which often feature myoclonus as part of the clinical picture.

EXPERIMENTAL MYOCLONUS PRODUCED BY TRANSMISSIBLE AGENTS

Luttrell et al.[2,3,4] injected Newcastle disease virus into cats and produced repetitive myoclonic movements in head, neck or limbs, the pattern depending on the route of administration. Newcastle disease virus is an epizootic infection of chickens that causes encephalomyelitis in pigeons, turkeys, ducks and some wild birds when administered orally, by aerosol or parenterally. Mammals including mice, rats, cats and monkeys, are also susceptible to the virus especially when injected intracerebrally. Kittens are more easily infected than adult cats, the kittens being more susceptible to intranasal and intraocular injection of the virus. Three to 4 days following intracerebral inoculation, encephalitis develops with fever, myoclonus, in some instances extensor spasms and seizures, weakness of limbs and death within 24-48 hours. Detectable mental changes are exceptional and consciousness is usually preserved until terminal stages. Pathological changes of perivascular cuffing, focal and diffuse inflammatory changes and glial nodules are most prominent in the brainstem tegmentum and in the midzones and anterior horns of spinal cord. The cerebral cortex usually appears normal except for lesions in the olfactory cortex in animals inoculated intranasally.

Clinically, the involuntary myoclonic movements of animals infected with Newcastle virus are usually repetitive, rather regular, with rates varying from 40 to 120 per minute. The rhythm is, however, augmented by auditory stimuli such as a handclap or a metallic tap. The myoclonic movements are usually symmetrical and bilaterally synchronous.

The distribution and evolution of the myoclonic movements depend upon the route of inoculation. When the site of inoculation is intracerebral, intraocular or intranasal, myoclonus first appears in the muscles of the head, neck and forequarters, only subsequently spreading to trunk and hindlimbs. When lower thoracic cord is injected, the hindlimbs are affected first. The segments of brainstem and spinal cord that are infected with virus are capable of sustaining myoclonic movements even when surgically isolated from higher segments by brainstem or spinal cord transection. Thus it is clear that 'all the necessary integrants for development of myoclonus exist at the spinal level...'.[3] A similar statement can be made about experimentally produced tongue myoclonus, which persists when the brainstem is isolated by combined midbrain and high cervical transection.[4]

When myoclonus produced by Newcastle disease virus becomes generalized, the generalization of the movements does not necessarily imply that the viral infection has itself become widely disseminated. In Luttrell's experiments, after intraspinal inoculation, histological evidence of inflammation was only found in the injected segments during early stages of myoclonus. Myoclonus in limbs remote from the injected areas was abolished by midthoracic spinal cord transection. That is, after cervical spinal cord inoculation of virus had produced myoclonus in forelimbs followed by hindlimbs, thoracic cord transection abolished the hindlimb movements but had no effect on forelimb movements. The converse was also true in animals with injections into lumbar cord, where forelimb movements were abolished by thoracic cord transection. These experiments strongly imply that generalization of myoclonic movements can occur without widespread dissemination of the initiating pathogenetic factor.

The above-mentioned experiments of Luttrell's group have been of most significance in focusing attention on the possible sites of involvement in myoclonus associated with encephalomyelitis. It is of interest that some of these findings were anticipated a century ago in studies with dogs infected with a naturally occurring viral illness. Some scholarly research by Breazile et al.[5] uncovered early work by Chauvau, Gowers and others[6,7] showing that involuntary jerks in dogs, called at one time canine chorea and associated with canine distemper, persist in spite of transection of the spinal cord. Additional examples of canine distemper myoclonus were discussed by Breazile et al.[5] who observed the effects on the rate and intensity of the movements of (1) spinal cord transection between the last thoracic and first lumbar segments; (2) section of all dorsal roots caudad to the spinal cord transection; and (3) sequential section of each spinal cord segment caudad to the initial transection. The contractions in canine distemper myoclonus occur in rather regular bursts at rates between 60 and 80 per minute. Barbiturate anesthesia may reduce the rate but movements persist even at surgical levels of anesthesia. Hindlimb myoclonus actually increases in rate and intensity following spinal cord transection. Dorsal root section has no effect on myoclonic activity in the lumbar-innervated muscles, though activity in sacral segments did diminish after sacral root section combined with isolation of sacral spinal cord.

The aforementioned experimental studies have clearly shown that virus-induced myoclonic movements of the rhythmic variety can originate at spinal cord or brainstem levels. Information as to the physiological mechanism by which the movements are produced awaits further joint neurophysiological and neuro-virological studies. Techniques are now available for studying membrane properties of anterior horn cells and these have been applied to penicillin-induced myoclonic movements.[8,9]

VIRAL ENCEPHALOMYELITIS IN HUMANS

Encephalomyelitis is one of the illnesses most frequently associated with acute generalized myoclonic movements. A viral etiology may or may not be proved in the individual case. Even when proof is lacking, the acute appearance of generalized myoclonus in the absence of a known metabolic cause may, for some observers, suffice for the presumptive diagnosis of viral encephalomyelitis.[10]

Rhythmic myoclonus

The myoclonic movements of viral etiology are frequently rhythmic and, there-fore, resemble the movements produced in animals by Newcastle disease virus. This characteristic has prompted French workers to use the term 'clonismes' to distinguish them from the arrhythmic, asynergic jerks that occur in other dis-orders such as the progressive myoclonus epilepsy of Unverricht.[11] Rhythmic myoclonus of neck, limbs, face or trunk occurred in cases of encephalitis lethar-gica[12] but is clearly not confined to this type of encephalitis. A representative case history of virus-associated myoclonus is extracted from a previous report (Case 4, Ref. 1):

A 19 year old woman developed an upper respiratory infection several days after her husband and 15 month old infant had had similar mild transitory symptoms. She complained of severe frontal headache for 2 to 3 days, and then became restless and agitated. Two days later she developed auditory hallucinations, became febrile and had 3 generalized convulsions. On admission to the hospital, her temperature was 102°F. She was stuporous and her neck was rigid.

There were repetitive forceful muscular contractions of both eyelids, both arms and left leg. In the upper extremities the movements were characterized by strong flexion and external rotation of hand, forearm and arm. In the leg, they consisted of pronator-extensor spasms. Later the movements spread to involve tongue, jaw, trunk and remaining leg. They were generally synchronous, with a rate varying between 60 and 100 per minute. Diphenylhydantoin and phenobarbital had no effect on the movements which were, however, reduced in forcefulness but not in frequency by 5 to 12 ml of paraldehyde.

The cerebrospinal fluid contained 85 mononuclear cells and 16 mg/100 ml of protein. Serum agglutinations were negative for psittacosis, St. Louis encephalitis, mumps, lymphocytic choriomeningitis, eastern and western equine encephalitis, influenza, rickettsial pox, Rocky Mountain spotted fever and typhus. The elec-troencephalogram showed some diffuse slowing but no seizure discharges.

The patient died on the 8th hospital day following a rise in temperature. Autopsy showed consolidation of all lobes of the lung. Microscopic sections of brain revealed some polymorphonuclear cells in the superficial cortical vessels, and slight perivascular cuffing in a few brainstem vessels. Neurons in basal ganglia and brainstem were pale with clumping of Nissl substance.

Comment This 19 year old patient developed rhythmic myoclonus during the course of a febrile illness. The clinical picture and autopsy findings were compatible with a viral encephalomyelitis, though no specific serological etiology was found.

The characteristics of the rhythmic myoclonus due to a presumed virus infection were analyzed by Silfverskiöld[10] in 3 patients, aged 8 to 16 years. In no case were electroencephalographic abnormalities found that corresponded to the myoclonic jerks. The frequencies of the myoclonic jerks ranged from about 15 per minute to 70 or 80 per minute. During active or passive movements or during other activities involving attention, irregularly prolonged intervals appeared between myoclonic contractions. For example, one patient was able by the act of writing to suppress for 20 seconds the myoclonic jerks which normally occurred about 50 times per minute. The myoclonus disappeared not only from the right arm but was also absent from all extremities. However, the movements persisted during fist contraction, but diminished in amplitude of contractions when she relaxed.

When muscles in several limbs are involved, the myoclonic contractions in the different extremities are not necessarily synchronous. Case 1 of Silfverskiöld[10] usually had contractions that alternated in right and left arm and right and left leg. Electromyographic recording of Case 2 showed synchronous contractions in the muscles of a single limb, however. The EMG showed bursts of action potentials lasting 0.1 to 0.4 seconds and sometimes up to 2 seconds, correlating with irregularity in the intensity and duration of the contractions.

A variable distribution of rhythmic myoclonus is also common. One of Silfverskiöld's cases had contractions most marked in muscles of the neck, possibly indicating a segmental involvement of cervical spinal cord, while many patients will have myoclonus predominantly of the limbs. Case 5 of Swanson et al.[1] exhibited contractions of left leg, jaw and left abdominal muscles.

To close this section, it should be pointed out that the rhythmic type of myoclonus discussed above may occur in other pathological conditions. Garcin et al.[13] described a patient with an astrocytoma of the cervical spinal cord who developed 10-15 per second myoclonic jerks of muscles of the right arm and right diaphragm. The myoclonic movements were similar to those described in encephalomyelitis, though more sharply segmental. Finally, the rhythmic type of movement usually termed palatal myoclonus, which usually results from a defined structural lesion of brainstem or cerebellum, has not been discussed because of the infrequency of infectious causes of this movement disorder.

Opsoclonus

This term refers to rapid oscillations of the eyes, which resemble nystagmoid movements in being usually conjugate, but which differ from nystagmus in being more abrupt, coming in bursts and sometimes described as 'violent' and 'chaotic'.[14]

The term 'opsoclonus' was used by Orzechowski[15] to describe eye movements that occurred in patients with encephalitis. By 1960, 16 cases had been documented in the literature, though this number undoubtedly underestimates the frequency of the occurrence of the phenomenon.

The presence of opsoclonus in viral encephalitis has been suggested to indicate direct involvement by the infecting agent of brainstem structures.[1] Though it is true that most patients with opsoclonus have generalized myoclonic jerks, it is difficult to conceive of conjugate eye movements arising from structures caudal to the brainstem vestibular system. It is not so easy to dismiss supratentorial structures involved in conjugate eye movements as possible sites of involvement. The autopsied case of Cogan[16] who had opsoclonus and generalized myoclonic jerks had inflammation in hypothalamus, midbrain and pons with normal cerebral cortex and basal ganglia.

Opsoclonus is most often seen in young adults or children. Commonly there is a prodromal upper respiratory infection for several days followed by fever, headache, malaise and the onset of eye movements.[17] It is unusual for the ocular oscillations to occur in isolation, since most patients develop other motor abnormalities, including severe truncal ataxia, or truncal jerks, described as 'coarse movements of the head, trunk and limbs that are continuous so long as the patient is sitting or standing but are absent while the patient is recumbent... They have features resembling chorea, truncal ataxia, and myoclonus and are sometimes so bizarre as to suggest hysteria'.[17] It is interesting that limb ataxia is usually absent and the patients are often otherwise neurologically intact. Because of the acute nature of the illness, the other associated symptoms suggesting an infectious etiology and the frequent presence of mononuclear cells in the cerebrospinal fluid,[18] the etiology of the syndrome is usually thought to be viral. Baringer et al.[18] suggested the possible localization of the pathological process to be in the region of the cerebellar vermis.

Opsoclonus can occur in infancy in association with ataxia and myoclonic jerking of the limbs. An example of this syndrome in a 2 year old child was described as follows:[19]

> 'Constant involuntary conjugate eye movements occurred in rapid bursts, irregularly, and in various directions. Amplitude varied from jelly-like oscillations to jerks of up to 30°. Vertical movements were slower than horizontal, and at times, one globe appeared to move faster than the other. Complex patterns of vertical and horizontal movements presented a chaotic appearance. The lids fluttered and blinked much of the time. The bursts of eye movements and head shaking resembled a photomyoclonic response.'

In this case, the myoclonic symptoms began a week following a febrile illness and progressed. The movements did not begin to subside until 4 years had passed.

It should be pointed out that this syndrome is sometimes included under the category of acute cerebellar ataxia which usually occurs in childhood. In the series of Weiss and Carter[20], 7 of 18 children had violent tremors, involving head and neck and, to a lesser degree, the extremities; 2 had sudden random eye movements and 2 had 'abnormal rhythmic eye movements, nystagmus'.

Etiology of opsoclonus-ataxia syndrome

Though a viral etiology has often been presumed, culture or serological confirmation has usually been lacking. Cases in infancy have been reported in association with tumors, especially neuroblastoma, and an immunological abnormality has been suggested.[21] A 63 year old man with opsoclonus, ataxia and myoclonic jerks of chin, cheeks, shoulders and feet had an occult bronchogenic carcinoma and evidence of chronic inflammatory changes in brainstem.[22] Although reported cases have not demonstrated opsoclonus or myoclonus, infection with *Mycoplasma pneumoniae* has been found in some cases of acute cerebellar ataxia,[23] so it would seem reasonable to include serologic diagnosis of infection with this organism in evaluation of patients with acute myoclonus.

Segmental origin of myoclonus in encephalomyelitis

The experimental work on encephalomyelitis and the association of segmental myoclonus of a limb with spinal cord tumor is convincing evidence that myoclonic movements, particularly those with rhythmicity, can arise at spinal cord level. The evidence is less convincing that the myoclonic movements of the limbs associated with a viral infection always arise from the spinal level. The 3 cases of Campbell and Garland[24] are often cited as proof that myoclonic movements of the legs can result from localized viral infection of spinal cord. The problem with Campbell and Garland's cases is the possible additional role of radiotherapy in the production of the movements. Case 1 received approximately 1,000 r to the middorsal and cervical spine 2 months prior to the onset of contractions of legs, chest and sternomastoid muscles. Case 3 also received a course of deep X-ray therapy to the thoracic region 3 months prior to onset of leg twitching. Only Case 2, who developed spasms of the abdominal muscles during an acute illness associated with a normal cerebrospinal fluid, had not received radiation therapy. Pathological examinations were carried out in cases 1 and 3, where inflammatory changes in spinal cord were found in appropriate areas. While supporting the concept that myoclonus can arise at the spinal level, the possible role of X-ray damage makes the role of viral myelitis uncertain in these cases.

Prognosis of myoclonus

The prognosis of encephalomyelitis associated with myoclonus is very variable, ranging from very benign[17,18] to fatal (Cases 4 and 5 of Ref. 1). If the patient survives the acute illness, chances appear to be excellent that the myoclonic jerks will regress or disappear altogether. The movements may disappear within days or a few weeks as the acute illness subsides (Case 6 of Ref. 1) or they may persist for months before improvement.[10] The acute syndrome of opsoclonus and truncal myoclonus also appears to have an excellent prognosis, with recovery being complete in 2-12 weeks.[18] However, the syndrome of acute cerebellar ataxia of childhood is not always benign, and neurologic deficits have, on rare occasions, persisted for several years.[20]

MYOCLONUS ASSOCIATED WITH 'SLOW-VIRUS' DISEASES

In recent years, several progressive diseases in which involuntary myoclonic movements are a prominent feature, have been shown to be in all likelihood caused by viral infection of the central nervous system. The two conditions to be considered here are Jakob-Creutzfeldt disease and subacute sclerosing panencephalitis (SSPE). In both conditions the anatomical basis for the myoclonus very likely differs from that in acute viral encephalitides since electroencephalographic abnormalities often occur in association with the myoclonic movements.

JAKOB-CREUTZFELDT DISEASE

This rare subacute disease of the nervous system usually progresses to death within a period of months to a very few years after onset. The disease usually affects middle to older age individuals and causes a constellation of signs and symptoms referable to widespread dysfunction of the central nervous system. Dementia, other disorders of higher cortical function, movement disorders, myoclonus, ataxia, and amyotrophy are found in variable proportions in these patients. Myoclonic jerks are often a prominent feature, especially in late stages of the disease. Over the past 50 years, many individual cases and small series of patients have been reported. Many of these reports have attempted to define separate clinico-pathologic entities, the result of which has led to some confusion. Authors writing in more recent times have tended to group the various clinical subtypes into a single disease entity, namely Jakob-Creutzfeldt disease. This recent trend will be adhered to for this review.

Historical background

In 1920, H. G. Creutzfeldt[25] reported a 23 year old female who had a progressive neurologic course over a period of 7 years. The patient's symptoms started with gait difficulty at age 16. By the age of 20 years, she also had mental changes. She continued to show progression of her clinical state over the next 3 years to the point that she was severely demented and demonstrated ataxia, myoclonus, paresis, 'pathologic' reflexes, and seizures. Four months before she died, continuous fluttering of facial muscles was noted as well as tic-like twitches of the arms. At times twitches were more marked in the upper extremities and face, at times more in the legs. In her last month, she exhibited movements that were rapid and 'blitzartig', sometimes followed by a period of increased tone and felt to represent cortical seizure activity. At autopsy, this patient's brain revealed enlarged lateral ventricles. Microscopically, there was disappearance of ganglion cells of the cortex, thalamus, dentate nucleus, and grey matter of the spinal cord. Neuronal chromatolysis was a prominent cellular alteration and there was microglial proliferation. Reactive gliosis and status spongiosus were not described. The author commented on the similarities of this case to that of the 'pseudosclerosis' of Westphal-Strumpell.

The following year, Jakob[26,27] described 3 further cases, 2 of whom showed involuntary movements towards the end of their disease. The first patient exhibited trembling movements of arms and hands, resembling chorea. The second had tic-like movements beginning in the right orbicularis oculi, later involving the left side of the face and accompanied by grinding of the teeth. The third case showed no involuntary twitches and had a great deal of muscular atrophy. Later, Jakob[28] added 2 more cases and gave a rather complete clinical and pathological description of this disease. In addition to the description of the neuronal changes in specific areas of the brain and spinal cord, Jakob noted marked proliferation of reactive glial cells in those regions of the nervous system which showed neuronal alterations. Like Creutzfeldt before him, Jakob related the similarities of his cases to the 'pseudosclerosis' of Westphal-Strumpell and named this specific disease spastic pseudosclerosis.

In 1929, Heidenhain[29] reported 3 new cases, 2 of whom had either cortical blindness or a visual agnosia as one of their major symptoms. Myoclonus developed during the course but the visual symptoms dominated the clinical picture. In addition to reporting these clinical variants, this author described the microscopic spongiosis of the cerebral cortex. Although Heidenhain related his 3 cases to those previously reported by Jakob, certain subsequent authors have attempted to separate the visual form into a separate syndrome. In this same year, 1929, A. Meyer[30] described a 55 year old male who presented clinically with a syndrome closely resembling amyotrophic lateral sclerosis, but in addition had significant dementia as an early part of his disease. This author proposed a classification consisting of two types: one resembling amyotrophic lateral sclerosis and the other resembling the presenile dementias.

It was S. A. K. Wilson[31] who proposed the topographic term 'cortico-striato-spinal' degeneration and criticized the choice of the earlier designations of this disease: spastic pseudosclerosis and 'cortico-pallido-spinal' degeneration. His criticisms of the earlier designations were based on the following: " 'pseudosclerosis' itself is a worthless term, having nothing to commend it; hence tacking on of the adjective 'spastic' merely adds confusion, for it irrationally mixes clinical and pathological notions (under no circumstances can a 'sclerosis' be 'spastic'), apart from the fact that the syndrome has nothing whatever to do with hepato-lenticular disease." Wilson's criticism of the use of 'cortico-pallido-spinal' degeneration was based on the improper use of the term 'pallido' since the "striatal lesions are not confined to globus pallidus."

Clinical features — general

1. Incidence The incidence and prevalence of Jakob-Creutzfeldt disease has not been established for any population to date. Part of the difficulty in establishing either of these parameters is possibly due to the lack of recognition of this disease by physicians and also to the relative lack of agreement even among experts as to what constitutes Jakob-Creutzfeldt disease. About 200 cases have now been reported in the literature, but these reports usually come from very specialized centers dealing with diseases of the nervous system and in no measurable way reflect the true frequency of this disease.

2. Age of onset About 90% of the reported cases of this disease have had the clinical onset of symptoms during the 4th, 5th, and 6th decades of life. A smattering of cases have been reported in both younger and older individuals; the youngest of whom was 16 years of age while the oldest was 79 years.

3. Sex distribution Of the 6 initial cases reported by Jakob and Creutzfeldt, 4 were women and 2 men. In a recent review by Van Rossum[32] in 1967, there again was an excess of females (63:52). In a review of the pathologically proven cases in the literature, May[33] found an equal distribution of males to females (68 : 69).

4. Familial cases The famous Backer family has been demonstrated to have had multiple family members affected over at least two generations.[34,35,36] A second well-studied family (Family B) has been described,[37] in which 3 sisters developed clinical and pathologic changes consistent with Jakob-Creutzfeldt disease. The familial nature of this second family is not as convincing as the Backer family, since it is based on historical evidence that the father suffered from the same disease, although he had never been examined either clinically or pathologically. The inheritance pattern of this disease in these two families has been reported to be consistent with a simple autosomal dominant gene. The role of a dominant genetic inheritance pattern for Jakob-Creutzfeldt disease is still open to considerable doubt in view of the more recent finding that the disease can be transmitted to subhuman primates (see section on transmission experiments).

5. Duration of illness About 65% of the pathologically proven cases are fatal within 1 year, while about 90% prove fatal in under 2 years. The extremes of survival are from less than 1 month to more than 6 years.

Clinical features — neurologic manifestations

The neurologic manifestations in any given case of Jakob-Creutzfeldt disease appear to result from a number of related factors. The variability of each of these factors determines the clinical subgroup (see below) into which the patient falls. Some of the factors responsible for the clinical subgroups include: (1) the anatomical sites of the brain and spinal cord first affected; (2) the rate of progression of the disease to other anatomical areas; (3) the length of time the patient has had symptoms prior to being seen by his physician; (4) the stage in the illness when the patient becomes comatose; and (5) the length of time the patient survives his illness. Three stages in the course of the disease have been described:[38,39,40] (1) the initial or prodromal stage; (2) middle or full stage; and (3) advanced or terminal stage.

1. Initial stage The onset is usually insidious and the great majority of patients have reported rather vague symptoms including anxiety, fear, depression, lack of concentration, emotional slowness, easy fatigability, sleeplessness, euphoria, loquacity, boastfulness, poorly described difficulties with gait and speech, and many other non-specific complaints. In the older literature, many of the patients who were seen during this stage of their illness were diagnosed as having a functional psychiatric illness. Fisher[40] noted that most of his patients had at least 3 or 4 of the following signs and symptoms when first seen by a physician: forgetfulness, 'dizziness', disturbances of gait, ease of startle, clumsiness of a limb, impaired vision, hallucinations, cerebellar ataxia, twitching or insomnia. The length of this initial stage may be quite variable, but most patients progress to the next stage in a matter of weeks.

2. *Middle stage*   As Fisher[40] pointed out, this stage can be an admixture of almost every unilateral or bilateral cortical or cerebral disturbance ever described. It is the myriad of symptoms and signs that occur in this stage that led to a variety of classifications and subclassifications of Jakob-Creutzfeldt disease.

Alemá and Bignami[41] classified Jakob-Creutzfeldt disease into five clinical types: amyotrophic, myoclonic, transitional, dyskinetic, and amaurotic; while Garcin et al.[42] proposed the following classification also based on clinical symptoms: 'classic' form of Jakob-Creutzfeldt, and amyotrophic, thalamic, amaurotic and subacute spongiform encephalopathic forms. Both of these proposed clinical classifications are based on a fairly rigid and static view of a single or at most a few clinical symptoms to separate the various types. In actuality, the disease process is not static, but progressive. Using the rigid classifications when new symptoms may come to the fore, the patient would then have to change from one clinical type to another.

Case report
This 47 year old man, Case 6 of Table 1, was admitted to hospital on December 14, 1971, with a history of progressive right hemiparesis of 1 month duration. His wife noted that during this same time he had frequent brief little jerks of his right hand. At this time, the patient had a slight drift with pronation of the right arm and impaired coordination of the fingers when attempting to do repetitive finger movements. Proprioception was reduced in the right great toe. The cerebrospinal fluid was normal, as was an arteriogram. By December 29, the patient demonstrated alterations in his affect and his mental state was definitely abnormal. Myoclonic movements of the right arm were observed by his physicians for the first time. An electroencephalogram done at this time showed 'diffuse high voltage slowing'. By January 10, a right homonymous hemianopsia was noted and the patient had developed bilateral spasticity and myoclonus. The myoclonus was stimulus sensitive and during periods when the patient was relatively free of these movements they could be elicited by a loud noise or a tap on a tendon with a reflex hammer.
By February 4, the patient was comatose and the myoclonus was more prominent in the left arm and face. On February 8, 1972, a parietal cortex biopsy was performed for histology and electron microscopy. Frozen samples were sent to the National Institute of Neurological Diseases and Stroke for attempts to transmit this disease to subhuman primates.
The patient remained in a comatose state, the myoclonus progressively disappeared, and on May 11, 1972, the patient died.

Table 1 demonstrates the sequence in the development of the various symptoms in 6 pathologically proven cases seen at the University of Washington and affiliated

TABLE I

Clinical summary of 6 verified cases of Jakob-Creutzfeldt disease

Case	Age	Duration (months)	Dementia	Myoclonus	Rigidity and tremor	Ataxia	UMN	LMN	Cortical blindness
1	71	9	1	3	4	1	3	4	2
2	68	14	2	0	0	0	0	1	0
3	66	7	1	2	0	2	3	0	4
4	63	18	–	2	0	0	aphasia(1)	0	2
5	56	3	1	2	3	0	aphasia(1)	0	3
6	47	6	2	1	0	0	1	0	3

Zero (o) indicates no symptoms. The earliest symptom in each case is indicated by the number 1. The numbers 2, 3, and 4 indicate the sequence in the development of subsequent symptoms in each case. Because of a severe aphasia in Case 4, the presence of dementia could not be adequately determined (–).

hospitals over the past few years. The presenting features differed for each given case, but as the disease progressed all of the patients developed dementia and 5 out of 6 of the patients demonstrated the following symptoms at some time during the course of the illness: myoclonus, cortical blindness, other symptoms of cortical damage including aphasia, hemisensory defects, hemiparesis, quadriparesis and concomitant signs of spasticity and reflex changes. Three of these 5 patients also had symptoms and signs referable to lesions of the basal ganglia and cerebellum. Case 2 remained clinically pure and only had dementia and signs of motor neuron disease. While the clinical symptoms and signs were referable to the spinal cord and cerebral cortex, pathologic alterations consisting of neuronal loss with reactive gliosis were noted in the caudate nucleus, putamen, globus pallidus, thalamus, and substantia nigra. Similar pathologic alterations were present in our case with dementia and amyotrophy. It may be that this form represents a specific subtype of Jakob-Creutzfeldt disease, but it is more likely that when the main brunt of the disease affects the anterior horn cells and the descending corticospinal tracts, symptoms which we would expect from lesions of the corpus striatum and cerebellum cannot manifest themselves clinically.

3. Terminal stage After a variable amount of time, different for each given case, the majority of patients with Jakob-Creutzfeldt disease become mute, unresponsive, rigid, with myoclonic jerks, show either 'decorticate' or 'decerebrate' postures and some develop major motor seizures. Again, the length of time that a given patient remains in this terminal phase is somewhat variable. The patient may remain comatose for several months or, rarely, for more than a year.

Clinical features of the myoclonus seen in Jakob-Creutzfeldt disease

Fisher[40] has emphasized the diagnostic significance of an augmented startle reaction as an early sign of this disease and has suggested that this is a manifestation of a stimulus-sensitive myoclonus. While myoclonic activity may be a presenting symptom in patients with this disease, it more commonly occurs during the evolution of the disease. The myoclonic movements themselves may be quite variable in extent from the random, irregular quick movements of muscle fascicles to involvement of the entire body. Frequently, spontaneous myoclonic jerks begin in a single extremity, and with time spread to the face or other extremity on the same side or to the other side. It has frequently been noted that as the myoclonic activity progresses to new areas the movements frequently decrease in the initial area of involvement. During much of the clinical course the myoclonic jerks are stimulus-sensitive and can frequently be elicited by a variety of stimuli including: loud sharp noises, flashing lights, passive movement of a limb, stimulation of the skin with a pin or other sharp object, and by striking a tendon with a reflex hammer. At a time when spontaneous myoclonic activity is limited to a single limb an applied stimulus may bring about generalization to the entire body or more extensive myoclonic activity in other areas of the body which have not previously demonstrated spontaneous myoclonic activity. As the patient progresses (usually in a comatose state at this time), the spontaneous myoclonic activity usually stops and in the terminal stages of the disease can no longer be elicited by sensory stimulation.

Laboratory studies

1. Cerebrospinal fluid   The cerebrospinal fluid is normal in the vast majority of patients with Jakob-Creutzfeldt disease. When abnormalities have been described they have been limited to an increase in the cerebrospinal fluid protein with elevations to 121 mg percent having been reported.[43] Siedler and Malamud[44] in their review found increases in CSF total protein in only 11% of 62 patients and in only 1 case was the value above 100 mg percent.

2. Pneumoencephalogram and arteriogram   The value of these two diagnostic techniques in demonstrating pathologic alterations of the brain would depend greatly upon the stage of the illness when the study was done. Early in the course, one would not be too surprised if the study proved normal, while later in the course these studies would demonstrate ventricular enlargement and cortical atrophy. The majority of cases reported in the literature who were studied with these techniques have shown ventricular enlargement and/or cortical atrophy (either diffuse or limited to specific cortical areas).

3. Electromyography   Those cases demonstrating clinical features of motor neuron disease have been shown to have denervation and fasciculation potentials as well as an increase in the duration and mean voltage of the individual motor action potentials, consistent with anterior horn cell disease.

4. Electroencephalography   Electroencephalographic abnormalities have been described in nearly every case of Jakob-Creutzfeldt disease where an EEG has been recorded. The nature of the abnormalities described in the earlier literature has been inconsistent. Pallis and Spillane[45] described runs of bilateral, synchronous, high voltage polyphasic complexes at a frequency of 2 per second and uninfluenced by sensory stimuli. Lesse et al.[46] described slow spikes and spike-waves at a frequency of about 70-75 per minute; at times myoclonic jerks were associated with these complexes.

Enough cases have now been described who had serial recordings throughout the course of their disease to demonstrate an evolution in EEG pattern as the disease progresses. The earliest changes are limited to the background rhythms. There is gradual and diffuse slowing which is certainly not specific but suggests diffuse dysfunction of the cerebrum. Asymmetries in the background slowing are common and have been emphasized by Pallis and Spillane[45] and Burger et al.[47] The periodicity usually develops late in the illness, but as the rate of the progression of the disease is so variable, this change can occur as early as the second week. When the periodicity first appears it may either be intermittent or continuous. If intermittent, the periodic discharges become constant within a couple of weeks. Myoclonic jerks are frequently seen in association with the periodic discharges, but not invariably so.

At times the myoclonic jerks precede the discharges, at times are synchronous with these discharges, and at other times occur after the discharges. Some of the myoclonic jerks appear synchronous with the well established discharges, but in Fig. 1 recorded from Case 6 in Table 1, there are 2 or more discharges per myoclonic jerk as measured by EMG activity from the left side of the face. Fig. 2 (Feb. 4, 1972) demonstrates the tight coupling of the periodic discharges to flashes which are at a frequency of 1 flash per second, whereas at faster flash

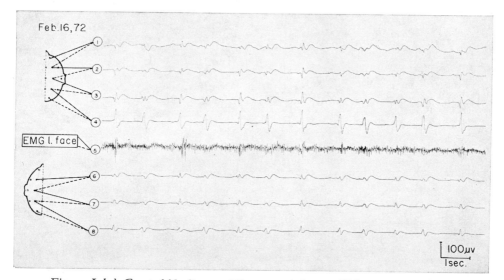

Fig. 1. Jakob-Creutzfeldt disease. Electroencephalogram (Feb. 16, 1972) showing periodic diphasic and triphasic waves; simultaneous electromyogram to record myoclonus. Note that each cortical response is not accompanied by a myoclonic jerk.

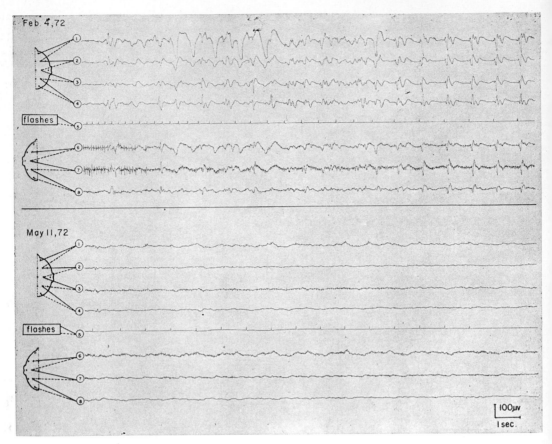

Fig. 2. Jakob-Creutzfeldt disease.   Electroencephalographic tracing dated Feb. 4, 1972,
demonstrates the irregularity of the periodic complexes at fast flash frequencies, but as the flash
frequency approaches 1/sec, there is a one-to-one relationship between the flash and the cortical
response. The background activity ceases as the complexes become regular. Terminal electroen-
cephalogram (May 11, 1972). There is no evidence of either spontaneous or evoked periodic com-
plexes.

frequencies the periodicity is not as regular and does not appear to influence the
timing of the periodicity. Fig. 2 (May 11, 1972) demonstrates the electroencephalogram during the terminal phase of the illness. Electrical brain activity is
difficult to recognize at this stage and flashes had no discernible effect.

In their review of the electroencephalographic characteristics in Jakob-
Creutzfeldt disease, Burger et al.[47] demonstrated the periodicity to be from
0.5 to 1.6 seconds with a mean of 1.0 seconds in 6 patients, and a period which
varied from 2.5 to 4.0 seconds in 1 patient. One further case never developed a
periodic type of discharge, but recordings were not made during the last 2
months of life. While some variation in the shape of the waves occurs, they are
generally described as being triphasic with an average duration of 360 msec and

an average amplitude of 100 μvolts. Suppression of background activity between the periodic discharges is common.

Nelson and Leffman[48] examined the effects of evoked potentials from photic, auditory, and somatosensory stimuli on the electroencephalogram and on the interactions of the stimuli presented in various combinations as well as the effects of certain pharmacologic substances, including amobarbital, pentylene-tetrazole, and chlorpromazine. They concluded that the widespread discharges in Jakob-Creutzfeldt disease were cortical potentials produced by an ascending diffuse projection system from somewhere in the rostral brainstem.

Rayport[49] studied pathologically verified cases of Jakob-Creutzfeldt disease with scalp, pial, and intracerebral recordings. From the surface he recorded high voltage positive-negative waves or triphasic waves occurring at 0.5 to 20 times per second. In white matter the complexes were of lower voltage and of simpler form, whereas in deep nuclear structures (globus pallidus) the discharges were similar to those recorded in the cortex. This was interpreted as demonstrating both cortical and subcortical foci. Lesions in both these regions were felt to be necessary for the periodicity to develop.

At the present time, periodicity of the electroencephalogram is poorly understood. But while this type of EEG pattern has been described rarely in other conditions, including cerebral anoxia, cerebral lipidosis, postictal states, head injury, and acute necrotizing encephalitis, its diagnostic usefulness in Jakob-Creutzfeldt disease should not be underestimated.

Pathology

1. Macroscopic The brain weight varies greatly from case to case. Most brains weigh between 1,100 grams and 1,450 grams while exceptional cases have been reported down to 950 grams. In some cases very little is seen upon gross inspection, while in many other cases cortical atrophy, ventricular enlargement and moderate to severe reductions in the sizes of the caudate, putamen, globus pallidus, and medial thalamus are evident (Fig. 3). In those cases where amyotrophy is present the spinal cord is small and the anterior roots are atrophic.

2. Microscopic The cerebral cortex reveals a severe loss of neurons in a diffuse pattern as well as in a patchy distribution. The cellular changes may involve widespread areas including prefrontal, central temporal, hippocampal, parietal, and occipital cortex. Portions of the basal ganglia, medial thalamus, subthalamic nuclei, midbrain, cerebellum, and spinal cord are all regularly involved. Besides neuronal loss there are frequently cellular alterations in the remaining neurons including shrunken hyperchromatic, broken cells as well as large swollen neurons with marginated Nissl substance and eccentrically-placed dark-staining nuclei. Lipofuscin pigment is frequently noted in these large swollen cells. Marked proliferation of astrocytes is also present and may even be the most striking feature in this disease. In fact, Foley and Denny-Brown[50] considered the marked astrocytosis to be the primary defect in Jakob-Creutzfeldt disease. The astrocytes are of the reactive type with a marked increase in their fibrillary processes.

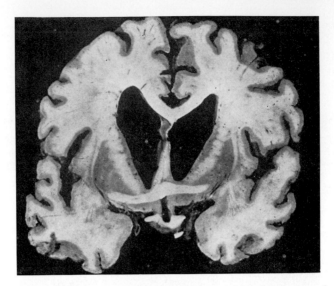

Fig. 3. Jakob-Creutzfeldt disease. This brain demonstrates marked thin-
ning and granular appearing changes of the cerebral cortex, as well as severe atrophy
of the caudate nucleus. The lateral ventricles are markedly enlarged.

Microglial cells are much less abundant and do not seem to play a major role in this disease.

Status spongiosus is present in the majority of cases, but not invariably so (Fig. 4). Microscopic cystic spaces and occasionally gross cystic changes occur in addition to the other cellular changes. These changes are usually found in the middle to deeper cortical layers, but may also be present in the basal ganglia, thalamus, midbrain, and cerebellar nuclei. Prior to electron microscopy, these cysts were thought to occur in the ground substance of the brain.

Senile plaques and Alzheimer's neurofibrillary tangles have usually been absent in Jakob-Creutzfeldt disease, but recently Hirano et al.[51] have described 2 cases which, in addition to the customary changes of Jakob-Creutzfeldt disease, also had far too many senile (argentophilic) plaques and neurofibrillary tangles to be accounted for by the age of the patients. The significance of these findings is difficult to assess since these changes have been so infrequently described in this disease.

Of even more interest have been recent reports of kuru-plaques in the cerebellum of each of 2 patients. One case was reported as a case of Jakob-Creutzfeldt disease with kuru-plaques[52] while the other was reported as a case of kuru in a North American.[53] The kuru-plaque is similar to a senile plaque except that it occurs primarily in the cerebellum, stains strongly with periodic acid Schiff stain, weakly with Congo-Red stain and weakly with argentophilic stains, and can thereby be distinguished from typical senile plaques. Since our present understanding of kuru suggests that it is limited to a single area of the world, it is likely that this change is not as specific for kuru as previously thought (it has

Fig. 4. Jakob-Creutzfeldt disease. Light microscopic picture showing the microcystic changes (status spongiosus) and reactive astrocytosis of the cerebral cortex.

been described in scrapie in sheep) and it now appears to be a rare finding in Jakob-Creutzfeldt disease.

Electron microscopy Examination with electron microscopy of the areas showing status spongiosus has led to a much better understanding of this process. Status spongiosus had been thought to consist of microcysts of the 'ground substance' of the brain. Electron microscopy has clearly demonstrated that these cystic collections are membrane bound and frequently displace organelles from their path. Gonatas et al.[43] demonstrated that the astrocytes are more frequently affected, but were able to show 1 example of a cystic alteration in a presynaptic terminal while the postsynaptic membrane was normal. Bignami and Forno[54] confirmed the cystic alterations in astrocytes and were able to recognize many more examples of cysts in small myelinated axon terminals containing synaptic vesicles. Again, the postsynaptic membrane and process was normal. Fig. 5 is an electronmicrograph of a portion of parietal cortex from a case of Jakob-Creutzfeldt disease. The type of cell or cellular process in which the large cystic structure is present is impossible to recognize, but the smaller cyst is obviously of neuronal origin and most likely represents a dendritic process, for a normal

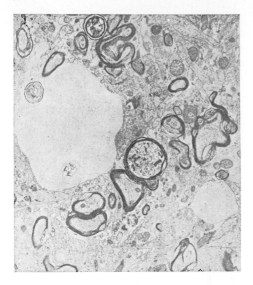

Fig. 5. Jakob-Creutzfeldt disease. Electronmicrograph of status spongiosus demonstrating the membrane bound cystic spaces. Larger cyst is in an unrecognized cell process, but small cyst is in a dendrite. Note the presynaptic terminal with many vesicles abutting the smaller cyst, which has a slightly thickened subsynaptic membrane as part of its wall.

appearing presynaptic terminal abuts the cystic space and upon careful inspection the postsynaptic specialization of the membrane can be recognized in the cyst adjacent to the presynaptic terminal. This is the first description of dendritic involvement by this process. (Full details of these electron-microscopic findings will be reported elsewhere by Sumi, Shaw and Leech.)

Pathologic chemistry Before a viral etiology was suspected, Jakob-Creutzfeldt disease was considered to be a degenerative disease. A number of biochemical and histochemical analyses were carried out with findings that probably reflect the neuronal loss and gliosis that occurs in this disease. Korey et al.[55] found in a formalin-fixed brain a marked reduction in lipids and ganglioside content of gray matter. There was also a less definite increased amount of cerebroside. Suzuki and Chen[56] described the following: the lipid to protein ratio increases as the disease progresses in both gray and white matter. Total lower phase glycolipids increase as the pathological changes advance, while ethanolamine phosphatides decrease and cholesterol remains constant. Gangliosides are severely reduced particularly in morphologically devastated cortical areas. The overall ganglioside pattern is normal. These abnormalities, though more severe, are very similar to those found in Alzheimer's disease.

Histochemical studies[57,58] have demonstrated a marked reduction in a number of cerebral enzymes, including DPN diaphorase, lactic dehydrogenase, enzymes responsible for oxidative metabolism and acetylcholinesterase and monoamine oxidase. It is probable that here, too, a reduction in the staining of these enzyme activities may only reflect a measure of the cellular loss and destruction of the brain in this disease.

Pathogenesis Gibbs et al.[59] reported on the first successful transmission of Jakob-Creutzfeldt disease to the chimpanzee. A 5% homogenate of brain tissue in phosphate buffer, pH 7.4, was utilized for inoculation. Inoculations of 0.2 ml intracerebrally and 0.3 ml intravenously were given to a chimpanzee. There was a latency period of 13 months which was followed by the appearance of a subacute, progressive, non-inflammatory, degenerative brain disease. Subsequently, this same group has transmitted a number of other similar cases to the chimpanzee.[60] Again, there is a latency period of 12-14 months followed by a rapidly progressive mental and neurological disturbance leading to total incapacitation within 2 months after the onset of the illness. To date, a total of 14 cases of Jakob-Creutzfeldt disease have been transmitted to chimpanzees. The pathologic changes in the recipient chimpanzee are identical to those of Jakob-Creutzfeldt disease. Similar histologic findings are noted in all of the transmissible spongiform encephalopathies such as kuru, scrapie, and mink encephalopathy. The transmissible agent is able to pass through a millipore filter of 220 nm and is stable to storage at −70°C. The virus also persists for many months in vitro in tissue culture of human brain cells without losing its virulence for the chimpanzee.[61]

Bots et al.[62] described particles resembling virions in brain biopsies of 2 patients with Jakob-Creutzfeldt disease. These particles were hexagonal having a dense core surrounded by a membrane. They had a diameter of 65-85 nm and were primarily seen in the cytoplasm of astrocytes.

Now that it has been demonstrated that Jakob-Creutzfeldt disease is transmissible, it seems that it will be possible to clarify some of the questions regarding whether the disease is a single entity or a syndrome. To date, careful clinicopathological studies of the cases that have been transmitted to experimental animals have not been reported. It would be of interest to determine if all the supposed clinical subtypes behave in a similar or different manner when transmitted to experimental animals.

SUBACUTE SCLEROSING PANENCEPHALITIS (SSPE)

This progressive encephalitis, probably caused by the measles virus, usually affects children and adolescents. Early mental changes and absence attacks progress to severe mental disturbances, movement disorders, 'myoclonic' jerks, and signs of diffuse neurologic dysfunction. After a variable period of time the patient demonstrates a decorticate posture, is blind, and is without evidence of mental function. Death may occur as early as 6 weeks or as late as 10 years, but the illness proves fatal in the vast majority of patients within 1 year of the onset of symptoms.

History

In 1933, and again in 1934, Dawson[63, 64] reported 2 subacute progressive cases of encephalitis in children from Tennessee. Both had involuntary jerking movements and progressive mental deterioration. The pathology was characterized by Cowdry type A intranuclear inclusions in many cortical neurons. Dawson attempted to transmit the illness to rabbits, mice, guinea pigs, monkeys, dogs and chickens, but with no success. Because of his inability to transmit the disease to experimental animals, Dawson concluded that the encephalitis was not the result of herpes simplex infection. Cases similar to those described by Dawson were reported by Akelaitis and Zeldis[65] and by Brain et al.[66]

In 1945, L. van Bogaert[67] reported 3 cases of what he termed *subacute sclerosing leukoencephalitis*. There was a diffuse inflammatory exudate in the white matter in certain areas of the cerebral hemispheres. There was a slight demyelination and a marked fibrous gliotic reaction of the white matter which was out of proportion to the demyelination. Inflammatory lesions were also noted in the cerebral cortex, thalamus, and brainstem.

Both forms were known to affect the same age group and to have indistinguishable clinical features, as well as to be similar neuropathologically. Following the recognition of Cowdry type A intranuclear inclusions in the neurons and oligodendroglia in subacute sclerosing leukoencephalitis, this condition was considered to be the same disease as Dawson's inclusion encephalitis.

It is of interest that the descriptions of subacute inclusion body encephalitis had been reported mainly from the United States, Canada and England, while the descriptions of subacute sclerosing leukoencephalitis had been reported from Europe. It has been suggested by Forno[68] that this may be due to the common practice of staining pathologic specimens with hematoxylin and eosin in the United States, which would demonstrate the inclusion bodies, whereas in Europe it is common practice to use more specialized stains which would not necessarily stain the inclusion bodies.

Clinical features

1. Age of onset   The great majority of patients reported with SSPE have had the onset of their symptoms between the ages of 5 and 15 years. A few cases have been as young as 3 years while a few have been as old as 22 years of age. Pette and Doring[69] described a condition which they called *nodular panencephalitis* in 4 patients. Three of these patients were 61, 59 and 56 years old. It is difficult to place these older patients in the SSPE group since Cowdry type A intranuclear inclusions were not described, and subsequent to their report the histologic material from these cases was destroyed during World War II.

2. Sex ratio   In reviewing over 200 cases of SSPE in various series and cases that we have seen, there are far more males with this condition than females; a ratio of about 2.5 to 1. At this time, it is not clear whether this is the result of a sampling bias or if it is a valid observation. A ready explanation for this observation, based on our present understanding of the etiology of SSPE, is not at hand.

3. Familial cases   A familial incidence of SSPE is a distinct rarity. Only a few reports are available in which more than 1 child in a family has had SSPE.[70,71]

4. Course of the illness   By far the greatest number of cases have a subacute course and die within 1 year. A smaller number of patients stabilize and exist in a vegetative state for many years. In the small series of Freeman[72] 5 out of 6 patients were still alive 2 years after the onset of their symptoms, although they were neurologically devastated. These differences in survival times obtained from different parts of the world may reflect the quality of care and not the natural history of the illness.

Remissions in the course of SSPE are rare, although they have been reported by many authors, but well documented by only Landau and Luse[73] and Resnick et al.[74] In 1956, Kurtzke[75] reported a case who recovered from inclusion body encephalitis. The description of the illness and subsequent recovery more closely suggests herpes simplex encephalitis rather than SSPE. Cobb and Morgan-Hughes[76] reported 2 cases of SSPE who recovered with intellectual deficits as residuals. Both of these cases were atypical in that at no time did they have the repetitive movement disorder and their electroencephalograms were not typical for SSPE.

A certain amount of skepticism has to remain as to whether any person with documented SSPE has ever recovered.

Neurologic manifestations

The slowly progressive clinical course has been divided into at least 3 clinical stages.[72,77]

1. First stage (onset) SSPE usually has an insidious onset and earliest symptoms are usually of 2 types: (1) symptoms referable to intellectual function; or (2) the onset of brief absence and akinetic attacks. Major motor seizures are, rarely, the earliest manifestation of this illness, but are not really a prominent feature at any stage of the disease. The earliest manifestation noted by the family or teachers is a change in behavior and a decreased ability to learn new material in school. The child becomes irritable, has a short attention span, refuses to listen or obey, has temper tantrums (not previously manifest in the child's normal development) and he develops difficulties in doing his school work. In our experience, deterioration of work in school has usually been the symptom responsible for the child being seen by his physician. Older children and adolescents may show a gradual withdrawal from social activities and spend a large amount of their time alone, seemingly being either depressed or preoccupied with themselves. Difficulties with sleeplessness may occur during this stage and rather commonly visual hallucinations, or less often, auditory hallucinations are noted. There is a gradual decline in both speech and writing ability and many children become unable to dress themselves. These symptoms are thought to be due to a general decline in mental function rather than to a specific aphasia or apraxia.

Major motor seizures can initiate the onset of the illness, but as mentioned earlier, they are infrequent. Absence (petit-mal-like) attacks and akinetic attacks are rather common. These attacks usually precede in time the development of the more characteristic complex periodic movements (to be described later in detail). As the disease progresses the absence and akinetic attacks are reduced in number and in most cases disappear.

2. Intermediate (middle) stage This stage of the disease is characterized by what is probably the most clinically dramatic feature of this illness, namely, the periodic movement disorder, which has frequently been described as 'myoclonic jerks'. There is usually further intellectual deterioration and this leads to an inability of the patient to care for his personal needs. The child becomes incapable of feeding or dressing himself and usually is incontinent of urine and feces. Volitional activity decreases and the child becomes confined to either a wheelchair or bed. Alterations in his level of consciousness occur and the child frequently becomes lethargic or stuporous. When aroused, the speech is frequently slow and unintelligible but a specific aphasia appears to be very rare.

While choreiform, athetoid and ballistic movements, as well as a fine, rapid tremor, have been described, these are very rare in the authors' experience.

The most frequently described movement disorder has been the so-called 'myoclonic jerks'. These movements have variously been described as 'sudden involuntary flexor jerks', 'intermittent clonic spasms of the flexors', 'constant flexor jerks', or merely 'occasional twitching movements of the limbs'. From the various descriptions, it can be seen that these movements are quite dissimilar to the fast-lightning movements seen in Jakob-Creutzfeldt disease, Tay-Sachs disease and some of the other lipidoses, as well as other diseases of the nervous system, which have been called 'myoclonic jerks'. The typical movement of this disorder may be described as showing a rapid onset of the movement which is followed by a slower dystonic phase. The entire movement may last up to 1 second or so. The jerks may be either mild or severe. They may be limited to a single limb, but more commonly involve the trunk, eyes and face, as well as the limbs. In the extremities the movement almost invariably involves the more proximal flexor groups, while in the trunk, flexion may occur, but extension with torsion is more commonly seen. The eyes are usually conjugately deviated either laterally or upward during the movement. The periodic recurrence of such movements has been an important and almost specific feature of this illness. When well established, the intervals between the movements are usually about 6 seconds, but intervals from 3 seconds to 20 seconds are not too unusual. The periodicity of the movements is not altered by extraneous stimuli such as light flashes, loud noises, or somatosensory stimuli and this lack of response distinguishes this type of movement from stimulus-sensitive myoclonus. The involuntary movements may not be a prominent feature although present to a degree in every case reported to date. When the movements are slight, they may be restricted to the proximal muscles of a single limb and the child may confuse the examiner by continuing the movement in a semi-purposeful manner, making the recognition of the involuntary component difficult to recognize. In the later stages of the disease, the periodic movements decrease in amplitude and finally disappear. For some time after the disappearance of the movements from the trunk and limbs, periodic conjugate ocular spasms may continue.

Expressionless facies and a poverty of spontaneous movements are commonly seen. The children demonstrate decorticate posturing and cortical blindness late in this stage.

3. Terminal (final) stage This stage is marked by the absence of any discernible intellectual function and marked rigidity progressing to a terminal decerebrate stage. During this stage there is frequently evidence of hypothalamic dysfunction such as episodes of hyperthermia, disturbances of pulse and blood pressure, and profuse diaphoresis. Death usually results within a year of the onset of symptoms.

Laboratory studies

Serum The serum is usually chemically normal except for minor elevations of alkaline phosphatase. Antibody titers to measles virus are usually very high when the patient is first seen.[78,79,80]

Cerebrospinal fluid The cerebrospinal fluid may have either a normal or a slightly elevated total protein. Classically, a first zone Lange colloidal gold curve has been present. The gamma globulin has been elevated in almost all of the cases studied. The gamma globulin has been from 18 to near 60 percent of the total CSF protein. The gamma globulin fraction has been shown to consist mainly of IgG by immunoelectrophoresis. Antibody titers to measles virus in the cerebrospinal fluid have been high except for a few instances where the titers were initially normal, but became elevated as the disease progressed.

Electroencephalographic studies

Alterations in the electroencephalogram in subacute sclerosing panencephalitis have been described by Radermecker[81], Cobb and Hill[82] and many other authors. The changes which have been noted can be divided into 2 types: (1) changes in background rhythms; and (2) the periodic complexes.

1. Background rhythms Early in the course of the disease alpha activity is present, but increased amounts of theta activity are usually noted. This slower activity may either be diffuse or be limited to one or the other hemisphere. On occasion, higher voltage slow activity (3 c/s) has been seen in the frontal regions. As the disease progresses the background rhythms become slower and of higher voltage. At this stage, it is not uncommon to see focal sharp waves interrupt the basal activity. As the disease continues in its relentless progression, the background activity gradually decreases in amplitude to become almost isoelectric.

2. Periodic complexes The periodic complexes seen in the electroencephalograms of patients with subacute sclerosing panencephalitis are a characteristic if not constant feature of this form of encephalitis. The periodic complexes consist of multiphasic complexes lasting 1 to 2 seconds. They are usually of high amplitude, the voltage ranging from 100 to 250 μvolts. The periodicity varies from 5 to approximately 15 seconds, but the interval is usually constant for a given patient. The periodic complexes usually appear to be quite synchronous with the periodic involuntary movements (Fig. 6). With rare exceptions, the complexes cannot be initiated or modified by photic stimulation, loud noises, or somatosensory stimuli (pin pricks or tapping the tendons). The intravenous administration of sodium pentobarbital and diazepam has no effect upon the well established periodicity.[83,84] Again, this is unlike the stimuli-sensitive periodic pattern of 1 per second seen in Jakob-Creutzfeldt disease where Nelson and Leffman[48] were able to abolish the complexes and myoclonic jerks with intravenous amobarbital. From numerous studies where simultaneous electromyography and electroencephalography have been accomplished, it is clear that the periodic complexes

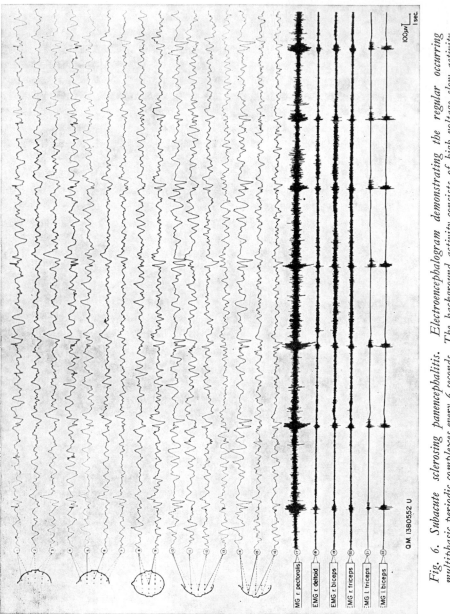

Fig. 6. Subacute sclerosing panencephalitis. Electroencephalogram demonstrating the regular occurring multiphasic periodic complexes every 6 seconds. The background activity consists of high voltage slow activity in the delta frequency. Simultaneous electromyograms demonstrate the synchronous muscle contractions.

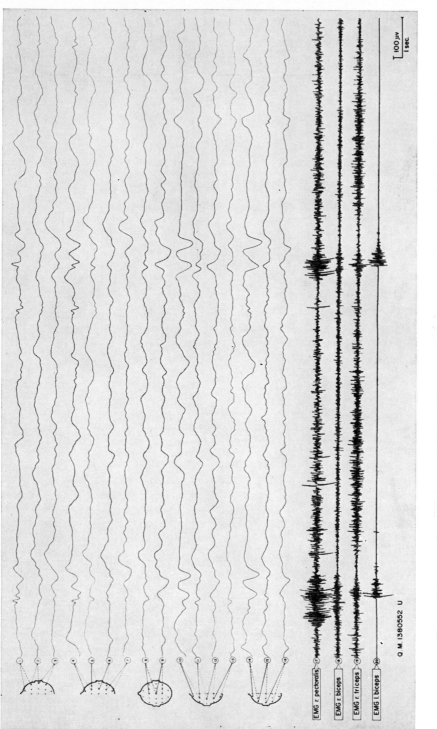

Fig. 7. Subacute sclerosing panencephalitis. Electroencephalogram at a faster speed shows that each multiphasic periodic complex is over a second in duration. Also, note that the muscle contraction in the right pectoralis muscle precedes the onset of the periodic complex.

are not the cause of the movements, for it has frequently been shown that the movement starts before the complex (Fig. 7). Lombroso[85] has also demonstrated that lateral eye movements frequently precede, by up to 1 second, the movement as recorded by EMG and the periodic complexes as recorded by the EEG. It is also clear that although the periodic movements cease during sleep, the periodic complexes of the EEG go on unaltered, demonstrating that proprioception impulses from the muscles are not responsible for the periodic complexes seen on the EEG.

The origin of the periodic complexes is not clear. Many authors have speculated that they depend upon a thalamic or mesencephalic reticular source,[83,85,86,87,88] whereas others propose that the complex originates within the cerebral cortex itself.[46,89]

The dissociation of the movements from the EEG complexes during sleep has already been alluded to. A pharmacologic dissociation has also been accomplished, but this time the complexes disappeared while the movements continued. Fenÿo and Hasznos[83] were able to do this with mephenesin, a drug known to block thalamic outflow (arousal reaction and recruiting response).

Farrell et al.[84] demonstrated that elevations in the body temperature in patients with SSPE abolished both the periodic complexes and the movements. They felt that this was due to an effect of temperature on altering synaptic activity and this resulted in an unbalancing of the factors required for periodicity.

Depth recordings in 5 different patients have not settled the question as to the origin, but available evidence including the dissociation of the EEG complexes, the eye movements and the movement disorder suggests a brainstem source for these phenomena. It is also clear that damage to the cortex and sclerosis of the white matter contribute to this interesting phenomenon of periodicity.

Pathology

Grossly, the brain is usually firmer than normal. The gyri may be narrowed and the sulci widened, the amount depending upon the duration of the illness.

Microscopic examination — the meninges show little evidence of inflammation by lymphocytes, plasma cells or histiocytes, although it is common to see perivascular cuffing by small mononuclear cells. Many areas of the cortex are damaged showing various stages of neuronal degeneration. In some cases, Alzheimer's neurofibrillary tangles have been noted.[90] Reactive microglial cells are common both diffusely and with glial nodule formation. Hyperplasia of astrocytes with its resulting fibrillary gliosis is a prominent feature. Focal areas of necrosis of the cortex are not uncommon. Cowdry type A intranuclear inclusion bodies are found in neurons but also in oligodendroglia. Typical Cowdry type A intranuclear bodies (Fig. 8) demonstrate a homogeneous rather hyaline appearance, are round to oval and vary from 3-10 μ, with an average of about 6 μ. The chromatin of the nucleus is beaded and marginated along the nuclear membrane while there is a clear halo separating the chromatin from the inclusion. Electronmicrographs of the intranuclear inclusions by Herndon and Rubinstein[90] and Shaw[91] have demonstrated tubules of 150-180 Å diameter (Fig. 9) consistent with the internal

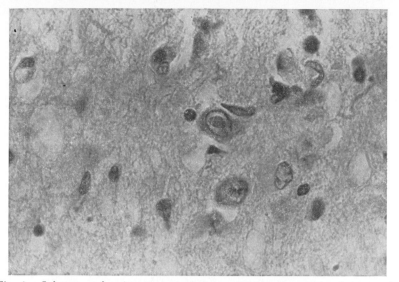

Fig. 8. Subacute sclerosing panencephalitis. Light microscopic demonstration of a typical Cowdry type A intranuclear inclusion body. The cell is most likely a neuron.

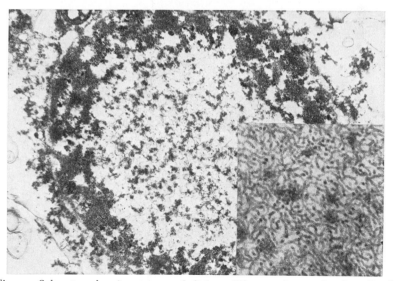

Fig. 9. Subacute sclerosing panencephalitis. Electronmicrograph of a Cowdry type A inclusion body. The nuclear chromatin is granular and marginated and many small filamentous processes are seen in the center of the inclusion. Insert shows the details of the viral tubules (150-180 Å), seen in SSPE. These tubules are consistent with the measles-distemper group of myxoviruses.

components of large myxovirus. Herndon and Rubinstein[90] recognized 3 types of inclusions, 2 intranuclear and 1 cytoplasmic, and related these to the various life cycles of the myxovirus group.

Involvement of white matter is quite variable from mild to severe. Widespread isomorphic gliosis is much more prominent than is demyelination, although the latter does occur in more severe cases. Cellular infiltrates which occur in the involved white matter are frequently made up of round cells, including plasma cells and macrophages filled with breakdown products.

Deeper nuclear structures showing similar changes to those noted in the cerebral cortex include: the thalamus, basal pontine nuclei, inferior olivary nuclei and midbrain. The caudate, lenticular nuclei, cerebellum and spinal cord are much less frequently involved.

Chemical alterations of the myelin isolated from cases of SSPE have been reported by Norton et al.[92] The yield of myelin was about one-third the normal amount. There was an increase in cholesterol and a concomitant reduction in cerebrosides, sulfatides, and ethanolamine phosphatides. The lipid to protein ratio was normal. Abnormal gangliosides were noted in the myelin. Normally, GM_1 ganglioside is the major constituent of myelin, but in SSPE there was a shift to the more minor ganglioside components.

Etiology

From the earliest description of SSPE by Dawson in 1933, this encephalitis has been considered to be a viral disease and not to be due to herpes simplex virus, although the same type of intranuclear inclusions are seen in that disease. High or rising antibody titers to measles virus in both the serum and cerebrospinal fluid were established in all cases of SSPE. Electron microscopy of the intranuclear inclusions seen by light microscopy reveals the presence of viral particles and tubules resembling the helical virions of the measles-distemper group of myxoviruses. Early attempts to isolate the virus met with failure until Chen et al.[93] propagated a 'defective' measles virus from a brain biopsy in tissue culture. Horta-Barbosa et al.[94] subsequently reported the isolation of a complete virus from a brain biopsy specimen, but only when the cells grown from the biopsy specimen were repeatedly cultured and co-cultured with HeLa cells. This same group[95] has been able to isolate a suppressed measles virus from lymph node biopsies from patients with SSPE. The SSPE virus has been transmitted to hamsters,[96] calves and lambs[97] and these animals demonstrated myoclonic jerks, ataxia, irritability and blindness.

While minor immunologic abnormalities have been reported in some patients with SSPE[98], it is still not clear whether the isolated virus is a normal measles virus in an immunologically deficient patient, or if there are subtle differences between the virus which causes SSPE and measles virus.

Treatment

A variety of therapies have been tried without success. Thymectomy was the first reported attempt at therapy. Neither BUDR,[99] amantadine,[100] or interferon induction utilizing pyran copolymer[72] have been successful in altering the course of the disease when measured against proper controls.

OTHER INFECTIOUS CAUSES OF MYOCLONUS

Though we have stressed the occurrence of myoclonus in diseases of probable viral origin, it should not be surprising that myoclonic movements may sometimes occur in association with other non-viral central nervous system infections. A patient with pneumococcal meningitis (Case 7 in Ref. 1) developed rapid, irregular, asynchronous jerks of right lower face, tongue, platysma, right deltoid, biceps, small hand muscles, abdomen, occasionally right leg, and infrequently left shoulder. The movements disappeared within 3 days as his infection was controlled with antibiotics. A patient with coccidioidal meningitis developed generalized sudden arrhythmic movements of small amplitude in all extremities.[101] A startle response was easily elicited and myoclonic jerks were seen especially in the arms and left leg. No electroencephalographic correlates of the myoclonic jerks were seen in either of these cases. Undoubtedly, other examples could be found of myoclonus occurring during the course of acute or chronic meningitis, though the occurrence is not common. It should again be stressed that the occurrence of myoclonus results 'from a wide diversity of central nervous system diseases or toxic-metabolic disorders, and that temporally myoclonus may emerge as an acute, intermittent or chronic disorder'.[1]

SUMMARY

Myoclonic movements may occur during the course of a variety of probable infectious disorders of the central nervous system. The character of the myoclonus, and the probable site of its origin differ among the clinical conditions. Repetitive rather rhythmic myoclonic movements of the limbs can be produced experimentally by inoculation of experimental animals with Newcastle disease virus. These movements resemble those occurring in canine distemper and in some human cases of viral encephalomyelitis. Electroencephalographic correlates are absent and experimental evidence suggests this type of movement may originate at spinal cord level.

Other patterns of involuntary movements may occur with probable viral illnesses, including opsoclonus, which is often associated with irregular jerks of the limbs or severe truncal ataxia. The origin of the eye movements may be brainstem, though other sites including cerebellar vermis have been suggested.

Two 'slow virus' infections, Jakob-Creutzfeldt disease and subacute sclerosing panencephalitis, are reviewed. The myoclonic movements in the former condition are usually random and asynchronous, whereas those in the latter condition are slower and more regular. In both conditions characteristic EEG discharges occur that are often synchronous with the involuntary movements. Hence the myoclonus in these disorders probably arises from levels in high brainstem or above.

Since myoclonic movements can occur in a wide variety of metabolic disorders, it is not surprising that they have been observed in cases of bacterial or fungal meningitis.

The precise pathogenesis of myoclonus occurring in infectious conditions is amenable to further study in appropriate animal models.

ACKNOWLEDGMENTS

We are very grateful to Dr. S. M. Sumi for providing us with the pathological and electron-microscopic materials on cases of Jakob-Creutzfeldt disease, to Dr. C.-M. Shaw for the electron-microscopic material on the patient with subacute sclerosing pan-encephalitis, to Dr. G. E. Chatrian for the electroencephalographic tracings of the case of SSPE, and to Dr. H. A. Leffman for the electroencephalographic tracings of the case of Jakob-Creutzfeldt disease.

REFERENCES

1. SWANSON, P. D., LUTTRELL, C. N., and MAGLADERY, J. W. (1962): Myoclonus — A report of 67 cases and review of the literature. *Medicine, (Baltimore), 41,* 339-356.
2. LUTTRELL, C. N., and BANG, F. B. (1958): Newcastle disease encephalomyelitis in cats: I. Clinical and pathological features. *Arch. Neurol. Psychiat., 79,* 647-657.
3. LUTTRELL, C. N., BANG, F. B., and LUXENBERG, K. (1959): Newcastle disease encephalomyelitis in cats. II. Physiological studies on rhythmic myoclonus. *Arch. Neurol. Psychiat., 81,* 285-291.
4. FELDBERG, W., and LUTTRELL, C. N. (1958): Observations on intraventricular perfusions in cats with myoclonus. *J. Physiol., (Lond.), 143,* 68-75.
5. BREAZILE, J. E., BLAUGH, B. S., and NAIL, N. (1966): Experimental study of canine distemper myoclonus. *Amer. J. vet. Res., 27,* 1375-1379.
6. CHAUVAU, A. (1862): Effet produit par l'isolement de la moelle épinière sur un chien choréique. *C.R. Soc. Biol. (Paris), 14,* 107-108. (Cited by Breazile, 1966).
7. GOWERS, W. R. (1875): Chorea in a dog; no emboli; persistence of movements after section of the cord. *Lancet, 75,* 610. (Cited by Breazile, 1966).
8. KAO, L. I., and CRILL, W. E. (1972): Penicillin-induced segmental myoclonus. I. Motor responses and intracellular recording from motoneurons. *Arch. Neurol. (Chic.), 26,* 156-161.
9. KAO, L. I., and CRILL, W. E. (1972): Penicillin-induced segmental myoclonus. II. Membrane properties of cat spinal motoneurons. *Arch. Neurol. (Chic.), 26,* 162-168.
10. SILFVERSKIÖLD, B. P. (1962): Rhythmic myoclonus in three girls. *Acta neurol. scand., 38,* 45-59.
11. VAN BOGAERT, L., RADERMECKER, J., and TITECA, J. (1950): Les syndromes myocloniques. *Folia psychiat. neerl., 53,* 650-690.
12. REIMOLD, W. (1925): Über die myoklonische Form der Encephalitis. *Z. ges. Neurol. Psychiat., 95,* 21-36.
13. GARCIN, R., RONDOT, P., and GUIOT, G. (1968): Rhythmic myoclonus of the right arm as the presenting symptom of a cervical cord tumor. *Brain, 91,* 75-84.
14. SMITH, J. L., and WALSH, F. B. (1960): Opsoclonus-ataxic conjugate movements of the eyes. *Arch. Ophthal., 64,* 244-250.
15. ORZECHOWSKI, K. (1927): De l'ataxie dysmétrique des yeux: remarques sur l'ataxie des yeux dite myoclonique (opsoclonie, opsochorie). *J. Psychol. Neurol., 35,* 1-18. (Cited by Smith and Walsh, 1960).
16. COGAN, D. G. (1954): Ocular dysmetria; flutter-like oscillations of the eyes, and opsoclonus. *Arch. Ophthal., 51,* 318-335.
17. COGAN, D. G. (1968): Opsoclonus, body tremulousness, and benign encephalitis. *Arch. Ophthal., 79,* 545-551.
18. BARINGER, H. R., SWEENEY, V. P., and WINKLER, G. F. (1968): An acute syndrome of ocular oscillations and truncal myoclonus. *Brain, 91,* 473-480.
19. CHRISTOFF, N. (1969): Myoclonic encephalopathy of infants. A report of two cases and observations on related disorders. *Arch. Neurol. (Chic.), 21,* 229-234.

20. WEISS, S., and CARTER, S. (1959): Course and prognosis of acute cerebellar ataxia in children. *Neurology (Minneap.)*, *9*, 711-721.

21. DYKEN, P., and KOLÁŘ, O. (1968): Dancing eyes, dancing feet: infantile polymyoclonia. *Brain*, *91*, 305-320.

22. ROSS, A. T., and ZEMAN, W. (1967): Opsoclonus, occult carcinoma, and chemical pathology in dentate nuclei. *Arch. Neurol. (Chic.)*, *17*, 546-551.

23. STEELE, J. C., GLADSTONE, R. M., THANASOPHON, S., and FLEMING, P. C. (1972): Acute cerebellar ataxia and concomitant infection with *Mycoplasma pneumoniae*. *J. Pediat.*, *20*, 467-469.

24. CAMPBELL, A. M. G., and GARLAND, H. (1956): Subacute myoclonic spinal neuronitis. *J. Neurol. Neurosurg. Psychiat.*, *19*, 268-274.

25. CREUTZFELDT, H. G. (1920): Über eine eigenartige herdförmige Erkrankung des Zentralnervensystems. *Z. ges. Neurol. Psychiat.*, *57*, 1-18.

26. JAKOB, A. (1921): Über eigenartige Erkrankungen des Zentralnervensystems mit bemerkenswerten anatomischen Befunde (spastische Pseudosklerose. — Encephalomyelopathie mit disseminierten Degenerationsherden). *Z. ges. Neurol. Psychiat.*, *64*, 147-229.

27. JAKOB, A. (1921): Über eine der multiplen Sklerose klinisch nahestehende Erkrankung des Zentralnervensystems (spastische Pseudosklerose) mit bemerkenswerten anatomischen Befunde. Mitteilung eines vierten Falles. *Med. Klin.*, *47*, 372-376.

28. JAKOB, A. (1923): Die extrapyramidalen Erkrankungen, mit besonderer Berücksichtigung der pathologischen Anatomie und Histologie und der Pathophysiologie der Bewegungsstörungen. *Monogr. Psychiat. (Berl.)* *37*, 215-245.

29. HEIDENHAIN, A. (1929): Klinische und anatomische Untersuchungen über eine eigenartige organische Erkrankung des Zentralnervensystems in Praesenium. *Z. ges. Neurol. Psychiat.*, *118*, 49-114.

30. MEYER, A. (1929): Über eine der amyotrophischen Lateralsklerose nahestehende Erkrankung, mit psychischen Störungen. Zugleich ein Beitrag zur Frage der spastischen Pseudosklerose (A. Jakob). *Z. ges. Neurol. Psychiat.*, *121*, 107-128.

31. WILSON, S. A. K. (1940): Syndrome of Jakob: Cortico-striato-spinal degeneration. In: *Neurology*, *Vol. 2*, pp. 907-910. Editor: A. N. Bruce. Edward Arnold and Co., London.

32. VAN ROSSUM, A. (1967): Spastic pseudosclerosis (Creutzfeldt-Jakob disease). In: *Handbook of Clinical Neurology*, *Vol. 6*, pp. 726-760. Editors: P. J. Vinken and G. W. Bruyn. North Holland Publ. Co., Amsterdam.

33. MAY, W. W. (1968): Creutzfeldt-Jakob disease. I. Survey of the literature and clinical diagnosis. *Acta neurol. scand.*, *44*, 1-32.

34. KIRSCHBAUM, W. R. (1924): Zwei eigenartige Erkrankungen des Zentralnervensystems nach Art der spastischen Pseudosklerose (Jakob). *Z. ges. Neurol. Psychiat.*, *92*, 175-220.

35. MEGGENDORFER, F. (1930): Klinische und genealogische Beobachtungen bei einem Fall von spastischen Pseudosklerose Jakobs. *Z. ges. Neurol. Psychiat.*, *128*, 337-341.

36. JACOB, H., PYRKOSCH, W., and STRÜBE, H. (1950): Die erbliche Form der Creutzfeldt-Jakobschen Krankheit. *Arch. Psychiat. Nervenkr.*, *184*, 653-674.

37. MAY, W. W., ITABASHI, H. H., and DE JONG, R. N. (1968): Creutzfeldt-Jakob disease. II. Clinical, pathologic, and genetic study of a family. *Arch. Neurol. (Chic.)*, *19*, 137-149.

38. JANSEN, J., and MONRAD-KROHN, G. H. (1938): Über die Creutzfeldt-Jakobsche Krankheit. *Z. ges. Neurol. Psychiat.*, *163*, 670-704.

39. JERVIS, G. A., HURDUM, H. M., and O'NEILL, F. J. (1942): Presenile psychosis of

the Jakob type. Clinico-pathologic study of one case with a review of the literature. *Amer. J. Psychiat.*, *99*, 101-109.

40. FISHER, C. M. (1960): The clinical picture of Creutzfeldt-Jakob disease. *Trans. Amer. neurol. Ass.*, *85*, 147-150.

41. ALEMÁ, G., and BIGNAMI, A. (1959): Polioencefalopatia degenerativa subacuta del presenio con stupore acinetico e rigiditá decorticatà con mioclonie (varietà 'mioclonica' della malattia di Jakob-Creutzfeldt). *Riv. sper. Freniat.*, *83* (*Suppl. IV*), 1485-1622.

42. GARCIN, R., BRION, S., and KHOCHNEVISS, A. (1963): Le syndrome de Creutzfeldt-Jakob et les syndromes cortico-striés présenium. *Rev. neurol.*, *109*, 419-441.

43. GONATAS, N. K., TERRY, R. D., and WEISS, M. (1965): Electronmicroscopic study in two cases of Jakob-Creutzfeldt disease. *J. Neuropath. exp. Neurol.*, *24*, 575-598.

44. SIEDLER, H., and MALAMUD, N. (1963): Creutzfeldt-Jakob disease. Clinico-pathologic report of 15 cases and review of the literature (with special reference to a related disorder designated as subacute spongiform encephalopathy). *J. Neuropath. exp. Neurol.*, *22*, 381-402.

45. PALLIS, G. A., and SPILLANE, J. D.: A subacute progressive encephalopathy with mutism, hypokinesia, rigidity and myoclonus: A clinical and pathological account of 3 cases. *Quart. J. Med.*, *26*, 349-373.

46. LESSE, S., HOEFER, P. F. A., and AUSTIN, J. H. (1958): The electroencephalogram in diffuse encephalopathies. Significance of periodic synchronous discharges. *Arch. Neurol. Psychiat.*, *79*, 359-375.

47. BURGER, L. J., ROWAN, A. J., and GOLDENSOHN, E. S. (1972): Creutzfeldt-Jakob disease. An electroencephalographic study. *Arch. Neurol. (Chic.)*, *26*, 428-433.

48. NELSON, J. R., and LEFFMAN, H. (1963): The human diffusely projecting system. Evoked potentials and interactions. *Arch. Neurol. (Chic.)*, *8*, 544-556.

49. RAYPORT, M. (1963): Electroencephalographic, corticographic and intracerebral potentials in two anatomically verified cases of Creutzfeldt-Jakob disease. *Electroenceph. clin. Neurophysiol.*, *15*, 922.

50. FOLEY, J. M., and DENNY-BROWN, D. (1957): Subacute progressive encephalopathy with bulbar myoclonus. *J. Neuropath. exp. Neurol.*, *16*, 133-136.

51. HIRANO, A., GHATAK, N. R., JOHNSON, A. B., PARTNOW, M. J., and GOMORI, A. J. (1972): Argentophilic plaques in Creutzfeldt-Jakob disease. *Arch. Neurol. (Chic.)*, *26*, 530-542.

52. CHOU, S. M., and MARTIN, J. D. (1971): Kuru plaques in a case of Creutzfeldt-Jakob disease. *Acta neuropath. (Berl.)*, *17*, 150-155.

53. HOROUPIAN, D. S., POWERS, J. M., and SCHAUMBURG, H. H. (1972): Kuru-like neuropathological changes in a North American. *Arch. Neurol. (Chic.)*, *27*, 555-561.

54. BIGNAMI, A., and FORNO, L. S. (1970): Status spongiosus in Jakob-Creutzfeldt disease: Electron microscopic study of a cortical biopsy. *Brain*, *93*, 89-94.

55. KOREY, S. R., KATZMAN, R., and ORLOFF, J. (1961): A case of Jakob-Creutzfeldt disease. 2. Analysis of some constituents of the brain of a patient with Jakob-Creutzfeldt disease. *J. Neuropath. exp. Neurol.*, *20*, 95-104.

56. SUZUKI, K., and CHEN, K. (1966): Chemical studies on Jakob-Creutzfeldt disease. *J. Neuropath. exp. Neurol.*, *25*, 396-408.

57. FRIEDE, R. L., and DE JONG, R. N. (1964): Neuronal enzymatic failure in Creutzfeldt-Jakob disease – Familial study. *Arch. Neurol. (Chic.)*, *10*, 181-195.

58. ROBINSON, N. (1969): Creutzfeldt-Jakob's disease: A histochemical study. *Brain*, *92*, 581-588.

59. GIBBS, C. J., JR., GAJDUSEK, D. C., ASHER, D. M., ALPERS, M. P., BECK, E., DANIEL, P. M., and MATTHEWS, W. B. (1968): Creutzfeldt-Jakob disease (spongi-

form encephalopathy). Transmission to the Chimpanzee. *Science, 161,* 388-389.

60. LAMPERT, P. W., GAJDUSEK, D. C., and GIBBS, C. J., JR. (1971): Experimental spongiform encephalopathy (Creutzfeldt-Jakob disease) in chimpanzees. Electron microscopic studies. *J. Neuropath. exp. Neurol., 30,* 20-32.

61. LAMPERT, P. W., GAJDUSEK, D. C., and GIBBS, C. J., JR. (1972): Subacute spongiform virus encephalopathics: Scrapie, Kuru and Creutzfeldt-Jakob disease: A review. *Amer. J. Path., 68,* 626-646.

62. BOTS, G. Th. A. M., DEMAN, J. C. H., and VERJAAL, A. (1971): Virus-like particles in brain tissue from two patients with Creutzfeldt-Jakob disease. *Acta neuropath. (Berl.), 18,* 267-270.

63. DAWSON, J. R. (1933): Cellular inclusions in cerebral lesions of lethargic encephalitis. *Amer. J. Path., 9,* 7-16.

64. DAWSON, J. R. (1934): Cellular inclusions in cerebral lesions of epidemic encephalitis. Second Report. *Arch. Neurol. Psychiat., 31,* 685-700.

65. AKELAITIS, A., and ZELDIS, L. (1942): Encephalitis with intranuclear inclusion bodies. *Arch. Neurol. Psychiat., 47,* 353-366.

66. BRAIN, W. R., GREENFIELD, J. G., and RUSSELL, D. S. (1948): Subacute inclusion encephalitis (Dawson type). *Brain, 71,* 365-385.

67. VAN BOGAERT, L. (1945): Une leuco-encéphalite sclérosante subaiguë. *J. Neurol. Neurosurg. Psychiat., 8,* 101-120.

68. FORNO, L.: personal communication.

69. PETTE, H. and DORING, E. (1939): Über ein heimische Panencephalomyelitis vom Charakter der Encephalitis japonica. *Dtsch. Z. Nervenheilk., 149,* 7-44.

70. LORAND, B., NAGY, T., and TARISKA, S. (1962): Subacute progressive panencephalitis. *Wld Neurol., 3,* 376-394.

71. KENNEDY, C. (1968): A ten-year experience with subacute sclerosing panencephalitis. *Neurology (Minneap.), 18 (part 2),* 58-59.

72. FREEMAN, J. M. (1969): The clinical spectrum and early diagnosis of Dawson's encephalitis. *J. Pediat., 75,* 590-603.

73. LANDAU, W. M., and LUSE, S. A. (1958): Relapsing inclusion encephalitis (Dawson type) of eight years' duration. *Neurology (Minneap.), 8,* 669-676.

74. RESNICK, J. S., ENGEL, W. K., and SEVER, J. L. (1968): Subacute sclerosing panencephalitis. *New Engl. J. Med., 279,* 126-129.

75. KURTZKE, J. F. (1956): Inclusion body encephalitis: A non-fatal case. *Neurology (Minneap.), 6,* 371-376.

76. COBB, W. A., and MORGAN-HUGHES, J. A. (1968): Non-fatal subacute sclerosing leukoencephalitis. *J. Neurol. Neurosurg. Psychiat., 31,* 115-123.

77. FOLEY, J., and WILLIAMS, D. (1953): Inclusion encephalitis and its relation to subacute sclerosing leucoencephalitis: A report of five cases. *Quart. J. Med., 22,* 157-194.

78. CONNOLLY, J. H., ALLEN, I. V., HURWITZ, L. J., and MILLAR, J. H. D. (1967): Measles virus antibody and antigen in subacute sclerosing panencephalitis. *Lancet, 1,* 542-544.

79. LENNETTE, E. H., MAGOFFIN, R. L., and FREEMAN, J. M. (1968): Immunologic evidence of measles virus as an etiologic agent in subacute sclerosing panencephalitis. *Neurology (Minneap.), 18 (part 2),* 21-29.

80. ADELS, B. R., GAJDUSEK, D. C., GIBBS, C. J., JR., ALBRECHT, P., and ROGERS, N. G. (1968): Attempts to transmit subacute sclerosing panencephalitis and isolate a measles related agent with a study of the immune response in patients and experimental animals. *Neurology (Minneap.), 18 (part 2),* 30-51.

81. RADERMECKER, J. (1949): Aspects électroencéphalographiques dans trois cas d'encéphalite subaiguë. *Acta neurol. belg., 49,* 222-232.

82. COBB, W., and HILL, D. (1950): Electroencephalogram in subacute progressive encephalitis. *Brain, 73*, 392-404.

83. FENŸO, E., and HASZNOS, T. (1964): Periodic EEG complexes in subacute panencephalitis: Reactivity response to drugs and respiratory relationships. *Electroenceph. clin. Neurophysiol., 16*, 446-458.

84. FARRELL, D. F., STARR, A., and FREEMAN, J. M. (1971): The effect of body temperature on the 'periodic complexes' of subacute sclerosing leucoencephalitis (SSLE). *Electroenceph. clin. Neurophysiol., 30*, 415-421.

85. LOMBROSO, C. T. (1968): Remarks on the EEG and movement disorder in SSPE. *Neurology (Minneap.), 18 (part 2)*, 69-75.

86. PETSCHE, H., SCHINKO, H., and SEITELBERGER, F. (1961): Neuropathological studies on Van Bogaert's subacute sclerosing leucoencephalitis. In: *Encephalitides*, pp. 353-384. Editors: L. Van Bogaert et al. Elsevier, Amsterdam.

87. COBB, W. (1966): The periodic events of subacute sclerosing leucoencephalitis. *Electroenceph. clin. Neurophysiol., 21*, 278-294.

88. PETRE-QUADENS, O., SFAELLO, Z., Van BOGAERT, L., and MOYA, A. (1968): Sleep study in SSPE (first results). *Neurology (Minneap.), 18 (part 2)*, 60-68.

89. BOGACZ, J., CASTELLS, C., SAN JULIAN, J., and AVELLANAL, C. (1959): Non-epidemic progressive subacute encephalitis (Van Bogaert). II. Serial EEG abnormalities and deep electrography. *Acta neurol. lat.-amer., 5*, 158-183.

90. HERNDON, R. M., and RUBINSTEIN, L. J. (1968): Light and electron microscopy observations on the development of viral particles in the inclusions of Dawson's encephalitis (subacute sclerosing panencephalitis). *Neurology (Minneap.), 18 (part 2)*, 8-20.

91. SHAW, C-M. (1968): Electron microscopic observations in subacute sclerosing panencephalitis: A supplementary report. *Neurology (Minneap.), 18 (part 2)*, 144-145.

92. NORTON, W. T., PODUSLO, S. E., and SUZUKI, K. (1966): Subacute sclerosing leukoencephalitis. II. Chemical studies including abnormal myelin and an abnormal ganglioside pattern. *J. Neuropath. exp. Neurol., 25*, 582-597.

93. CHEN, T. T., WATANABE, I., ZEMAN, W., and MEALLY, J., JR. (1969): Subacute sclerosing panencephalitis: Propagation of measles virus from brain biopsy in tissue culture. *Science, 163*, 1193-1194.

94. HORTA-BARBOSA, L., FUCCILLO, D., SEVER, J. L., and ZEMAN, W. (1969): Subacute sclerosing panencephalitis: Isolation of measles virus from a brain biopsy. *Nature. (Lond.), 221*, 974.

95. HORTA-BARBOSA, L., HAMILTON, R., WITTIG, B., FUCCILLO, D. A., SEVER, J. L., and VERNON, M. L. (1971): Subacute sclerosing panencephalitis: Isolation of suppressed measles virus from lymph node biopsies. *Science, 173*, 840-841.

96. LEHRICH, J. R., KATZ, M., RORKE, L. B., BARBANTI-BRODANO G., and KAPROWSKI, H. (1970): Subacute sclerosing panencephalitis: Encephalitis in hamsters produced by viral agents isolated from human brain cells. *Arch. Neurol. (Chic.), 23*, 97-102.

97. THEIN, P., MAYR, A., MEULEN, V., KOPROWSKI, H., KÄCKELL M. Y., MÜLLER, D., and MEYERMANN, R. (1972): Subacute sclerosing panencephalitis. Transmission of the virus to calves and lambs. *Arch. Neurol. (Chic.), 21*, 431-434.

98. GERSON, K. C., and HASLAM, R. H. A. (1971): Subtle immunologic abnormalities in four boys with subacute sclerosing panencephalitis. *New Engl. J. Med., 285*, 78-82.

99. FREEMAN, J. M. (1969): Treatment of Dawson's encephalitis with 5-bromo-2'-deoxyuridine. *Arch. Neurol. (Chic.), 21*, 431-434.

100. HASLAM, R. H. A., McQUILLEN, M. P., and CLARK, D. B. (1969): Amantadine therapy in subacute sclerosing panencephalitis. A preliminary report. *Neurology (Minneap.), 19*, 1080-1086.

101. Case records of the Massachusetts General Hospital, 1971, *285*, 621-630.

Infantile spasms

MAURICE H. CHARLTON

*University of Rochester School of Medicine and Dentistry,
and Strong Memorial Hospital,
Rochester, N.Y., U.S.A.*

The form of epilepsy now known as infantile spasms ('spasmes en flexion', 'Blitz-Nick- und Salaamkrämpfe') was first described by West in 1841.[1] His letter to the Lancet is reproduced here *in toto*, not merely for historical interest, but because its clinical picture of the seizures is as valid as any current description, and more literate and more dispassionately humane.

ON A PECULIAR FORM OF INFANTILE CONVULSIONS

To the Editor of the Lancet

Sir: – I beg through your valuable and extensively circulating Journal, to call the attention of the medical profession to a very rare and singular species of convulsion peculiar to young children.

As the only case I have witnessed is in my own child, I shall be very grateful to any member of the profession who can give me any information on the subject, either privately or through your excellent Publication.

The child is now near a year old; was a remarkably fine, healthy child when born, and continued to thrive till he was four months old. It was at this time that I first observed slight bobbings of the head forward, which I then regarded as a trick, but were, in fact, the first indications of disease; for these bobbings increased in frequency, and at length became so frequent and powerful, as to cause a complete heaving of the head forward towards his knees, and then immediately relaxing into the upright position, something similar to the attacks of emprosthotonus: these bowings and relaxings would be repeated alternately at intervals of a few seconds, and repeated from ten to twenty or more times at each attack, which attack would not continue more than two or three minutes; he sometimes has two, three, or more attacks in the day; they come on whether sitting or lying; just before they come on he is all alive and in motion, making a strange noise, and then all of a sudden down goes his head and upwards his knees; he then appears frightened and screams out: at one time he lost flesh, looked pale and exhausted, but latterly he has regained his good looks, and, independent of this affection, is a fine grown child, but he neither possesses the intellectual vivacity or the power of moving his limbs, of a child of his age; he never cries at the time of the attacks, or smiles or takes any notice, but looks placid and pitiful, yet his hearing and vision are good; he has no power of holding himself upright or using his limbs, and his head falls without support.

Although I have had an extensive practice among women and children, and a large circle of medical friends, I have never heard or witnessed a similar complaint before. The view I took of it was that, most probably, it depended on some irritation of the nervous system from teething; and, as the child was strong and vigorous, I commenced an active treatment of leeches and cold applications to the head, repeated calomel purgatives, and the usual antiphlogistic treatment; the gums were lanced, and the child frequently put into warm baths. Notwithstanding a steady perseverance in this plan for three or four weeks, he got worse, the attacks being more numerous, to the amount of fifty or sixty in the course of a day. I then had recourse to sedatives, syrup of poppies, conium, and opium, without any relief: at seven months old he cut four teeth nearly altogether without any abatement of the symptoms, and, up to this period, he was supported solely at the breast; but now, at the eighth month, I had him weaned, as he had lost flesh and appeared worse; I then only gave alternatives, and occasionally castor-oil. Finding no benefit from all that had been done, I took the child to London, and had a consultation with Sir Charles Clarke and Dr. Locock, both of whom recognised the complaint; the former, in all his extensive practice, had only seen four cases, and, from the peculiar bowing of the head, called it the 'salaam convulsion'; the latter gentleman had only seen two cases; one was the child of a widow lady, it came on while she was in Italy, and, in her anxiety, she consulted the most eminent professional gentlemen of Naples, Rome, Florence, Genoa, and Paris, one of whom alone seemed to recognise the complaint. In another case, mercury, corrosive sublimate, opium, zinc, and the preparation of iron, were tried without the slightest advantage; and, about six months from the commencement of the symptoms, a new one was added; there began a loss of motion in the whole of the right side, and the child could scarcely use either arm, hand, or leg. Sir Astley Cooper saw the child in this state; he had never seen or heard of such a case, and gave it as his opinion, that 'it either arose from disease of the brain and the child will not recover, or it proceeds merely from teething, and, when the child cuts all its teeth, may probably get well'; some time after, this child was suddenly seized with acute fever; the head became hot, and there were two remaining teeth pressing on the gums; the child was treated accordingly; leeches to the head, purged, and lowered; the gums were freely lanced; in a few days the teeth came through and the child recovered, and from that time the convulsive movements never returned. Sir C. Clarke knows the result of only two of his cases: one perfectly recovered; the other became paralytic and idiotic; lived several years in that state, and died at the age of 17 years. I have heard of two other cases, which lived one to the age of 17, the other 19 years, idiotic, and then died. I wrote to Drs. Evanson and Maunsell, of Dublin; the former gentleman being in Italy, the latter very kindly replied, he had seen convulsive motions in one finger, arm, or leg, but had never witnessed it to the extent of my poor child. As there has been no opportunity of a post-mortem examination, the pathology of this singular disease is totally unknown.

Although this may be a very rare and singular affection, and only noticed by two of our most eminent physicians, I am, from all I have learnt, convinced that it is a disease (*sui generis*) which from its infrequency, has escaped the attention of the profession. I therefore hope you will give it the fullest publicity, as this paper might rather be extended rather than curtailed. I am, Sir, one of your subscribers from the commencement, your faithful and obedient servant.

Tunbridge, Jan. 26, 1841.   *W. J. West.*

P.S.   In my own child's case, the bowing convulsions continued every day, without intermission, for seven months; he had then an interval of three days free; but, on the fourth day, the convulsions returned, with this difference: instead of bowing, he stretched out his arms, looked wild, seemed to lose all animation, and appeared quite exhausted.

After West's initial description, little contribution was made to the subject until the past two decades. This recent surge of interest was well reviewed by Jeavons and Bower in their monograph of 1964.[2] The present chapter will concentrate on contributions made to our knowledge since that time, and incorporate the author's own experience of 195 cases, published in summary form elsewhere.[3,4] Since many of the more recent contributions to the subject concern etiology, and since one's view on this affects some of the more commonly held views on infantile spasms, it seems justifiable to reverse the usual procedure of a medical text and to discuss etiology before clinical presentation.

ETIOLOGY

Jeavons and Bower, in reviewing the literature before 1964, found that about one third of all cases (34.7%) had a significant history of pre- or perinatal difficulty, and this was corroborated by their own findings (39 of 112 cases). In 57 of our 195 cases a significant history of pre- or perinatal difficulty was obtained. There were 9 cases of prematurity, 6 breech deliveries, 6 cases of hemorrhage in the first trimester of pregnancy, 4 cases of toxemia, 4 cesarean sections, 3 histories of habitual abortion, 2 histories of maternal infection during pregnancy, and 1 case each of maternal trauma during pregnancy, maternal diabetes, hyperemesis gravidarum, abruptio placentae and pre-eclampsia. Histories of dystocia and marked neonatal distress of uncertain cause were obtained in the remaining cases in this category. It is likely that pre- and perinatal distress account for an even larger percentage of the total cases of infantile spasms, since there is a male preponderance (75-62) even among the patients where no history of pre- or perinatal difficulty was obtained. Schütze and Fischer state that they were able to elicit significant histories of pre- and perinatal difficulty in 56% of their 36 patients.[5]

The general thrust of more recent literature has been to isolate specific causes of infantile spasms in the remaining two-thirds of patients. These causes may be classified as

1. Heredodegenerative diseases.
2. Developmental defects.
3. Biochemical causes, including deficiency states, inborn errors of metabolism and storage diseases.
4. Infections.
5. Immunologic causes.
6. Trauma.
7. Miscellaneous, including neoplastic and vascular.

1. Heredodegenerative diseases

Undoubtedly the most important entity within this category is tuberous sclerosis.[6] Jeavons and Bower reported only 2 cases in their series of 157 patients, but 13% of our patients (25 cases) were found to have tuberous sclerosis. Several points are worth emphasizing in this regard. Intracranial calcifications are rarely found on the skull X-ray at an age when the child is susceptible to infantile spasms, and were present in none of our cases. The diagnosis may depend on characteristic skin lesions. There was no suspicion of tuberous sclerosis initially in some of our 25 cases, and the diagnosis only became apparent on long term follow-up. On occasion an adequate etiology (e.g. birth trauma) was assumed to have been found initially, but was later rejected when the tuberous sclerosis became apparent.

Von Recklinghausen's disease has been found to be associated with infantile spasms.[7] Three cases of the 250 reported instances of incontinentia pigmenti have suffered from spasms.[8] The Sjögren-Marinesco syndrome of ataxia, congenital cataracts and retardation was found in our series in 2 cases, a pair of siblings. Mongolism was found in 2 cases. It has recently been suggested that mongoloid patients may not be as exempt from the occurrence of seizure disorders as hitherto supposed.[9]

2. Developmental defects

Perhaps on account of the high visibility of the neuropathological findings, there have been several recent publications on developmental defects as the cause of infantile spasms, well reviewed by Jellinger.[10] Agenesis of the corpus callosum, ulegyria, (poly)porencephaly, agyria, lissencephaly, pachygyria, micropolygyria, megalencephaly, cortical dysplasia, schizencephaly, and malformation of the lenticular nuclei have been found at post mortem. Elsewhere, arachnoid cyst of the temporal region has been reported[11] and, in our own series, a Sturge-Weber syndrome was found.

In this regard it seems worth quoting the remarks of Crome and Stern concerning 'the unsolved problems of brain showing no detectable abnormality'.[12] They refer to the case described by Gonatas and Goldensohn.[13] 'A biopsy specimen of the brain was obtained from a child aged $2\frac{1}{2}$ years who suffered from mental retardation, epilepsy and blindness, and whose EEG showed typical features of hypsarrhythmia. The only "abnormality" seen by light microscopy was a finding so common in all specimens as to have no pathological significance. Electron microscopy revealed, however, striking enlargement and other structural abnormalities of many presynaptic axon terminals.'

3. Biochemical abnormalities (including deficiency states, inborn errors of metabolism and storage diseases)

The earliest entity to be associated with infantile spasms was phenylketonuria.[14] Early detection and dietary treatment have made this less common as a cause of spasms. Lipidoses have been found to be associated with spasms.[15] Attention continues to be drawn to the two entities of pyridoxine dependency and pyridoxine deficiency states as etiologic. These are dealt with in the chapter 'The Therapy of Myoclonus' pp. 121-160. One case of hepatolenticular degeneration was included in Zellweger's series.[16] Two of our cases were reported to suffer from hypoglycemia, and Jeavons and Bower cite leucine-sensitive hypoglycemia as etiologic. Leigh's syndrome[17] and Alpers' disease have been reported.[18] Inborn errors of metabolism might be suspected in 2 of our cases where there was parental consanguinity, and 2 other pairs of siblings were concordant for the occurrence of infantile spasms. A further case had a sibling with documented Lowe's syndrome.

4. Infections

Feldman and Schwartz[19] reported on cases of cytomegalic inclusion disease: This infection is likely to be overlooked if patients receive only routine microscopic screening of their urine, without culture. Toxoplasmosis has been found in association with infantile spasms: 1 of our patients had chorioretinitis without any specific etiologic agent being found. Jeavons and Bower found 1 case associated with measles, and 1 such case was present in our own series. Meningococcal meningitis has been reported,[20] but bacterial meningitis seems to be rare as a cause of infantile spasms: in no case were we able to elicit a history of such infection, and in no case was the cerebrospinal fluid productive of such a diagnosis in respect of its cell content, protein, glucose and serology.

5. Immunologic

The most important question here is the relationship of infantile spasms to inoculation with pertussis vaccine. Jeavons and Bower were unable to reach a conclusion in this matter. A large series would be necessary for statistical proof, since the age of onset of infantile spasms is the age at which immunization tends to be administered. Individual cases may be impressive, but also misleading. In 4 of our cases the onset of spasms closely followed immunization with DPT and smallpox vaccine. One of these patients later proved to have tuberous sclerosis, and another had chorioretinitis on neurological examination. It is possible that a febrile response to the vaccine may have triggered the spasms, without being the primary cause. The subject has recently been discussed by Gordon,[21] who is aware of the other known neurologic complications of vaccination. In this light he reviews his own experience of 50 patients over a period of 10 years. Eight of these children developed infantile spasms within a few days of inoculation, but did not differ clinically or electroencephalographically from his other cases, and he concludes that 'it is difficult to produce acceptable evidence of a serious risk from whooping cough immunization, sufficient to advise against the use of the newer vaccine adsorbed on aluminum hydroxide'.

One of our patients had associated Rh incompatibility.

6. Trauma

Only in 1 of our cases was there suggested a relationship to head trauma, and the negative experience, i.e. the large number of serious head injuries which are not followed by spasms, might be considered significant. However, Todt and Schmidt have recently written on spasms following skull injuries in a small child.[22]

7. Miscellaneous

Jeavons and Bower mention 1 case in which spasms followed subarachnoid hemorrhage from an intracranial aneurysm, and 1 of our cases was found at autopsy to have a left hemispheric glioma.

CLINICAL COURSE

In 1948 Zellweger published 32 cases of his own and reviewed 62 cases from the literature. His paper was important for reintroducing (after Feré in 1883)[23] the dichotomous concept that infantile spasms might be classified as idiopathic (or cryptogenic) and symptomatic. This concept was developed by the work of Jeavons and Bower, and has attained wide currency. Essentially, the dichotomy is between the child who develops normally until the time of the attacks, who has no evidence of neurological disease, and (most important for the maintenance of the dichotomy) has a good prognosis for treatment. It is further claimed that the cryptogenic group show a later age of onset than those with documented pre- and perinatal damage, and that this fact further justifies the distinction of the two categories.

Review of the more recent literature, the author's own experience, certain theoretical considerations, and, indeed, certain admissions by its advocates, all suggest that the dichotomy may have been overemphasized.

The recent literature has shown an increasing number of diverse causes for the clinical occurrence of infantile spasms. It is therefore no longer tenable to have 2 broad categories of pre- and perinatal damage and 'cryptogenic', to which are appended further minor categories of cases to which a specific etiology can be assigned. It has become apparent that not merely gross static changes (such as congenital anomalies), but abnormalities hard to detect by conventional neuropathological techniques, unsuspected inborn errors of metabolism and storage disease of insidious development may all underly the occurrence of infantile spasms. Such patients may be grossly asymptomatic during the first few months of life: later the intrinsic progression of their biochemical or structural lesion may be masked by the retardation induced by the spasm or the effects of drug toxicity. It seems that a further search for specific etiologies for the cryptogenic cases is the most pressing need in this area (Fig. 1).

Several other facts cast out on the value of the dichotomy. Although Jeavons and Bower call attention to the male preponderance in their pre- and perinatal damage group, they admit an unexplained male preponderance in the cryp-

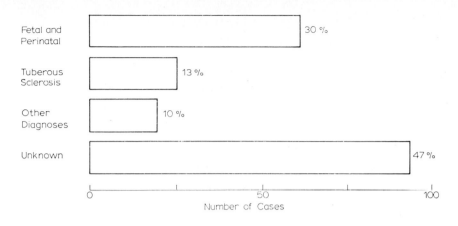

Fig. 1. Etiology of infantile spasm.

togenic group. This is also the author's experience, with 37 males to 21 females in the pre- and perinatal group, and 77 males to 60 females in the remaining patients. At the least this suggests that in both series unsuspected cases of pre- and perinatal damage are concealed in the cryptogenic group. No distinction as regards electroencephalographic findings can be made between the two groups. While the histogram of the age of onset for all patients is similar to that of previous authors, we were not able to find any significant difference in the age of onset of those cases with pre- and perinatal damage, as compared with those without evidence of such damage, among our patients (Fig. 2). It is even doubtful whether being placed in the symptomatic category carries any serious prognosis as far as retardation is concerned. Nineteen of our patients classified as of normal intelligence included 3 cases of tuberous sclerosis, 4 of pre- and perinatal difficulties, and 1 biochemical problem (hypoglycemia).

Despite our ignorance of etiology in many cases, and the clinical disagreement mentioned above, there is remarkable agreement on the general clinical presentation, electroencephalographic findings, and prognosis of infantile spasms. They are regarded as a non-specific response of the immature nervous system to serious injury of varying etiology, the age of onset of the spasms being determined by factors of cerebral development. The peak age of onset is between 3 and 6 months, but it must be emphasized that they can occur within the first days of life, and 1 of our patients began to have spasms at the age of 18 months. There is agreement that the age of onset is difficult to document: the early attacks may be unnoticed or misdiagnosed by parents as colic. Weeks or even months may elapse before diagnosis is made and treatment instituted. This is especially distressing if one believes that early treatment contributes significantly to a lesser degree of retardation.[24] In some cases diagnosis is delayed because of the coexistence of other forms of seizure which may be easily recognized and lead one to overlook the more dangerous infantile spasms. About 50% of the patients will have another form of epilepsy in addition to their spasms; the other

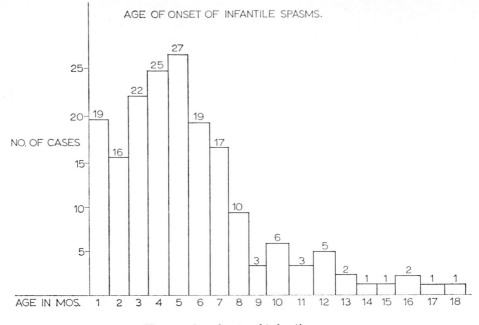

Fig. 2. Age of onset of infantile spasms.

may antedate, coincide with, or follow the onset of the spasms. The predominant type is grand mal, although focal motor and psychomotor attacks may be seen. Petit mal was not found by the author, although the significance of this finding is dubious since the 3 cycles per second spike and wave pattern and its clinical correlates are not normally seen within the first 2 years of life.[25]

The age specificity for the onset of infantile spasms, despite the varying etiologies, is supported by the electroencephalographic evidence. The hypsarrhythmic pattern of discharge is correlated in its appearance with the age groups susceptible to infantile spasms. Some authors stress that hypsarrhythmia may be found in children without spasms, and even without seizures of any type.[26] Criteria for characterizing a tracing as showing hypsarrhythmia or 'modified hypsarrhythmia' may differ. The author has seen hypsarrhythmia in the tracing of a child without spasms or seizures, but who subsequently developed infantile spasms. About two thirds of patients with infantile spasms, if untreated, have a hypsarrhythmic tracing, and in our series hypsarrhythmia was present in 118 of 176 EEGs. None of the remaining tracings could be classified as normal. The presence of hypsarrhythmia did not apparently carry a worse prognosis for mental development. Of around 19 patients classified as of normal intelligence, 11 had hypsarrhythmic EEGs. This finding is in disagreement with the beliefs of other authors concerning hypsarrhythmia, whether the patient suffers from infantile spasms or not. It is possible that the presence of 'suppression bursts' on a hypsarrhythmic tracing is correlated with a poorer prognosis for mental function. Whereas 73 of our 118 hypsarrhythmic records showed 'suppression bursts' only 3 of the 11 patients with both normal intelligence and hypsarrhythmia demonstrated the suppression bursts. However, this finding should be interpreted with caution. Suppression bursts may only be elicited by a sleep tracing, the number of patients involved may be insufficient for statistical purposes, and among the retarded patients the degree of retardation is rarely determined with psychometric accuracy.

It is apparent that whatever the child's level of function before the onset of infantile spasms, the diagnosis alone implies a grave outlook for future intellectual function (Fig. 3). In 174 of our patients for whom information on psychomotor performance was available, only 10% were judged to be of normal intelligence. Of the remainder over 70% were severely impaired, and 25% of these were in institutions. The percentage of patients of normal intellect in our cases is in accordance with the findings of previous authors. Only 1 patient (with tuberous sclerosis) was said to be of above normal intelligence. The hope of most pediatric neurologists is that by earlier recognition and treatment they might arrest or revert the retardation which may be caused by the seizures themselves.

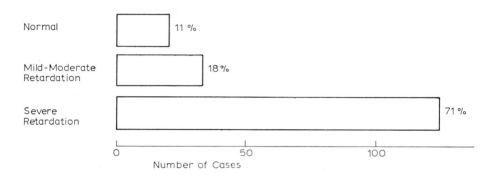

Fig. 3. Evaluation of psychomotor retardation.

Apart from the grave prognosis for intellectual function, there is a risk of death. This may be due to associated problems, e.g. coexistent cardiac anomalies. If the child has a progressive metabolic disease of which the spasms are symptomatic, the primary problem may be lethal. One of our patients died of a glioma. Death may be secondary to severe retardation and the consequent inability of the child to handle secretions — a problem sometimes made more difficult by the administration of anticonvulsant drugs. Occasionally death may ensue from the coexistence of grand mal seizures.

ACKNOWLEDGEMENT

The author wishes to acknowledge the help of Dr. James Mellinger in collecting the original cases, of Dr. William Tasker in drawing his attention to the earlier literature, and of Dr. Niels Low in first arousing his interest in the complexities of this problem.

REFERENCES

1. WEST, W. J. (1841): On a peculiar form of infantile convulsants. *Lancet*, *1*, 724.
2. JEAVONS, P. M. and BOWER, B. D. (1964): Infantile spasms. *Clinics in Developmental Medicine*, *No. 15*. William Heinemann Medical Books, London.
3. MELLINGER, J. F. and CHARLTON, M. H. (1969): Infantile spasms – an analysis of 195 cases. In: *Proceedings, Mediterranean-Middle Eastern Paediatric Congress, Athens 1969*.
4. CHARLTON, M. H. and MELLINGER, J. F. (1970): Infantile spasms and hypsarrhythmia. *Electroenceph. clin. Neurophysiol.*, *29*, 999.
5. SCHÜTZE, I. and FISCHER, H. U. (1972): Über Blitz-Nick- und Salaamkrämpfe. *Z. ärtzl. Fortbild.*, *66*, 150.
6. GASTAUT, H., ROGER, J., SOULAYROL, R., SALAMON, G., REGIS, H. and LOSS, H. (1965): Infantile myoclonic encephalopathy with hypsarrhythmia (West's syndrome) and Bourneville's tuberous sclerosis. *J. neurol. Sci.*, *2*, 140.
7. POU-SERRADELL, A. and SALEZ-VASQUEZ, R. (1971): Manifestations neurologiques (centrales) et non tumorales au cours de la neuro-fibromatose de Recklinghausen. *Rev. neurol.*, *129*, 431.
8. SIMONSSON, H. (1972): Incontinentia pigmenti, Bloch-Sulzberger's syndrome, associated with infantile spasms. *Acta paediat. scand.*, *61*, 612.
9. COLEMAN, M. (1971): Infantile spasms associated with 5-hydroxtryptophan administration in patients with Down's syndrome. *Neurology (Minneap.)*, *21*, 911.
10. JELLINGER, K. (1970): Neuropathological aspects of hypsarrhythmia. *Neuropaediatrie*, *1*, 277.
11. JEAVONS, P. M. and BOWER, B. D.: Loc cit. 38.
12. CROME, L. and STERN, J. (1967): *The Pathology of Mental Retardation*, p. 148. J. and A. Churchill Ltd., London.
13. GONATAS, N. K. and GOLDENSOHN, E. S. (1965): Unusual neocortical presynaptic terminals in a patient with convulsions, mental retardation and cortical blindness: an electron microscopic study. *J. Neuropath. exp. Neurol.*, *24*, 575.
14. LOW, N. L., BOSMA, J. F. and ARMSTRONG, M. D. (1957): Studies on phenylketonuria. VI. EEG studies in phenylketonuria. *Arch. Neurol. Psychiat.*, *77*, 359.
15. HARRIS, R. and PAMPIGLIONE, E. (1962): EEG and histopathology of 11 children with infantile spasms. *Electroenceph. clin. Neurophysiol.*, *14*, 283.
16. ZELLWEGER, H. (1948): Krämpfe im Kindesalter. *Helv. paediat. Acta, Suppl. 5*.
17. RICHTER, R. B. (1957): Infantile subacute necrotizing encephalopathy with predilection for the brain stem. *J. Neuropath. exp. Neurol.*, *16*, 281.
18. LAURENCE, K. M. and CAVANAUGH, J. B. (1968): Progressive degeneration of the cerebral cortex in infancy. *Brain*, *91*, 261.
19. FELDMAN, R. A. and SCHWARTZ, J. F. (1968): Possible association between cytomegalovirus infection and infantile spasms. *Lancet*, *1*, 180.
20. JEAVONS, P. M. and BOWER, B. D.: Loc cit. 38.
21. GORDON, N. (1970): Reactions to triple immunisation. *Neuropaediatrie*, *1*, 119.
22. TODT, H. and SCHMIDT, G. (1971): B. N. S. Krämpfe nach Schädeltrauma bei einem Kleinkind. *Kinderärztl. Prax.*, *39*, 289.
23. FERÉ, C. (1883): Le tic de salaam. Les salutations neuropathiques. *Pros. Med.*, *11*, 970.
24. OATES, R. K. and STAPLETON, T. (1971): Hypsarrhythmia developing in hospital: recovery with early treatment. *Aust. paediat. J.*, *7*, 209.
25. LIVINGSTON, S. and PRUCE, I. M. (1972): *Comprehensive Management of Epilepsy in Infancy, Childhood and Adolescence*, p. 58. Charles C. Thomas, Springfield, Ill.
26. FRIEDMAN, E. and PAMPIGLIONE, S. (1971): Prognostic implications of electroencephalographic findings of hypsarrhythmia in first year of life. *Brit. med. J.*, *4*, 323.

The therapy of myoclonus

GARY J. MYERS

Department of Pediatrics and Neurology, The University of Rochester School of Medicine and Dentistry, and Strong Memorial Hospital, Rochester, N.Y., U.S.A.

INTRODUCTION

(Some of the drugs mentioned in this chapter are at present available only on an investigative basis, and not for practitioners to prescribe. In addition, as the author makes clear, the value of some prescription drugs in myoclonus has not been definitely established. *Editor*.)

A general approach to the therapy of myoclonus is a subject which has not received much attention in the literature. Although numerous authors have reported therapy in selected diseases or groups of diseases and others have commented on it in the course of reporting some other aspect of myoclonic syndromes, an overview of the subject is not available. This chapter attempts to bring together some of these data and to discuss both general and specific aspects of therapy as they relate to myoclonus. An understanding of the general aspects of myoclonus, particularly useful therapeutic measures and the spectrum of diseases producing it are important in any approach to therapy. However, the cornerstone of therapy is the establishment of an accurate diagnosis. Only when this has been achieved can a specific mode of therapy be selected.

Myoclonus is a nonspecific symptom present in a variety of neurologic diseases. It is defined as a sudden, involuntary, nonrhythmic contraction of a group of muscles, a single muscle, or a part of one muscle.[1,2] It represents a muscle spasm which can be of variable intensity and whose manifestations may range from a muscle twitch to a sudden propulsive force that hurls the patient to the floor. The clinical differentiation of myoclonus from other forms of neuronal hyperexcitability such as seizures or fasciculations is often difficult and may require neurophysiological studies.[3]

Although myoclonus is seen in all age groups it is most frequent in infancy, childhood, and adolescence. Why myoclonus and myoclonic syndromes should occur more frequently in this age group is unknown. Development of cortical control is incomplete during early life and this may account for the spontaneous myoclonic jerks often seen in premature infants and the stimulus-sensitive myoclonic responses present in some full term babies.[4] Possible reasons for this predilection might be the rapid proliferation of neurons prenatally, and glia postnatally, with an increase in their susceptibility to systemic and local insults,

TABLE I

Disorders associated with myoclonus which are presently not treatable

I. *Metabolic/Degenerative*
  *Alper's disease[5]
  *Lipidoses[6]
  *Globoid leukodystrophy (Krabbe)[7]
  *Sudanophilic leukodystrophy[8]
  *Lafora body disease[9]
  *Ramsay Hunt syndrome[10]
  *Schilder's disease[2]
  *Huntington's chorea[11]
  **Syringomyelia[2]
  **Thalamic degeneration[12]

II. *Infectious*
  *Subacute sclerosing panencephalitis[13]
  Von Economo's encephalitis[2]
  *Other encephalitides (with or without polymyoclonus)[2]
  **Creutzfeldt-Jakob (Jones-Nevin)[14]
  **Amyotrophic lateral sclerosis[15]
  **Tabes dorsalis[16]

III. *Congenital*
  *Lissencephaly[17]
  *Polymicrogyria[18]
  *Schizencephaly[18]
  *Pachygyria[18]
  *Ulegyria[18]
  *Porencephaly[18]
  *Anencephaly (pontine)[19]
  *Myelomeningocele[20]
  *Hydranencephaly[4]
  *Holoprosencephaly[21]
  *Agenesis of corpus callosum[22]

IV. *Miscellaneous*
  Head trauma[23]
  Spinal cord trauma[24]
  *Infantile hemiplegia[25]
  *Sturge-Weber[26]
  *Tuberous sclerosis[27]
  *Linear nevus sebaceous[28]
  Spinal cord tumor[16]
  Meningeal gliomatosis[29]

*mainly pediatric;   **mainly adult

or some unique metabolic or physiological susceptibility of the newborn. If developmental malformations and metabolic abnormalities are excluded, this preponderance is less striking, and it may reflect the limited ways the fetal and neonatal brain can respond to various insults. Tables 1 and 2 list the diseases which have been associated with myoclonus and those which occur mainly in the pediatric or adult age ranges are indicated. The age of onset of myoclonus varies from birth to the geriatric period. Even the fetal brain may be capable of myoclonic seizures.[61] One infant had myoclonic seizures during delivery, and 'fluttering' fetal movements had been noted since 6 months of gestation. The other extreme of the age spectrum is a patient 86 years of age who developed benign myoclonus without any obvious cause.[2] There is also a wide range of severity among the myoclonic syndromes. Benign or essential myoclonus has persisted unchanged for over 50 years without seriously affecting a patient's life style,[62] whereas subacute sclerosing panencephalitis (SSPE) or progressive myoclonic epilepsies caused by the cerebral lipidoses and Lafora body disease can lead to death within months or years.[63]

Myoclonus has many and varied etiologies. Tables 1 and 2 attempt to divide these into causes which are treatable and those that are only treated symptomatically. Any division of this type is clearly arbitrary, but gains merit by directing attention toward the large number of etiologies for which treatment may be

TABLE 2

Disorders associated with myoclonus which are treatable

I. *Metabolic*
  Hypoglycemia[21]
  Hypocalcemia[21]
  Hypernatremia[30]
  Uremia[31]
  Hypoxia[21]
  Hyperoxia[21]
  Cellular water intoxication[21]
  *Wilson's disease[2]
  *Menkes's kinky hair syndrome[32]
  *Phenylketonuria[23]
  *Maple syrup urine disease[2]
  *Leigh's disease[18]
  *Pyridoxine insufficiency[33]
  *Hyperornithemia, hyperammonemia
      and homocitrullinuria[34]
  **Hyperthyroidism[35]
  *Kernicterus[36]

II. *Infectious*
  Bacterial meningitis[3]
  Bacterial sepsis[3]
  Tetanus[3]
  Malaria[2]
  Smallpox[2]
  Herpes encephalitis[37]
  *Toxoplasmosis[38]
  *Syphilis (infants)[38]
  **Whipple's disease[39]
  **Multiple sclerosis[2]
  **Spinal neuronitis[40]

III. *Miscellaneous*
  *Petit mal seizures
  *Lennox-Gastaut syndrome[41]
  *Infantile spasms
  Myoclonus preceding grand mal seizures
  Epilepsia partialis continua[42]
  *Infantile polymyoclonia with or
      without neuroblastoma[43]
  Subdural hematoma[18]
  **Stiff man syndrome[44]
  *Tic de Gilles de la Tourette[45]
  *Neonatal polycythemia[46]
  Arachnidism[47]
  Hyperekplexia (jumping, myriachit, latah)[48]
  **Behçet's disease[2]

Neuromyasthenia[49]

IV. *Intoxications or drug reactions*
  Mercury[2] and its salts[21]
  Lead[2]
  Alcohols[50]
  Ethylene glycol[50]
  Metaldehyde[50]
  Methyl bromide[51]
  Chloralose[50]
  Strychnine[52]
  Pentetrazole[21]
  Phenol[20]
  Camphor[21]
  Picrotoxin[21]
  Bemegride[21]
  Sodium santonin[2]
  Menthol[50]
  Borates[50]
  Fluoroacetate[21]
  Organophosphates[21]
  Organochlorines (DDT)[21]
  Paradichlorobenzene[50]
  Penicillin[53]
  Carbamazepine[54]
  Diphenylhydantoin[55]
  Phenobarbital (addiction or with-
      drawal)[56]
  Amphetamine[50]
  Lithium carbonate[57]
  Amitriptyline[58]
  Imipramine[21]
  Piperazine[59]
  Dextropropoxyphene[50]
  Codeine[50]
  Insulin[50]
  Biguanides[50]
  Sulfamides[50]
  Cycloserine[21]
  Nicotine[50]
  Nikethamide[50]
  Apresoline[50]
  Theophylline[50]
  Tris-aminomethane (THAM)[50]
  Isoniazid[50]
  Hydrazides[60]

*mainly pediatric;   **mainly adult

beneficial. Included as treatable causes are such conditions as hypoglycemia and hypoxia, where myoclonus may be a late manifestation, and other diseases for which treatment is available, but of questionable value. The physician treating a patient with myoclonus should be particularly aware of those diseases for which specific therapy is available. Some examples of these important etiologies are the pyridoxine depletion states,[33] polymyoclonia and opsoclonus with neuroblastoma,[43] hepatolenticular degeneration,[2] aminoacidurias,[2] uremia,[31] and various intoxications[50] or drug reactions.[58] In many of these the myoclonus is reversible with appropriate medical care, but the effects on central nervous system function may not improve if the correct diagnosis is missed and specific treatment not given early enough. As an example, in pyridoxine dependency, children treated late may be severely retarded while those receiving early pyridoxine supplements may develop normally.[64]

The neurophysiology of myoclonus has been discussed in a previous chapter. Still, it is worth reiterating the usual distinction made between seizures, myoclonic jerks, and fasciculations since all represent neuronal discharges which under most circumstances are abnormal. Those discharges arising primarily from cortex are labeled seizures, discharges from anterior horn cells are referred to as fasciculation, and those from interneurons of the brainstem or spinal cord are called myoclonus.[3] Diffuse neuronal degeneration has been suggested as a common etiology in myoclonic syndromes,[65] but Luttrell et al. found the cerebral cortex uniformly spared in experimental myoclonus produced with Newcastle disease virus.[66] The contrast in these findings probably indicates that myoclonus, can arise at many levels in the central nervous system (CNS). Diffuse neuronal effects may account for the frequency of myoclonus seen in intoxications, since many of the drugs which produce myoclonus in man (Table 2) cause generalized convulsions in larger doses.[21] The mechanisms of drug-induced myoclonus are variable. Some act directly upon the CNS (strychnine, pentetrazole) while others induce hypoglycemia (insulin, THAM), cause pyridoxine deficiency (thiazides, isoniazid), or lead to myoclonus by unknown mechanisms (piperazine, imipramine).[50]

EVALUATION OF PATIENTS

In order to arrive at a definite diagnosis, a thorough evaluation of the patient is necessary. This requires a careful history with special attention to details of the pregnancy, birth and perinatal periods, motor and mental development, and exposures to drugs, chemicals, and infectious agents. A detailed family history is often helpful in diagnosing such disorders as tuberous sclerosis, pyridoxine dependency, and diseases of the basal ganglia. In benign familial myoclonus or the familial system degenerations (Ramsay Hunt syndrome) this may be the only clue to the diagnosis. In addition to the general physical examination, a detailed neurological evaluation is essential. In children special attention during the examination should be directed to the head circumference and transillumination, skin lesions (depigmented areas, nevi, adenomas), and abdominal masses.

Laboratory evaluations of various kinds may be helpful in reaching a diagnosis.

TABLE 3

Laboratory determinations useful in determining the etiology of myoclonus

Blood:	sugar*, calcium*, urea nitrogen*, electrolytes*, arterial gases*, serology*, aminoacids**, heavy metals, thyroid function, screen for toxic substances, copper, ceruloplasmin, lysosomal enzymes, toxoplasmosis dye test, bilirubin.
Urine:	aminoacids**, heavy metals, screen for toxic substances, vanillylmandelic acid, homovanillic acid.
CSF:	protein*, sugar*, cell count*, gammaglobulin, colloidal gold, measles antibody titers, antibiotic levels.
X-rays:	skull*, chest, long bones, pyelogram.
Biopsies:	skin, nerve, muscle, liver, rectal, brain.
Other:	electroencephalogram*, electromyogram, electrocardiogram, brain scan (isotope), pneumoencephalogram, myelogram.

* indicated in most patients with myoclonus; **especially useful in children with myoclonus

The most useful kinds of tests will vary with the patient's age, symptoms, findings on examination, and the severity of the illness. Table 3 summarizes some of the most useful studies in investigating the etiology of myoclonus. Most patients should be screened for precipitating metabolic factors such as hypoglycemia, hypocalcemia, water intoxication, and uremia, and in children aminoacidurias. They should also have an evaluation of CNS functions with an electroencephalogram, a cerebrospinal fluid examination, and X-rays of the skull. If the history is suggestive or the onset of myoclonus abrupt, then a search for heavy metals, intoxicating chemicals or drugs, infectious agents, and other causes of myoclonus as outlined in Tables 1 and 2 should be instigated. Because of the poor prognosis and progressive deterioration in many of the disorders associated with myoclonus, extensive evaluations are often warranted. Even when a specific diagnosis is available, treatment is frequently difficult and at times symptomatic.

GENERAL ASPECTS OF THERAPY

Therapeutic drugs

A complete discussion of the medical therapy of myoclonus would require a review of most of the anticonvulsants available. Excellent discussions on the standard anticonvulsants are available,[67] and this discussion will be limited to two groups of drugs that are particularly useful in treating myoclonus. The benzodiazepine anticonvulsants will be covered since they have been consistently of value in myoclonus, and the adrenal corticosteroids and ACTH because of their frequent use and effectiveness in infantile spasms and polymyoclonia.

The benzodiazepines Although some authors[68] have considered myoclonus a focal type of epilepsy, the success in treating it with the commonly used anticonvulsants has been limited. However, some of the benzodiazepines have proven effective in treating myoclonic states. This group of drugs was first marketed as psychotherapeutic agents in 1959, but their value in convulsive disorders soon became apparent.[69] The most useful drugs clinically in the benzodiazepine group are diazepam, chlordiazepoxide, nitrazepam, oxazepam, flurazepam, and clonazepam. Diazepam, nitrazepam, and chlordiazepoxide have been useful in seizure disorders, clonazepam is currently under investigation and appears promising as an anticonvulsant, oxazepam is a psychotherapeutic agent, and flurazepam is an hypnotic. Of the anticonvulsant benzodiazepines, only diazepam and chlordiazepoxide are currently available in the United States. The structural formulae of the anticonvulsant benzodiazepine derivatives are given in Figure 1.

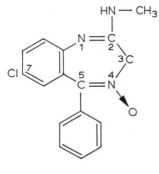

CHLORDIAZEPOXIDE

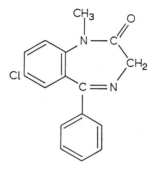

DIAZEPAM

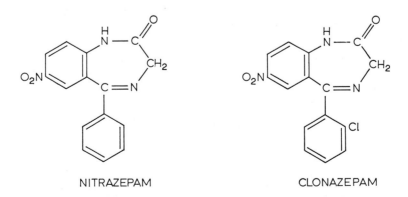

NITRAZEPAM   CLONAZEPAM

Fig. 1. Benzodiazepines useful in the treatment of myoclonus.

The mechanism of action for the benzodiazepines is not clear. Although they produce a sedative effect and are especially useful in seizure disorders aggravated by emotional stress,[70] they clearly have anticonvulsant properties.[69] In animal studies, diazepam suppresses seizure discharges arising from the hippocampus, amygdala, and septal areas.[69] Diazepam can also limit the spread from a seizure focus even though the focal discharge may continue.[69] Mattson reported a case of epilepsia partialis continua with a focal EEG discharge which persisted after diazepam therapy despite abrupt termination of the clinical seizures. Even though the benzodiazepines form a distinct chemical group, major stearic similarities between diphenylhydantoin and diazepam have been demonstrated.[71] Although this raises the possibility that both act on similar receptor sites, clinically diazepam is often effective in controlling myoclonus, while diphenylhydantoin rarely improves the myoclonus. Both in mice[72] and man[73] diazepam can block strychnine induced convulsions, and in the 'stiff man' syndrome[44] it may be beneficial. In all of these examples it seems to be acting at a spinal cord level. Diazepam thus appears to have three major actions, a sedative or antianxiety effect, a central anticonvulsant effect, and an effect at spinal cord levels.[74] Nitrazepam has actions similar to diazepam, but in small doses has a CNS stimulant effect not seen with other benzodiazepines. This may account for the grand mal seizures nitrazepam sometimes precipitates.[74] In animals nitrazepam is particularly active in suppressing temporal lobe seizure discharges,[74] but this does not appear to be the case in man.

Orally administered doses of benzodiazepines are adequately absorbed and produce therapeutic blood levels which vary with the specific compound. Diazepam and chlordiazepoxide reach peak blood levels from 1-2 hours after an oral dose while nitrazepam takes 3-4 hours.[69] In experimental animals maximum drug concentrations enter the cerebral gray matter within minutes of an adequate intravenous dose.[69] Chromatography using either gas or gas-liquid methods can be used to measure blood levels, but determining therapeutic levels has been hampered by the low serum concentrations needed for therapy. Although the optimum serum levels of these drugs needed for seizure control are not established, some information has been accumulated. Consistently decreased EEG paroxysms have been reported with serum diazepam levels above 0.25 µg/ml.[75] One patient had a photosensitive seizure discharge controlled with a serum diazepam level of 0.11 µg/ml.[69] When serum levels of both diazepam and its demethylated product are measured, they range from 0.1 to 2.3 µg/ml on oral doses of 5 mg 3 times a day in adults, and when the dose is increased to 10 mg 3 times a day these levels approach 1 µg/ml.[69] Serum levels after chronic administration are significantly higher than after single doses, presumably due to saturation of tissue stores. Data on therapeutic serum levels of the other benzodiazepines are not currently available. The liver is important in the excretion of all the benzodiazepines, but chlordiazepoxide can also be excreted primarily by the kidney.

During chronic administration of both nitrazepam and diazepam to animals and man, tolerance can appear. Livingston considered diazepam of limited value because of this. He reported 300 patients whom he treated with diazepam.[36] Many responded initially but relapsed after 2 or 3 months of treatment, and only

2 had permanent seizure control. Other authors have disagreed.[76,77] Weinberg and Harwell followed some patients on diazepam up to 12 months with sustained control, but 4 of their 14 patients did relapse on treatment.

Serious toxic reactions have not been a problem, but minor side effects such as drowsiness, dizziness, ataxia, and hypotonia are relatively common, especially in children taking over 1 mg/kg/day of diazepam.[69] Increased salivation and tracheobronchial secretions have been noted with nitrazepam and to a lesser extent with diazepam. The intravenous use of diazepam has been associated with respiratory depression on some occasions, and possible synergism with barbiturates was suspected;[78] however, Livingston[36] and others[79] have used diazepam and phenobarbital together without serious complications.

Corticotropin and adrenal hormones   A group of drugs which have been beneficial in myoclonic seizures, especially infantile myoclonic spasms, are the adrenal steroids and adrenocorticotropic hormone (ACTH). ACTH was used in seizure disorders with some transient success as early as 1950.[80] However, it became very popular in the treatment of infantile spasms after the work of Sorel and Dusaucy-Bauloye in 1958.[81] Following their success with ACTH, oral preparations of adrenal steroid hormones such as hydrocortisone, prednisolone, and prednisone were utilized and found to have similar effects.[82] Whether any of these preparations is superior in the treatment of myoclonic spasms or infantile polymyoclonia is currently an unanswered question.

The normal 24 hour adrenal output of cortisol (hydrocortisone) is 15 to 20 mg, and of corticosterone 2 to 4 mg.[83] These constitute the major glucocorticoid secretions, and when stimulated by ACTH their synthesis can increase from 5 to 10 fold. ACTH also increases the production of several weakly androgenic hormones and perhaps aldosterone,[84] but these are produced in smaller amounts, and it is not known if they have any effect on myoclonic seizures. There is no convincing evidence that ACTH is superior to currently used adrenal corticosteroid preparations. However, since ACTH is given by injections and is usually started in the hospital, compliance is good. The adrenal corticosteroids can be given orally though and are easier to utilize on an outpatient basis if the follow-up is reliable.

Both corticosteroids and ACTH have significant CNS effects and both increases and decreases in their levels have been associated with psychoses[85] and increased intracranial pressure.[86] How corticosteroids and ACTH affect the CNS is unclear, but it may be through changes in cerebral blood flow or alterations in relative electrolyte concentrations in intracellular and extracellular spaces. In adrenocortical insufficiency there is decreased cerebral blood flow which suggests that corticosteroids beneficially influence intracranial perfusion.[85] In excesses of desoxycorticosterone, the precursor of corticosterone, there is an increased ratio of intracellular to extracellular sodium and potassium, while the reverse is true with hypocorticism. Radioactive cortisol does cross the blood brain barrier and appears to increase brain excitability.[87] Other explanations based on genetic, psychological, and biochemical mechanisms have been proposed for the CNS effects of corticosteroids and are reviewed by Quarton et al.[85]

Another CNS effect of adrenal corticosteroids and ACTH is observed when the CNS is injured in the presence of elevated levels of these hormones. Rats given ACTH after a standardized thermal injury to the parietal cortex show a smaller cortical scar than those who are untreated.[88] This may result from the effects of elevated cortisone levels on neuroglial proliferation, either through a direct effect on neuroglia or an indirect effect acting through inhibition of connective tissue reaction to injury and consequent removal of a stimulus that provokes neuroglial reaction.

The toxicity of ACTH is primarily due to the increase in corticosteroids. These side effects are similar to those resulting from high doses of exogenous adrenal corticosteroids, and include hyperglycemia, increased susceptibility to infection, hypertension, myopathy, peptic ulcers, psychosis, hypokalemic alkalosis, osteoporosis, and skin changes. Alternate day oral corticosteroid therapy decreases some side effects.[89] The most frequent adverse reactions to prednisone are reportedly acute psychosis and gastrointestinal bleeding.[90] Eighteen percent of patients in one study had psychiatric complications when the dosage exceeded 80 mg of prednisone per day.[90]

In summary, the selection of either ACTH or corticosteroids at the present time must be done on grounds other than pharmacologic. Factors such as route of administration, patient's compliance, ease of follow-up, and ability of the patient, parent, or relatives to assist in the care are important. Despite this lack of scientific confirmation, empirically ACTH at times seems beneficial when corticosteroids have either not been successful or have not maintained their benefit.[91]

Surgical approaches to myoclonus

Myoclonus has been approached surgically with some encouraging results. In 1960 Hassler and his colleagues reported their experience with stereotactic surgery in the treatment of extrapyramidal motor disturbances.[92] They reported that in patients with myoclonus, unilateral stimulation of the anterior basal part of the ventral lateral thalamic nucleus at any frequency would produce typical myoclonic jerks. They reasoned that myoclonus may be due to uncontrolled impulses from efferent cerebellar pathways to the thalamus, and chose to destroy the posterior part of the ventral lateral nucleus of the thalamus. This nucleus is a relay for the major cerebellar efferent systems which reach it through fibers of the superior cerebellar peduncle. Some of their patients with myoclonic syndromes improved after coagulation of the posterior basal part of the ventral lateral thalamic nucleus, but they did not feel it was an indicated procedure in most patients with progressive myoclonic epilepsy because of the usual rapid progression of the primary illness. Hassler updated this experience in 1968 when he reported 16 patients with extrapyramidal myoclonus and 12 patients with 'myoclonic torticollis' whom he treated with coagulation of the nucleus ventralis oralis posterior and who improved clinically.[93]

Laitinen performed subventrolateral thalamotomies on 7 patients with severe progressive myoclonus epilepsy.[94] All of the patients had grand mal seizures in addition to frequent myoclonic jerks of the extremities and head. Six of these patients were in their teens, and in all the symptoms had started at about 10 years of age. In most of the patients the contralateral ataxia and intention tremor improved, and 4 of the patients regained the ability to feed themselves. Five patients had a reduced number of grand mal seizures in addition, but the myoclonus did not significantly improve. The long term results were less optimistic, but progression of the basic disease may have contributed to this.

Another surgical approach utilizing similar anatomical reasoning was taken by Spiegel, Wycis, and their colleagues.[95,96] They placed stereotactic lesions in Forel's field H (campotomy). A large number of fiber systems form or pass through this area, including pallidofugal, rubrothalamic, corticofugal, hypothalamofugal, cerebello-thalamic, and ascending fibers from the reticular formation. Their original report on campotomy in extrapyramidal disorders included 1 patient with localized myoclonus,[95] and in a follow-up report they related further experience with this lesion in myoclonic syndromes.[96] They described a 19 year old man with myoclonic jerks of the left neck, shoulder, arm, and diaphragm which were present since 11 years of age. The movements increased with anxiety and were absent during sleep. His neurological examination was otherwise normal. Following right campotomy the myoclonic jerks were markedly reduced, and he returned to work. Fifteen months later similar myoclonic jerks recurred on the opposite side, and he underwent a left campotomy. The second lesion was also successful, and on examination 4 years later he had only mild intermittent contractions of the right platysma. Another patient with a similar story also responded well to contralateral campotomy. Their third success was a 30 year old man with a 4 year history of bilateral myoclonic jerks of the arms, legs, and neck. Except for the myoclonus, he was neurologically intact. Preoperatively he was given a trial of diazepam, but the jerks persisted. Immediately following a left campotomy, there was a marked reduction of the myoclonic movements in the right side of the body, and 6 months later the movements of his left side had also decreased. He was maintained postoperatively on 15 mg a day of diazepam, however.

These initial results with surgical approaches to myoclonus in selected patients seem encouraging, but myoclonus secondary to diffuse neuronal disease is probably not amenable to this type of therapy. The surgical approaches have been directed toward ablation of the posterior ventral lateral thalamus and fiber systems entering it. Although they show some promise in selected patients, their usefulness is limited by the diffuse and progressive nature of many myoclonic syndromes.

EXPERIMENTAL MYOCLONUS

An understanding of experimental myoclonus and the factors influencing it is helpful in approaching the therapy of myoclonus. Myoclonus was produced in experimental animals as early as 1894 when Turtschaninow induced it with sodium santonin.[97] It was next reported by Muskens using the monobromide of camphor injected intravenously into cats.[98] Even in these early works it was apparent that small doses of the drug produced myoclonus and larger doses often led to grand mal seizures. Many authors have regarded myoclonus as an epileptic phenomenon because of this relationship with generalized seizures.[68,98]

Adrian and Moruzzi in 1939 showed that myoclonic jerks precede generalized convulsions when an agent interferes with the function of cortical control in a progressive and slow enough fashion.[99] They also noted that stimulus-sensitive myoclonus occurred prior to spontaneous myoclonus and that cerebral ischemia would temporarily prevent this response even though cortical potentials could still be recorded. Among the agents which can do this are anoxia, oxygen intoxication, hypoglycemia, pentetrazole, picrotoxin, and chloralose. When concentrations of these agents sufficient to produce myoclonus are reached, only a slight increase will result in a grand mal seizure.[19] Sound, light and touch are some of the sensory stimuli which precipitate myoclonic jerks in the preconvulsive phase of the intoxication. Gastaut has studied experimental myoclonus and noted that the electrical discharge of myoclonus appears first in the mesencephalon and thalamus, that the spike and wave discharges are present in gray matter throughout the brain, that myoclonic jerks occur even in the rhombencephalic animal, and that stimulation of the midline anterior thalamic nuclei produces an electrical discharge pattern identical to that of a myoclonic discharge.[19]

Alvord and Fuortes studied myoclonus produced by light chloralose anesthesia and compared it to the effects of strychnine in the spinal cat.[52] They found that strychnine enhances intersegmental spread of reflexes throughout the spinal cord while chloralose acts primarily through supraspinal structures. This differentiation between myoclonic jerks arising in spinal and supraspinal structures was also found by Luttrell and Bang in a series of experiments utilizing Newcastle disease virus (NDV).[100,101] This virus can produce either segmental or central myoclonus depending upon the route of inoculation. Following intraventricular NDV inoculation diffuse central myoclonus occurs within 40 to 60 hours, while spinal inoculation results in segmental myoclonus. In the diffuse myoclonus preparation they studied the effects of chlorpromazine and paraldehyde given into the cerebral ventricles. Both drugs produced a marked attenuation of the myoclonus by this route, but the drugs were not given systemically. They also noted that while light ether anesthesia did not affect the myoclonus, asphyxia consistently reduced both its rate and force.[101]

Denny-Brown and Milhorat have approached the problem from the surgical aspect. In his monograph on diseases of the basal ganglia Denny-Brown noted that in primates after bilateral symmetric ablations of the centrum medianum, the nucleus ventralis lateralis oralis, or the globus pallidus, there was a tendency to have flexion myoclonus of all 4 limbs.[12] Contralateral spontaneous myoclonus and lowering of the myoclonic threshold in primates was also produced by Milhorat when he destroyed the midline thalamic nuclei.[102] In contrast, he found that lesions in the lateral thalamus did not produce myoclonus, and indeed abolished myoclonus produced 5-7 days earlier by an ipsilateral medial thalamectomy.[102,103] Destruction of the nonspecific interlaminar nuclei and the medial nuclei of the thalamus including the median dorsal nucleus appeared to be important in lowering the myoclonic threshold. He interpreted these findings to mean that myoclonus results from removal of normal inhibitory mechanisms.

Another experimental model with clinical applicability is that of urea infusions producing hyperosmolarity and myoclonus.[104] Urea readily crosses cellular membranes and when plasma concentrations reach 400 mosm it consistently produces coarse myoclonic jerks, whereas similar serum osmolalities produced by sodium chloride or sucrose result only in muscular twitching and at higher concentrations seizures, but do not lead to either reticular spike activity or myoclonic jerks. Electrophysiologically the myoclonus is associated with spikes and sharp waves originating in the lower brainstem reticular formation. Urea induced myoclonic jerks are similar to those seen in uremic patients.

These experimental situations suggest that therapy, whether medical or surgical, should be directed toward influencing the function of the reticular formation and thalamus in central myoclonus. The mechanism for segmental myoclonus remains obscure.

SPECIFIC ASPECTS OF THERAPY

Essential or benign myoclonus

The presence of a benign form of myoclonus which is neither progressive nor associated with other neurological or mental deficits has been well documented in the literature.[105,106] Other features of this entity are its familial occurrence, onset in the first or second decade of life, and normal EEG findings. The myoclonus is usually present only during waking hours, does not significantly interfere with normal life, and is frequently increased by anxiety. The presence of myoclonic jerks during waking hours differentiates them from those seen in most normal people when drowsy.[107] In several families they have started as early as $1\frac{1}{2}$ to 2 years of age[105,106] and in a single case they started at age 86.[2]

Because of their benign nature and relatively minimal interference with life styles, they have not received vigorous treatment. Mahloudji and Pikielny treated 1 patient with phenobarbital, but there was little effect.[106] Gilbert saw a 75 year old man with over 50 years of myoclonic jerking and noted some improvement when he was treated with diazepam.[62] Daube and Peters described 2 families who had many individuals involved.[105] In some of their patients they tried phenobarbital, meprobamate, chlordiazepoxide, diazepam, diphenylhydantoin, reserpine, and fluphenazine. They found variable responses to all of these drugs and concluded that the beneficial effects were proportional to the sedation achieved. Indeed alcohol was as helpful as other drugs, but no medications controlled the myoclonic jerks well enough for the patient to feel comfortable in public.

Surgical intervention in unequivocal cases of this myoclonic syndrome has not been reported, probably because of the benign nature of the disorder and its relative lack of interference with normal activities. The third case of Wycis and Spiegel in their report on campotomy was said to have essential myoclonus, but he was atypical in that his movements started at 26 years of age, the myoclonic jerks had progressively worsened, and there was no family history of the disorder.[95]

If the myoclonus is of sufficient frequency or intensity to require treatment, then diazepam or phenobarbital in standard therapeutic doses should be tried initially. Other antianxiety drugs might also be beneficial, since no specific action has been attributed to diazepam or phenobarbital in essential myoclonus.

Segmental myoclonus

Segmental myoclonus refers to myoclonic jerks occurring in the motor distribution of a spinal cord segment or a localized brainstem area. Unlike other types of myoclonus it is usually due to pathology at the involved level of the CNS. Myoclonus secondary to local spinal cord disease has been reported by several authors,[16,108] and experimentally produced by Luttrell and his colleagues.[101] Spinal cord tumors producing myoclonus have been reported by Penfield and Jasper,[108] and by Garcin et al.[16] Garcin and co-workers reported a 63 year old female with a 2 year history of rhythmic myoclonic contractions in the right arm which had started in the biceps. On examination she had a sensory loss over the right shoulder and arm, wasting of the shoulder and arm muscles, and a Brown-Séquard syndrome below this level. The myoclonus was continuous even during sleep, but could be transiently abolished by voluntary contraction of an involved muscle, or decreased by performing mental arithmetic. The myoclonus was most prominent in the C5 and C6 musculature, but was present in C4 and C7 segments to a lesser degree. At laminectomy she had a poorly demarcated astrocytoma extending from C3 to C5 which contained an old hematoma. Postoperatively the myoclonus decreased in frequency and became irregular and synchronous.

Similar segmental myoclonic syndromes have been recorded after other types of spinal cord disease. Patrikios reported a 49 year old male with a gunshot wound in the neck who had a Brown-Séquard syndrome below C4 from a predominantly right-sided spinal cord lesion.[24] This man developed rhythmic myoclonus in the C3 to C6 distribution on the left, and in the C6 to C8 segments to the right. The same author reported a 60 year old man with typical amyotrophic lateral sclerosis who had rhythmic myoclonus of the fingers.[15] Snyder and Appenzeller reported segmental myoclonus in a 2 year old boy who had a lower thoracic meningomyelocele with a flaccid paraplegia.[20] At 15 months of age this child developed intermittent rhythmic myoclonus of the lower extremities. On electromyogram the glutei showed rhythmic discharges of normal motor units. They attributed the myoclonus to isolation of a spinal cord segment in conjunction with possible deafferentation. Swanson et al. described segmental myoclonus in a 28 year old man who was otherwise normal.[3] His movements were restricted to the deltoid, forearm flexors, and upper abdominal muscles on the left, and had been present his entire life. They increased when he was nervous or used his left arm. No etiology was determined, but on the basis of electromyography they were felt to arise at the level of the spinal cord. Treatment was not commented upon. Recently a patient with myoclonic contractions of the periumbilical muscles was seen at this hospital. The movements had been present intermittently for 4 years and were an incidental finding when he was seen for a left hemisphere transient ischemic attack. Contractions occurred at a rate of 10-20 per minute and were confined to a focal area of musculature corresponding to the T9-T10 motor distribution on the left. A left carotid stenosis and an abdominal aortic aneurysm were found and both were repaired. The focal myoclonus was felt to be related to the aortic aneurysm.

Another category of segmental myoclonus is that secondary to infectious agents. That infectious agents can do this experimentally was shown by Luttrell et al.[101] Campbell and Garland described a segmental myoclonic syndrome in 3 patients which they named subacute myoclonic spinal neuronitis.[40] The outstanding clinical feature of their 3 patients was stimulus-sensitive myoclonus primarily in the muscles of the abdomen and lower extremities which was associated with painful muscle spasms. Their 2 patients who died had increased neuroglia and lymphocytic perivenous cuffing limited to the spinal cord, which suggested a viral etiology. Their only surviving patient (Case 2) had the onset of myoclonic spasms and fever over a 24 hour period with spasms persisting for 2 days and then steadily clearing over the following week. Both patients who died had received irradiation to their spinal cords months or years prior to this episode. Treatment in all 3 patients was mainly supportive. In the 2 patients who died muscle spasms were so severe that morphine was used for relief. In one of their patients (Case 3) who lived for 5 weeks after the illness started, they found that morphine, pethidine, thiopental, and bromethol gave only minimal relief from the painful muscle spasms. Consequently, spinal anesthesia was given and complete relief was obtained for 24 hours before the spasms recurred. When spinal anesthesia was repeated, relief again occurred, but following this curare was utilized to prevent the muscle spasms and respiratory support became necessary. Initially 30 mg of aqueous curare every 3 hours gave good relief, but later this was adjusted to 50 mg of curare in oil and 10 mg in aqueous solution at 3-hourly intervals. Despite the relief with this treatment, physical examination was never possible, presumably because of the painful spasms initiated by any stimulus.

A similar but less severe segmental myoclonus which appeared to be infectious was reported by Greenhouse.[109] It occurred in a 20 year old soldier who developed rhythmic myoclonus in the cervical segments following a respiratory infection. Initially there was a lymphocytic pleocytosis and an elevated protein in his CSF. The myoclonus persisted for 6 months before abating. The clinical similarity of Campbell and Garland's patients[40] to some patients with the 'stiff man' syndrome[110] raises the possibility that diazepam or other benzodiazepines might be helpful in acute spinal neuronitis, since these drugs affect spinal reflexes and diazepam has been useful in relieving painful muscle spasms in the latter disease.

Intoxications

As previously noted, myoclonus can be produced in animals or man by a variety of pharmacologic agents, most of which will cause generalized convulsions if given in large enough doses. Among these agents are such commonly used therapeutic drugs as penicillin, piperazine, tricyclic antidepressants, and the anticonvulsants diphenylhydantoin, phenobarbital and carbamazepine. In addition, a number of less common chemicals and pharmaceuticals have occasionally been reported to cause intoxications and myoclonus in man.

Piperazine, a frequently prescribed antihelminthic used to treat the gastrointestinal parasites Enterobius and Ascaris, can cause myoclonus in patients taking it therapeutically.[59,111] The hexahydrate form of piperazine is more soluble and better absorbed than other salts such as tartrate, citrate, and adipate. All of these forms seem to be effective against the helminths, but the more easily absorbed forms produce toxicity most frequently. Schuch et al.[111] observed abnormal EEG's in several patients after administering piperazine hexahydrate, and considered this a true neurotoxicity. They felt piperazine should be avoided in anyone with known disease of the CNS, and reported 2 cases with status epilepticus after therapeutic doses of piperazine hexahydrate, 1 of whom died. However, the majority of these patients show rapid clearing of their symptoms when piperazine is stopped.[59] Treatment consists of discontinuing the medication, supportive care, and evaluation of the renal status since renal insufficiency can both cause and prolong toxic accumulations.

The neurotoxicity of penicillin when placed in direct contact with the CNS has been apparent since 1945 when Johnson and Walker gave it directly into the lateral ventricle of a patient and observed unresponsiveness, shock, and later myoclonus.[112] It rapidly became apparent that intrathecal penicillin in sufficient doses would act similarly;[113] however, only in recent years with the use of very high intravenous doses of penicillin has toxicity been noted by this route. Very high serum penicillin levels have been used for gram-negative infections[114,115] during cardiopulmonary bypass,[116] and have been seen secondary to reduced excretion during renal failure.[53,117] The rarity of penicillin-induced myoclonus and convulsions may be related to penicillin's active transport across the blood brain barrier and its rapid clearance by the kidneys. Serum penicillin levels sufficiently high to overcome the active transport mechanisms of the blood brain barrier are seldom achieved, and toxicity is unusual. Lerner and co-workers have studied the CSF concentrations of penicillin associated with neurotoxicity and found levels of 12 units/ml and above were associated with either myoclonus or seizures.[118] Toxic levels of CSF penicillin were most frequently noted when it was infused constantly rather than intermittently, when renal function was compromised, or when other CNS irritating factors such as hyponatremia or meningitis were present. The use of probenecid may also increase CSF levels of penicillin since it inhibits renal excretion, competes with penicillin for serum protein binding sites, and inhibits the transport system which removes penicillin from the spinal fluid.[119] Characteristically the neurotoxicity of penicillin consists of myoclonic jerks of the face and upper extremities followed by generalized myoclonus, hyperreflexia, hallucinations, coma, and convulsions. Deaths have been reported, but the patients were seriously ill and the role of penicillin was unclear.[116] Neurotoxicity has also been reported with sodium cephalothin and carbenicillin.[53,117] In most cases discontinuing the antibiotic or reducing the dosage results in rapid clinical improvement over 24 to 72 hours.[117]

Myoclonus has also been associated with therapeutic doses of imipramine,[120] amitriptyline,[58] lithium carbonate,[57] diphenylhydantoin,[55] and carbamazepine.[54] In most instances reducing the dosage or discontinuing the drug has stopped the myoclonus.

A large number of intoxications in both children and adults can result in myoclonic symptoms (see Table 2). Their treatment consists of removing the source of intoxication, careful attention to maintenance of blood glucose, and prevention of anoxic episodes.

Posthypoxic action myoclonus

The myoclonic movement disorder seen after episodes of acute anoxia from any etiology has been termed action or intention myoclonus by Lance and Adams.[121] It is characterized by myoclonic jerks which are present at rest but increase markedly with any intentional or voluntary movement. It is usually associated with a mild cerebellar syndrome, and there may be lapses of postural control which can result in falls. Since voluntary movements strikingly increase the myoclonus, the symptoms are often disabling.

Lance and Adams in their original article commented on treatment in only 1 of their 4 cases.[121] That patient reported that, after a cocktail or two, his limbs became sufficiently steady for him to feed himself. He was treated with several medications but only mephobarbital in doses of 600-650 mg daily was effective, and with that dose he had to take dextroamphetamine to stay awake. Rosen et al. reported 2 patients with intention myoclonus who responded well to a combination of diazepam and phenobarbital.[122] The first was a 27 year old physician who developed intention myoclonus after a cardiac arrest. He failed to respond to large doses of standard anticonvulsants (diphenylhydantoin up to 600 mg/day, phenobarbital up to 180 mg/day, and primidone up to 1250 mg/day), but diazepam 5 mg 3 times a day produced striking relief, and the addition of phenobarbital 30 mg 4 times a day reduced the myoclonus to a rare episode when he was exhausted. Their other patient was a 27 year old woman with an intraoperative hypoxic episode which resulted in intention myoclonus. She responded well to diazepam 10 mg 3 times a day and improved further when phenobarbital 30 mg 3 times a day was added. Two months after starting treatment the diazepam was stopped for a re-evaluation and the myoclonus returned, but she again responded well when treatment was resumed.

A newer benzodiazepine derivative, clonazepam, has been used with success in postanoxic myoclonus by Boudouresques and co-workers.[123] One of their patients, a 54 year old school principal, improved on daily oral doses of phenobarbital 100 mg, carbamazepine 600 mg, diazepam 30 mg, and nitrazepam 5 mg, but continued to have difficulty in walking. When 6 mg a day of clonazepam was given along with 500 mg daily of primidone, there was striking improvement and he could walk without difficulty. Another patient had an equally good response, and both had EEG's that returned to normal after starting clonazepam. They postulated that clonazepam's action is both cortical and subcortical.

Although the benzodiazepines have been the most promising, other treatment regimens have succeeded. Hirose et al. treated a 44 year old woman with action myoclonus following a cardiac arrest.[124] Her myoclonic jerks were resistant to a variety of medications, but did respond to phenacemide. She unfortunately developed liver toxicity and the drug had to be discontinued. Following this, a stereotactic left thalamotomy was done, but the myoclonus persisted. She was then given diazepam 40 mg a day, phenobarbital 90 mg a day and primidone 250 mg a day with little change in the movement disorder. Eventually she needed institutional care. At a later time carbamazepine was added to her other medications and when it was increased to 800 mg a day, there was dramatic improvement. She was able to feed herself and could walk with minimal assistance. Attempts to lower the dosage of diazepam, phenobarbital, or carbamazepine resulted in exacerbations. She was followed for 8 months and maintained her improvement. Sherwin and Redmon treated a 62 year old man whose myocardial infarction and cardiac arrest was followed by intention myoclonus.[125] They found diazepam and chlorpromazine to be the most beneficial drugs. The latter was used to treat his anxiety and incidentally improved the movement disorder. On 400 mg a day of chlorpromazine his myoclonic jerks subsided and he was able to carry on activities, despite the development of mild extrapyramidal symptoms. Even on treatment the myoclonus could easily be induced with stimulation when he was anxious. He was given diazepam alone in doses up to 40 mg a day and had excellent control of the myoclonus, but subjectively he felt better on chlorpromazine and preferred to take it. The authors suggested two possible physiologic mechanisms for his benefit from chlorpromazine apart from its antianxiety effect. Chlorpromazine may selectively depress incremental cortical responses secondary to thalamic stimulation without affecting the reticular activating system, or it may produce a gating effect on brainstem collaterals and thus reduce the input from the proprioceptive afferents which can induce myoclonic jerks.

Lhermitte et al. did an extensive pharmacological evaluation of a 59 year old female who developed intention myoclonus after a cardiac arrest.[126] They found phenobarbital, diazepam, carbamazepine, alcohol, and 5-hydroxytryptamine (5HTP) to be the most effective drugs in reducing her myoclonus. They tested a number of drugs including chlorpromazine, levomepromazine, haloperidol, dihydroergotamine, and methyldopa which made the myoclonus worse. Methysergide, a drug that inhibits or blocks serotonin, also made the myoclonus worse and an anticholinergic (trihexyphenidyl) did not affect the movements. In view of Sherwin and Redmon's[125] success with chlorpromazine, the reverse effect in this patient is puzzling.[126] The myoclonus in this patient became so severe after the dose of chlorpromazine reached 20 mg a day that treatment with phenobarbital was required. The difference in dosage was large, however, and this may be important. The use of 5HTP and its relief of myoclonus is interesting. Initially the 5HTP was mixed in isotonic glucose and given in 3 doses totalling 100 mg a day. The patient's improvement was marked, and she continued to improve as the dose was increased to 200 mg daily, but beyond this there was little change although the dose was increased to 1 gram daily. When changed to 300 mg of 5HTP orally, the improvement persisted. The only complications with 5HTP were a mild hypotension and some gastrointestinal complaints. She was maintained on phenobarbital during all the medication trials except those with diazepam and alcohol. Lhermitte and co-workers concluded that myoclonus was facilitated by blocking catecholaminergic and serotoninergic synapses, while increasing the available serotonin inhibits myoclonic mechanisms. This same group later studied a second patient, and again methysergide, haloperidol and levomepromazine in therapeutic doses worsened the myoclonus.[127] This second patient also received L-DOPA in rapidly increasing doses up to 2.5 grams daily for a total of 10 days. Both objective and subjective improvement was noted, but agitation, insomnia, and gastrointestinal symptoms occurred. Iproniazid, a monoamine oxidase inhibitor, was also given to this patient in a dose of 100 mg daily and did produce improvement. A repeat trial with 5HTP again showed remarkable improvement, but not at a dose of 200 mg orally per day. An oral dose of 1.5 to 2 grams daily was required, and this resulted in orthostatic hypotension and transient tachycardia with incomplete bundle branch block. Their previous conclusion, that increasing catecholamine and serotonin levels inhibit myoclonus, was confirmed.

A surgical approach to this problem was taken by this same group.[128] They stereotactically stimulated the ventral lateral thalamus in a 34 year old female who suffered hypoxia after an overdose of nitrazepam, but were unable to produce myoclonus. In their study spikes from the ventral lateral nucleus of the thalamus followed cortical motor discharges, but never preceded them. They later ablated the patient's ventral lateral thalamic nucleus but she did not improve.

Subacute sclerosing panencephalitis

Subacute sclerosing panencephalitis (SSPE) is a progressive disease of the CNS characterized by dementia with personality change, motor deterioration, myoclonus, and a typical EEG pattern. It is considered uniformly fatal by some authors although survivors have been reported.[129,130] It is thought to be a slow virus infection caused by measles. Measles is a ribonucleic acid (RNA) containing member of the myxovirus group. The large myxoviruses are divided into two basic groups, the measles distemper-rinderpest group, and the mumps-Newcastle disease-Sendai-parainfluenza group. Myoclonic syndromes result from infections with at least two other members of these groups. Experimental Newcastle disease virus infection in cats,[100] and distemper virus infection in dogs produce myoclonus.[131]

Treatment of SSPE has generally been discouraging although some patients are reported to stabilize.[130,131] Thymectomy was an early treatment used in 1 patient who had progressive symptoms despite corticosteroid treatment, and who had thymic enlargement on chest X-ray.[132] Following thymectomy both motor signs and seizures improved, but the mental status did not change. The use of thymectomy was based on the assumption that SSPE is an autoimmune disease. With this same rationale, numerous authors have used corticosteroids or corticotropin,[63,129,133] but no significant benefit has been attributed to them. Hyperimmune gammaglobulin was used by Hanissian et al. in a 5 year old boy with X-linked hypogammaglobulinemia and SSPE, but the course of the disease was not altered and he died $2\frac{1}{2}$ years following the onset of SSPE after progressively deteriorating.[134] Haloperidol was given to a 19 year old girl with a progressive encephalitis resembling SSPE, but without inclusion bodies on brain biopsy.[135] Her movement disorder was markedly improved, but the follow-up was short.

Since the growth of measles virus from brain biopsy in a patient with SSPE,[136] a number of patients have been treated with antiviral drugs. The anti-RNA agents would appear to be the most logical choices, but both anti-RNA and anti-desoxyribonucleic acid (DNA) drugs have been tried. Amantadine is a synthetic antiviral agent which has anti-RNA properties and has been shown in tissue culture to prevent cellular penetration by certain virus strains.[137] Haslam et al. used it in an effort to prevent spread of virus from infected to uninfected brain cells.[138] The drug has been shown to cross the blood brain barrier in therapeutic doses. They treated 5 patients with oral amantadine hydrochloride in doses of 3.5 to 10 mg per kilogram daily and noted stabilization of the disease in all 5 patients; however, there was no neurological improvement. The other anti-RNA drug which has been utilized is 8-azaguanine, which was given intraventricularly to 6 patients with SSPE by Robb and Waters.[139] Although the patients tolerated the drug, there was no improvement.

The use of anti-DNA drugs in the treatment of SSPE was tried prior to the recognition of SSPE as a measles virus infection.[139,140] However, there is a theoretical basis for the use of these drugs to treat an RNA virus infection. The two anti-DNA drugs that have been tried are 5-iodo-2-deoxyuridine (5IUDR) and 5-bromo-2-deoxyuridine (5BUDR) which are thymidine analogues and appear to compete for incorporation into DNA. DNA which incorporates these drugs would be abnormal and could inhibit further synthesis of RNA. Ventricular perfusion in 3 patients with 5IUDR, was without benefit.[139,140] A double-blind study using the 5-bromo substituted 2-deoxyuridine was reported by Freeman.[141] Twelve patients with SSPE were in the study, but no benefit with 5BUDR could be shown. The use of cyclophosphamide has not been reported in man, but in the hamster model of this disease it can activate a latent measles virus infection.[142] This may be secondary to inhibition of intercellular antibody in the brain with resultant viral spread and activation of a previously latent infection, but the exact mechanism is unknown.

Freeman also tested pyran copolymer in patients with SSPE.[143] Pyran copolymer induces the production of interferon which in turn inhibits replication of RNA viruses. He reasoned that high levels of interferon might prevent the progression of SSPE, but although the 2 patients treated showed elevated serum and CSF interferon levels, there was no improvement.

At present there is no successful treatment available for SSPE, and medical efforts are mainly supportive. Indeed, it is unknown whether the disease is related to the replication of the measles virus, the host's immunologic response to the infection, or some other factor such as neuronal damage secondary to the elevated measles antibody titers in the CSF.

Polymyoclonia with opsoclonus

The syndrome of polymyoclonia and opsoclonus consists of truncal and extremity myoclonus associated with chaotic eye movements. It occurs in all age groups and has several etiologies. The infantile form of the disease presents a fairly uniform picture which has been descriptively called the dancing eyes and dancing feet syndrome by Dyken and Kolar.[144] Infantile polymyoclonia usually has a normal CSF and EEG, but occasional infants[145] and many adults[146] have a CSF pleocytosis suggesting the syndrome is related to a meningoencephalitis.[43,147] Among the patients with infantile polymyoclonus there is a high incidence of neural crest tumors. A careful and continued search for such tumors is important in these patients.

In 1962 Kinsbourne reported 6 patients with truncal and extremity ataxia associated with opsoclonus, and documented their excellent response to ACTH.[91] Ford added 3 more patients,[148] and in recent years numerous patients have been reported.[149,53] In patients treated with ACTH, remissions occur within a few days of starting the medication, and exacerbations may occur when the dose is lowered too far. The effectiveness of prednisone as compared to ACTH in some patients with polymyoclonia is particularly interesting. These cases confirm that corticosteroids or corticotropin are the treatments of choice in infantile poly-myoclonia, and other investigators[144,150] have agreed. The treatment does not prevent the neurological sequelae of the illness, however.[150,152] Corticosteroids are most effective in large doses, and when they fail or do not provide lasting benefit then ACTH in doses of 30-40 units daily should be used. Treatment may be beneficial even in long standing cases.[91,150] Table 4 outlines the doses of ACTH and corticosteroids used with success by various authors. It is important to appreciate that corticosteroids or ACTH may provide symptomatic relief even when a neuroblastoma is present.[147]

TABLE 4

Treatment schedules used in infantile polymyoclonia

ACTH 40 to 120 units a day i.m. for 2 to 4 weeks, then taper to maintenance.[91, 152, 153]

Prednisolone 30-50 mg a day orally, then taper to maintenance.[91]

Hydrocortisone 15 mg a day orally (later changed to ACTH).[144]

Dexamethasone 1.5 mg a day orally, then taper to maintenance (dose increased with fevers).[159]

A relationship between tumors and polymyoclonia has also been reported in adults,[154,155] but the association between neural crest tumors and infantile polymyoclonia is more commonly encountered. This latter relationship is frequent enough that neuroblastoma or other neural crest tumors should be seriously considered in any child with polymyoclonia and opsoclonus, especially when the CSF is normal. The diagnosis of neuroblastoma in these children is often difficult, and may require repeated evaluations over several months. The laboratory studies that are most helpful in diagnosing neuroblastomas are X-rays (chest, abdomen, kidneys and long bones), urinary catecholamine excretion, and bone marrow aspiration. There are now several reports of children extensively evaluated for neural crest tumors with negative results initially who later were found to have tumors.[43,147,156] One patient had the onset of symptoms at 2 years of age and when 6 years old a ganglioneuroblastoma with widespread metastases was found.[43] The presence of catecholamine metabolites in the urine, either vanillylmandelic (VMA) or homovanillic acid (HVA) has been variable, and several cases with tumors have had normal levels.[157,158] The VMA spot test has also varied in usefulness. Chest X-rays are often helpful since nearly half of the patients with polymyoclonia and neuroblastoma have had intrathoracic tumors.[159] One patient had an intraspinal neuroblastoma.[43] Bone marrow aspirations, long bone X-rays, and liver function tests are helpful only if metastases are present. One patient had CSF pleocytosis and was later found to have a neuroblastoma.[156] In several cases the difficulty in diagnosing a neuroblastoma was impressive.[156,158] Removal of the neuroblastoma has improved symptoms in some patients,[156,160] but resulted in only partial relief of symptoms in others.[144,161] Two mg of diazepam intravenously produced transient symptomatic relief lasting 5 minutes in a 13 month old boy with opsoclonus and a neuroblastoma.[160]

Treatment of infantile and adult polymyoclonia should start with a careful evaluation of CSF looking for pleocytosis and a search for evidence of a tumor mass. In children the most common tumors are those of the neural crest, but adults can have tumors of the lung,[154] breast,[162] or uterus.[163] In any age group the tumor may be found months or years after symptoms appear. Symptomatic relief is often provided by ACTH in doses of 40 units a day for 2 to 4 weeks, but may require continued maintenance at a lower dosage for long periods of time. Periodic re-evaluations for a tumor are indicated in any patient whose symptoms persist.

Infantile spasms

It is important to stop these seizures, if possible, since this allows the child to reach his maximum potential, improves the psychosocial atmosphere for the child in the home, and may prevent further brain damage. In recent years it has become easier to control these seizures, but whether a concomitant improvement has occurred in the long term outlook with treatment is still debatable. In those patients where a specific etiology, such as pyridoxine dependency, is found and treatment begun early, the outcome may be very good.[64]

Although the treatable causes of infantile spasms are uncommon, they are important for the physician to recognize, since early diagnosis and proper treatment may stop the seizures, prevent brain damage, and permit the child to develop normally. Table 5 outlines some of the treatable causes of myoclonic seizures in infants. Early and vigorous treatment of any disorder in infancy which can produce brain damage is essential in preventing infantile spasms. Perinatal hypoglycemia and hypoxia are common factors in patients who later develop

TABLE 5

Treatable causes of infantile spasms

Hypoglycemia[21]
Hypoxia[21]
Lead[2]
Kernicterus[36]
Menkes's kinky hair syndrome[32]

Meningitis, purulent[3]
Syphilis[38]
Toxoplasmosis[38]

Phenylketonuria[23]
Maple syrup urine disease[2]
Leigh's disease[18]
Pyridoxine insufficiency[33]
Hyperornithemia, hyperammonemia
    and homocitrullinuria[34]

Neonatal polycythemia[46]
Subdural hematoma[18]

infantile spasms, and are common problems in newborn nurseries. Neonatal meningitis, although less common, should receive thorough treatment for similar reasons. The association of neonatal polycythemia with myoclonic or generalized convulsions is not widely appreciated,[46] but when central hematocrits above 65 to 70 are associated with any CNS symptoms, treatment consisting of a partial exchange transfusion using fresh frozen plasma, or phlebotomy, is indicated. Several defects in amino acid metabolism produce myoclonic seizures and retardation. Phenylketonuria is the most common, but maple syrup urine disease and the urea cycle defect described by Shih et al.[34] can also produce infantile spasms. Since these are treatable with dietary modifications, they should be looked for in these patients. Menkes's kinky hair syndrome has been associated with seizures and myoclonus also, and appears to be a defect in copper metabolism which may soon be treatable.[32] Pyridoxine and thiamine have been implicated in infantile spasms also. Leigh's disease may be related to abnormal thiamine metabolism and although it seldom causes seizures, it is reported to be associated with infantile spasms.[18]

Vitamin B_6 or pyridoxine deficiency or dependency is an uncommon but treatable cause of myoclonic spasms and generalized seizures in infancy.[166,169] Vitamin B_6 is a coenzyme precursor which in biological systems exists in several forms extracellularly (pyridoxal, pyridoxol, and pyridoxamine), and different forms intracellularly (pyridoxal-5-phosphate and pyridoxamine-5-phosphate).[166] The intracellular forms are coenzymes for many apoenzymes involved in the metabolism of aminoacids, glycogen, and fatty acids. In the gray matter of the CNS they participate in the decarboxylation of glutamic acid to form the neuro-inhibitor gamma-aminobutyric acid (GABA). Low levels of GABA can lead to CNS hyperirritability, myoclonus, and convulsions. Since GABA levels in the CNS of immature brains are lower than those in adults, the infant may be at risk for any process which lowers GABA levels further. Vitamin B_6 deficiency is seen in diabetics, pregnancy, secondary to drugs (isoniazid,[50] penicillamine,[167] cycloserine), and due to insufficient intake.[168] Some infants appear to require larger than normal amounts of this vitamin, and this has been called vitamin B_6 dependency.[168] This type is usually familial.[64] In both types of pyridoxine insufficiency the response to adequate doses of pyridoxine is good, but in the dependency state high doses may be required. Pyridoxine in single doses of 50 mg intravenously or intramuscularly provides dramatic seizure relief in some patients.[169] Daily maintenance doses of 12.5[64] to 25 mg[169] in addition to that obtained from dietary sources may be needed, and higher doses may be required with fevers. This important cause of infantile spasms should not be overlooked since severe brain damage or death results in untreated patients.[64]

Prior to 1958 when Sorel and Dusaucy-Bauloye introduced the use of ACTH,[81] treatment of infantile spasms consisted mainly of anticonvulsants and antibiotics. Metharbital and mephobarbital were successful in some patients in oral doses of 25 mg 4 to 6 times daily for metharbital and 32 mg 3 to 4 times daily for mephobarbital.[164] Other drug choices which are occasionally helpful are diphenylhydantoin, phenobarbital, phenacemide, and trimethadione. Because of the possibility that some patients with infantile spasms had encephalitis, chlortetracycline was used by several authors,[170,171] and initial reports were encouraging. However, the first sustained optimism in the treatment came with the use of ACTH and corticosteroids. Sorel and Dusaucy-Bauloye reported 21 cases of infantile spasms, 7 of whom had received ACTH.[81] They used 4 to 10 units of long acting ACTH daily for 15 days, and followed this with a similar course 8 days later if there was no improvement. All 7 patients who received ACTH had hypsarrhythmic EEG's and in 5 of these the EEG rapidly returned to normal while 6 of these patients stopped having seizures. In 3 of the patients responding to ACTH the intellect returned to normal. The authors related this mental improvement to early treatment. Only 10 of the 14 patients not receiving ACTH were followed for longer than 1 month, and among these, 2 patients died and 8 were retarded. In 1 untreated patient the seizures stopped spontaneously, and 2 other untreated patients seemed improved on follow-up. Five of the 7 treated with ACTH seemed normal prior to the onset of seizures (1 had the onset after immunizations), and the other 2 were premature births. Many authors class patients who seem normal prior to the onset of their seizures into a cryptogenic group,[22] and these patients have a better prognosis than those whose spasms are related to other etiologies. Several authors quickly confirmed this success with ACTH,[82,172,173] but as follow-ups lengthened, many patients were seen to relapse both clinically and electroencephalographically. In 1963 Bray followed up 6 of the 7 patients reported by Low[82] to have a striking improvement after ACTH or cortisone therapy and found only 1 who was normal 4 years after treatment.[174] Jeavons in his monograph on infantile spasms noted that nearly 90% of patients show a favorable initial response to ACTH or corticosteroids as manifested by fewer seizures and an improved EEG, but that only rarely does the mental level improve.[22] Harris writing on the EEG changes in patients treated with ACTH found 6 of 75 children who had totally recovered on a 1 to 2 year follow-up, but many more had EEG improvement.[175] All of those who eventually recovered showed an early EEG response to ACTH. Jeavons et al. in 1970 followed up 98 of the 112 cases originally reported in 1964.[22,176] Eighteen of those patients had died (9 of whom received steroids), and 80 were over 5 years of age and had been followed for 4 to 12 years. Fifty-eight of the original group had received steroid or ACTH therapy, and within this group 8 patients were attending regular schools. However, 2 of the 21 patients who received no treatment and 4 of the 14 patients treated with chlortetracycline were also attending regular school classes. They felt that patients classed as cryptogenic or whose seizures followed immunization had the best prognosis, and that adrenal corticosteroids or other drugs had little effect upon the eventual intellect. They commented, as did Bray, that ACTH or adrenal steroid therapy was worth using since it frequently stops the seizures and improves the EEG. In view of the generally poor outlook in this disease, even questionable treatment seems warranted.

Varying dosage schedules for ACTH have been used. Jeavons and Bower recommended 20 to 30 units of ACTH gel daily, divided into 2 doses and given for 4 weeks or longer if improvement occurs.[22] They also used prednisolone 2 mg/kg/day orally on a 6 hourly schedule or 0.3 mg/kg/day of dexamethasone again given on a 6 hourly schedule. Other authors have used smaller[81,177,178] or larger[173,179] doses of ACTH. Low recommended 3 mg/kg/day of cortisone orally to start and tapered this to 1 mg/kg/day which he maintained for up to 4 weeks.[82] Snyder has treated patients with corticosteroids for as long as 1 year, but his results are comparable to those of others.[179]

The use of L-glutamine either alone or in conjunction with ACTH has been reported.[180,181] Farina and Renson treated 2 patients parenterally with 450 mg of L-glutamine daily for 3 weeks.[181] There were no side effects, but only 1 patient became seizure free. In the other patient the EEG improved, but the seizures did not change.

Since the introduction of the benzodiazepines, they have been used frequently in infantile spasms and with fair success. Weinberg and Harwell reported the use of diazepam in 14 infants using oral doses ranging from 5 to 40 mg daily.[77] All of their patients had a reduction in seizure frequency, and 8 patients had excellent seizure control while 2 had only moderate control. Drug tolerance was not noted during a 1 year follow-up. There was no change in mental status with seizure control. The use of nitrazepam has been reported extensively and it shows similar beneficial results.[182,185] Markham treated 17 children with infantile spasms using doses of 5 to 25 mg daily of nitrazepam and found that all had a reduced number of seizures. In 12 of these patients the results were considered excellent, while 2 had only a 30-60% reduction in spasms. His longest follow-up was 30 months, and he did find tolerance in a few patients. Gibbs and Anderson used nitrazepam in 22 children with infantile spasms who had not responded to ACTH either on their EEG's or clinically.[183] In oral doses of 5 to 20 mg per day 20 of their patients had a marked reduction in seizures;

however, 14 had an increase in grand mal seizures and in 6 of these nitrazepam had to be discontinued. Other authors have agreed with these results, and nitrazepam has been recommended by some as the drug of choice in infantile and childhood myoclonic seizure disorders.[184,185] Intravenous nitrazepam has been utilized and compared to diazepam,[186] and by this route they are similar, but when given orally nitrazepam appears to be more effective in seizure control. The newest anticonvulsant benzodiazepine, clonazepam, appears to be as beneficial as the other two.[187] In contrast to these authors, Livingston[36] treated over 300 children with infantile spasms and found that tolerance limited the value of diazepam in treating them. Despite tolerance many patients responded well to diazepam for several months and he considers diazepam the drug of choice in infantile spasms if ACTH cannot be started soon after the onset of seizures.

Other anticonvulsants such as bromides,[36] acetazolamide,[188] and amino-oxyacetic acid[189] have also been used, and occasionally these are successful. Livingston found the ketogenic diet to be the most useful anticonvulsant regimen in his series. Ketosis induced by a diet high in medium-chain triglycerides was used in 1 patient, but seizures persisted unchanged.[190]

The most beneficial therapy for infantile spasms when specific etiologies are not present appears to be ACTH or adrenal corticosteroids. This treatment does not alter the long term intellectual impairment, but is usually helpful in controlling the seizures. Diazepam or nitrazepam are second choices, but tolerance may limit their value. A ketogenic diet may be necessary if other therapies fail. Other medications may be helpful, but their effects are less predictable.

Myoclonic epilepsies

Nonprogressive myoclonic epilepsies Myoclonus is associated with a variety of epileptic phenomena which may improve, remain stable, or progress over the course of time. The presence of myoclonic jerks preceding grand mal seizures is well recognized.[68] In one series of 96 patients with myoclonus nearly half (45) had epilepsy.[2] In that series both the seizures and myoclonus had usually started within a year of each other. Control of the grand mal seizures may relieve the myoclonus also.[2] Myoclonic jerks are frequently associated with petit mal seizures and along with absences and astatic seizures constitute Lennox's petit mal triad. Treatment should be directed toward the petit mal seizures. Hyperekplexia or stimulus-sensitive myoclonus is less common, and may be precipitated by stimuli of many kinds (light, sound, touch).[191,192] Anticonvulsants are not usually helpful, but diazepam and chlordiazepoxide have improved some patients. The rhythmic myoclonic jerks of epilepsia partialis continua have responded to diazepam[69] and surgical excision of focally discharging cortical areas.[193] Most cases have multiple bilateral lesions though and are not amenable to surgery.[42]

True myoclonic epilepsy or massive myoclonic jerks occurring in older children is uncommon. Harper reported 14 such children and distinguished them from infantile spasms by their older age of onset, frequently normal intelligence, and an atypical spike wave pattern on EEG.[194] The seizures were resistant to therapy, but tended to improve as the children grew older. One of his patients responded well to a ketogenic diet and another to carbamazepine, but diazepam was the most useful drug in his patients. Huttenlocher reported 6 patients with myoclonic and akinetic seizures whom he treated with a medium chain triglyceride diet to induce ketosis.[190] Other authors have confirmed the value of diazepam and also nitrazepam in patients with myoclonic seizures of mixed types (minor motor, akinetic, atypical petit mal).[195,196] In Snyder's patients nitrazepam seemed more effective than diazepam, but Killian and Fromm found them to be about equal. Nitrazepam is usually started at a dosage of 0.5 mg/kg/day and diazepam at 1 mg/kg/day. These can then be increased. In one study the maximum dose was 5.1 mg/kg/day for diazepam and 2.5 mg/kg/day for nitrazepam.[196]

The distinction between progressive and nonprogressive myoclonic epilepsies is often difficult and best done by laboratory tests and follow-up; however, there are some suggestive clinical features that separate the Lennox-Gastaut syndrome from the lipidoses. In the Lennox-Gastaut syndrome the myoclonus decreases with stimulation, increases with fatigue, and consciousness is depressed during status epilepticus, while in patients with lipidoses the myoclonus increases with stimulation, decreases when tired, and consciousness is unchanged even with repeated seizures.[197] Gastaut and co-workers have studied the Lennox-Gastaut syndrome or atypical petit mal in 50 patients.[198] The syndrome consists of a severe seizure disorder, retardation or progressive dementia, and a typical EEG pattern. Therapy was difficult and protective headgear important. Standard grand mal and petit mal drugs except for trimethadione were not helpful. Therapy with ACTH or adrenal corticosteroids was at times spectacular, but relief was transient. Diazepam proved to be most helpful, and in 14% of the patients gave relief for over 6 months. With time the myoclonic seizures become less frequent. In the nonprogressive myoclonic epilepsies the anticonvulsant benzodiazepines are presently the therapy of choice.

Progressive myoclonic epilepsies The progressive myoclonic epilepsies are generally divided into 3 categories, Lafora body disease, lipidoses, and the familial system degeneration (Ramsay Hunt).[25] The Lennox-Gastaut syndrome or petit mal variant has several features in common with these (see Table 6), but is usually not included. The myoclonic seizures in all of these entities are difficult to control and become increasingly so as the disease progresses. The generalized seizures which are a part of all three types usually respond to standard anticonvulsants, at least early in the course of the disease.

Lafora body disease or the progressive myoclonic epilepsy of Unverricht-Lundborg has been treated with a variety of medications. Diphenylhydantoin, primidone, and mephenytoin have not been useful, but phenobarbital may be helpful early in the disease.[199] Riehl and co-workers studied a 12 year old girl with biopsy proven Lafora body disease using a series of CNS drugs and monitoring her EEG responses.[200] A 50 mg dose of secobarbital abolished both spontaneous cortical discharges and her myoclonus. Other drugs which suppressed EEG discharges were diphenhydramine, chlordiazepoxide, neostigmine, and amphetamine. On the basis of these results and intracortical EEG recordings during her brain biopsy they felt that the EEG findings resulted from cortical

TABLE 6

Typical features of the progressive myoclonic epilepsies and Lennox-Gastaut syndrome

	Lafora body	Lipidosis	Familial system degenerations	Lennox-Gastaut
Usual onset in years	10-20	Under 10	After 10	1 to 6
Course	Rapidly fatal	Rapidly fatal	Slowly progressive	Slowly progressive
Dementia	Rapidly progressive	Variable (severe to absent)	Low IQ, no progressive dementia	May develop low IQ
Neurological exam	Ataxia and dysarthria	May have ocular findings, ataxia, or dysarthria	May have pes cavus, extra-pyramidal signs, and severe ataxia or dysarthria	No special findings
Other seizures	Generalized	Generalized	Rare generalized	Generalized tonic, focal, or petit mal
Diagnostic aids	Liver, skeletal muscle, or brain biopsy	Leucocyte enzymes Brain biopsy	+ family history	Typical EEG (diffuse slow spike-waves)

deafferentation and discharges from deep, midline nuclear masses. Gath studied drug effects on somatosensory evoked potentials in 2 patients with presumed Lafora body disease.[201] Both patients had received standard anticonvulsants (diphenylhydantoin, primidone, carbamazepine, acetazolamide, and phenobarbital) with little benefit, but with either nitrazepam or diazepam 1 patient had a significant reduction in his somatosensory evoked potentials and an objective decrease in the myoclonus. The other patient did not improve with these drugs, but his disease was in a later stage. Petersen and Hambert studied the pharmacologic responses in Lafora body disease to clomethiazole, lidocaine, amobarbital sodium, diazepam, nitrazepam, and ACTH.[202,203] All of these drugs improved the patients' EEG's and reduced the myoclonus, but no single drug was effective in every case. There was no improvement in their single patient who received mephenesin. Seven patients had long term oral therapy with clomethiazole and 2 with nitrazepam.[203] The dose of clomethiazole ranged from 1 to 1.5 gram daily and in 5 of these patients the myoclonus decreased. They also treated 2 patients with nitrazepam and in both the myoclonus improved at doses from 5 to 15 mg 3 times a day. Tolerance was a problem with both these drugs. Other authors have confirmed the value of diazepam.[204] Phenacemide or phenylacetylurea was used by Bradshaw in doses of 250 to 500 mg 3 times a day and produced good relief from the myoclonic jerks, especially when combined with phenobarbital.[1]

This relief did not appear until 3 to 4 days after starting treatment, but long term treatment has been successful.[202] Kelly and Laurence reported 5 patients whom they treated with mephenesin, but large doses (up to 48.5 g daily) were required and side effects were a problem.[205] Immunosuppressive treatment with 6-mercaptopurine was used in a patient with a G hypergammaglobulinemia and presumed Lafora body disease.[205] The course stabilized, but follow-up was only 4 months. Laitinen did thalamotomies in some patients as previously discussed.[94]

The familial system degenerations with myoclonus (Ramsay Hunt syndrome) may become worse with anxiety, and sedation with chloral hydrate is one mode of therapy.[207] Bromides, primidone, and reserpine have been tried and are not useful.[207] Trimethadione has been of variable benefit, and the succinimides have occasionally been helpful.[208] Chlorpromazine improved 1 patient's myoclonus even though it activated the EEG, but a sibling who was asymptomatic developed myoclonus when given this drug.[209] Prochlorperazine helped 1 patient and mephenesin or phenacemide have occasionally helped. The most useful drugs have been the anticonvulsant benzodiazepines, nitrazepam and diazepam. May and White transiently abolished a marked photic sensitivity in 2 patients by using i.v. diazepam.[210] Significant benefit has also been seen with chlordiazepoxide. Two patients underwent unilateral thalamotomy, but the effect was transient and they eventually had bilateral ablations.[211] Diazepam used with the surgical approach improved results.

The lipid storage diseases associated with myoclonus are variable in their presentation and progression. They may survive for long periods of time. Richardson and Bornhofen reported a 9 year old girl with biopsy proven cerebral lipidoses whose seizures were better on phenobarbital, but other patients have not responded so well.[212] Chlordiazepoxide was helpful in 1 patient.[195] Most drugs have been helpful only for short periods, presumably due to progression of the disease.

TABLE 7

Effectiveness of anticonvulsants in 47 patients with myoclonic seizures or myoclonus*

	Control of seizures		
	Good	None	Effectiveness (%)
Trimethadione	2	14	13
Ethosuximide	3	11	21
Phenytoin	10	25	29
Carbamazepine	7	17	29
Sultiame	3	7	30
Primidone	13	21	35
Barbiturate	13	23	37
Diazepam	11	15	44
Nitrazepam	16	10	61

* modified from Lance.[213]

In the progressive myoclonic epilepsies the most useful drugs have been phenobarbital and the anticonvulsant benzodiazepines. The relative value of other anticonvulsants in myoclonic seizures is best illustrated by Lance's data (Table 7).[213] His data show the value of various anticonvulsants in 47 patients with myoclonus or myoclonic epilepsy from a variety of etiologies.

Myoclonic status epilepticus

Many patients with progressive myoclonic epilepsy eventually reach a stage where the seizures occur at frequent intervals. This is most commonly seen in the cerebral degenerative diseases such as the lipidoses, Schilder's disease, SSPE, and Lafora body disease. In these patients there may be 100 or more myoclonic seizures a day, but despite this frequency, consciousness may be preserved interictally. Under some circumstances such as in the Lennox-Gastaut syndrome, myoclonic seizures may occur so frequently that consciousness is depressed between seizures, and these can be classed as true myoclonic status epilepticus rather than serial myoclonic seizures. In some patients myoclonic petit mal status occurs. This differs in its lower morbidity or mortality than grand mal status.[212]

Treatment of myoclonic status is difficult if the underlying disease is a severe degenerative one, but when it is secondary to other disease processes the treatment may be successful. Lombroso reported 27 patients with status epilepticus of whom 6 were in myoclonic status.[214] In 5 of these patients seizure control with intravenous diazepam was prompt, while 1 patient with SSPE continued in status. In 1 patient the relief lasted only 15 minutes. Two patients with recurrent infantile spasms also had prompt, but temporary relief from seizures with diazepam. Doses of diazepam ranging from 2.5 to 10 mg were used. Control of myoclonic status was also reported by Sawyer et al. using diazepam.[215] They treated 26 patients with status epilepticus of whom 3 had myoclonic status. An 8 year old retarded male with seizures entered their hospital on 2 occasions with myoclonic status. Seizures were occurring every 2-3 seconds and consciousness was impaired interictally. One episode had persisted for 5 hours prior to treatment and the other for 4 days, but both responded to 5-6 mg of i.v. diazepam (0.26 to 0.3 mg/kg) with abrupt cessation of seizures. They also treated 2 adults in myoclonic status. One patient had an intracerebral hematoma and though 0.06 mg/kg of diazepam promptly stopped the seizures, he died $3\frac{1}{2}$ hours later. The other patient had a gram-negative sepsis with hypotension and had been in coma with continual myoclonic seizures for 12 hours. He died within minutes of receiving 0.18 mg/kg of diazepam intravenously. Gordon reported an 11 year old boy with recurrent seizures characterized by rigidity and generalized myoclonus who responded well to 10 mg of i.v. diazepam.[216]

The value of diazepam in doses of 5 to 10 mg has been documented in status epilepticus of either the grand mal or myoclonic type. It should be administered slowly i.v., and only that amount necessary to halt the seizure should be given. If relief is not obtained, the dose can be repeated in 20-30 minutes. At the same time more long-acting anticonvulsants such as phenobarbital should be started.

CONCLUSIONS

The therapy of myoclonus is often difficult due to the serious nature of many of the diseases associated with it. Despite this, many treatable conditions cause myoclonus. It is important to define the basic etiology of the process whenever myoclonus is observed. Therapy in myoclonic syndromes has been most success-ful using the benzodiazepines, ACTH or adrenal corticosteroids, phenobarbital, or stereotactic ablations of the posterior ventral lateral thalamus. Although these are the most consistently beneficial medications, a variety of other anticonvulsants occasionally relieve myoclonus.

REFERENCES

1. BRADSHAW, J. P. P. (1954): A study of myoclonus. *Brain, 77,* 138.
2. AIGNER, B. R. and MULDER, D. W. (1960): Myoclonus. Clinical significance and an approach to classification. *Arch. Neurol. (Chic.), 2,* 600.
3. SWANSON, P. D., LUTTRELL, C. N. and MAGLADERY, J. W. (1962): Myoclonus — A report of 67 cases and review of the literature. *Medicine (Baltimore), 41,* 339.
4. MYERS, G. J. Unpublished observations.
5. BLACKWOOD, W., BUXTON, P. H., CUMINGS, J. N., ROBERTSON, D. J. and TUCKER, S. M. (1963): Diffuse cerebral degeneration in infancy (Alper's disease). *Arch. Dis. Childh., 38,* 193.
6. BONDUELLE, M. (1969): The myoclonias. In: *Handbook of Clinical Neurology, Vol. 6,* pp. 761-781. Editors: P. J. Vinken and G. W. Bruyn. North Holland Publ. Co., Amsterdam.
7. PALINSKY, M., KOZINN, P. and ZAHTY, H. (1954): Acute familial infantile here-dodegenerative disorder of the central nervous system. *J. Pediat., 45,* 583.
8. SARNAT, H. B. and ADELMAN, L. S. (1973): Perinatal sudanophilic leukodystrophy. *Amer. J. Dis. Child., 125,* 281.
9. SCHWARZ, G. A. and YANOFF, M. (1965): Lafora's disease. Distinct clinico-pathologic form of Unverricht's syndrome. *Arch. Neurol. (Chic.), 12,* 172.
10. HARRIMAN, D. G. F., MILLAR, J. H. D. and STEVENSON, A. C. (1955): Progressive familial myoclonic epilepsy in three families: Its clinical features and pathological basis. *Brain, 78,* 325.
11. FAU, R., CHATEAU, R., TOMMASI, M. and GROSLAMBERT, R. (1971): Etude anatomo-clinique d'une forme rigide et myoclonique de maladie de Huntington infantile. *Rev. neurol. (Paris), 124,* 353.
12. DENNY-BROWN, D. (1962): *The Basal Ganglia and Their Relation to Disorders of Movements.* Oxford University Press, London.
13. FREEMAN, J. M. (1969): The clinical spectrum and early diagnosis of Dawson's encephalitis. *J. Pediat., 75,* 590.
14. MAY, W. W. (1968): Creutzfeldt-Jakob disease. Survey of the literature and clinical diagnosis. *Acta neurol. scand., 44,* 1.
15. PATRIKIOS, M. J. (1951): Sclérose latérale amyotrophique avec mouvement in-volontaire des doigts et du poignet gauche de caractère extrapyramidal. *Rev. neurol. (Paris), 85,* 60.
16. GARCIN, R., RONDOT, P. and GUIOT, G. (1968): Rhythmic myoclonus of the right arm as the presenting symptom of a cervical cord tumour. *Brain, 91,* 75.
17. DAUBE, J. R. and CHOU, S. M. (1966): Lissencephaly: Two cases. *Neurology (Minneap.), 16,* 179.

18. JELLINGER, K. (1970): Neuropathological aspects of hypsarrhythmia. *Neuropaediatrie, 1*, 277.

19. GASTAUT, H. and FISHER-WILLIAMS, M. (1959): The physiopathology of epileptic seizures. In: *Handbook of Physiology, Vol. 1*, pp. 329-363. Editor: J. Field. American Physiological Society, Washington, D.C.

20. SNYDER, R. D. and APPENZELLER, O. (1971): Segmental myoclonus in meningomyelocele. *Trans. Amer. neurol. Ass., 96*, 97.

21. GASTAUT, H. (1968): Seméiologie des myoclonies et nosologie analytique des syndromes myocloniques. *Rev. neurol. (Paris), 119*, 1.

22. JEAVONS, P. M. and BOWER, B. D. (1964): Infantile spasms. A review of the literature and a study of 112 cases. In: *Clinics in Developmental Medicine, No. 15*, pp. 1-79. W. Heinemann Medical Books Ltd., London, with the Spastics Society, London.

23. MILLICHAP, J. G., BICKFORD, R. G., KLASS, D. W. and BACKUS, R. E. (1962): Infantile spasms, hypsarhythmia, and mental retardation. A study of etiologic factors in 61 patients. *Epilepsia, 3*, 188.

24. PATRIKIOS, M. J. (1938): Sur un cas d'automatisme moteur particulier des membres supérieurs après traumatisme de la moelle cervicale. *Rev. neurol. (Paris), 69*, 179.

25. HALLIDAY, A. M. (1967): The clinical incidence of myoclonus. In: *Modern Trends in Neurology, Vol. 4*, pp. 69-105. Editor: D. Williams. Butterworth, London.

26. WRIGHT, F. S. (1969): Myoclonic seizures in infancy and childhood. *Postgrad. Med., 46*, 100.

27. RIZZUTO, N. and FERRARI, G. (1968): Familial infantile myoclonic epilepsy in a family suffering from tuberous sclerosis. *Epilepsia, 9*, 117.

28. MONAHAN, R. H., HILL, C. W. and VENTERS, H. D. (1967): Multiple choristomas, convulsions, and mental retardation as a new neurocutaneous syndrome. *Amer. J. Ophthal., 64*, 529.

29. CASTLEMAN, B. and KIBBE, B. U. (1958): Case records of the MGH. *New Engl. J. Med., 259*, 688.

30. DODGE, P., SOTOS, J. F., GAMSTORP, I., DEVIVO, D., LEVY, M. and RABE, T. (1962): Neurophysiologic disturbances in hypertonic dehydration. *Trans. Amer. neurol. Ass., 87*, 33.

31. LOCKE, S., MERRILL, J. P. and TYLER, H. R. (1961): Neurologic complications of acute uremia. *Arch. intern. Med., 108*, 519.

32. DANKS, D. M., CAMPBELL, P. E., STEVENS, B. J., MAYNE, V. and CARTWRIGHT, E. (1972): Menkes's kinky hair syndrome. An inherited defect in copper absorption with widespread effects. *Pediatrics, 50*, 188.

33. BEJSOVEC, M., KULENDA, Z. and PONCA, E. (1967): Familial intrauterine convulsions in pyridoxine dependency. *Arch. Dis. Childh., 42*, 201.

34. SHIH, V. E., EFRON, M. L. and MOSER, H. (1969): Hyperornithinemia, hyperammonemia and homocitrullinuria. A new disorder of amino acid metabolism associated with myoclonic seizures and mental retardation. *Amer. J. Dis. Child., 117*, 83.

35. WERK, E. E., SHOLITON, L. J. and MARNELL, R. T. (1961): The 'stiff man' syndrome and hyperthyroidism. *Amer. J. Med., 31*, 647.

36. LIVINGSTON, S. (1972): *Comprehensive Management of Epilepsy in Infancy, Childhood, and Adolescence*. Charles C. Thomas, Springfield, Ill.

37. MacCALLUM, F. O., POTTER, J. M. and EDWARDS, D. H. (1964): Early diagnosis of herpes-simplex encephalitis by brain biopsy. *Lancet, 2*, 332.

38. LIVINGSTON, S., EISNER, V. and PAULI, L. (1958): Minor motor epilepsy. Diagnosis, treatment, and prognosis. *Pediatrics*, *21*, 916.

39. STOUPEL, N., MONSEU, G., PARDOE, A., HEIMANN, R. and MARTIN, J. J. (1969): Encephalitis with myoclonus in Whipple's disease. *J. Neurol. Neurosurg. Psychiat.*, *32*, 338.

40. CAMPBELL, A. M. G. and GARLAND, H. (1956): Subacute myoclonic spinal neuronitis. *J. Neurol. Neurosurg. Psychiat.*, *19*, 268.

41. GASTAUT, H., ROGER, J., SOULAYROL, R., TASSINARI, C. A., REGIS, H. and DRAVET, C. (1966): Childhood epileptic encephalopathy with diffuse slow spike-wave (otherwise known as 'Petit Mal Variant') or Lennox syndrome. *Epilepsia*, *7*, 139.

42. JUUL-JENSEN, P. and DENNY-BROWN, D. (1966): Epilepsia partialis continua. *Arch. Neurol. (Chic.)*, *15*, 563.

43. BRAY, P. F. ZITER, F. A., LAHEY, M. E. and MYERS, G. G. (1969): The coincidence of neuroblastoma and acute cerebellar encephalopathy. *J. Pediat.*, *75*, 983.

44. GORDON, E. E., JANUSZKO, D. M. and KAUFMAN, L. (1967): A critical survey of Stiff-Man syndrome. *Amer. J. Med.*, *42*, 582.

45. SHAPIRO, A. K., SHAPIRO, E. and WAYNE, H. (1973): Treatment of Tourette's syndrome with haloperidol, review of 34 cases. *Arch. gen. Psychiat.*, *28*, 92.

46. OSKI, F. A. and NAIMAN, J. L. (1972): *Hematologic Problems in the Newborn*. Second Edition. W. B. Saunders Co. Philadelphia, Pa.

47. BOGEN, E. (1926): Arachnidism; spider poisoning. *Arch. intern. Med.*, *38*, 623.

48. GASTAUT, H. and VILLENEUVE, A. (1967): The startle disease or hyperekplexia. *J. neurol. Sci.*, *5*, 526.

49. HENDERSON, D. A. and SHELOKOV, A. (1959): Epidemic neuromyasthenia-clinical syndrome? *New Engl. J. Med.*, *260*, 757.

50. MOENE, M. M. Y., CUCHE, M., TRILLET, M., MOTIN, J. and MICHAEL, D. (1969): Problèmes diagnostiques posés par l'intoxication aiguë au chloralose (à propos de 6 cas). *J. Méd. Lyon*, *50*, 1483.

51. LANGLOIS, M., VERCEL, R. M. and KAHLIL ET BERENI, R. (1963): Sur quatre cas d'intoxication collective par le bromure de méthyle. Considérations cliniques et électroencéphalographiques. *Rev. neurol. (Paris)*, *108*, 305.

52. ALVORD, E. C. and FUORTES, M. G. (1954): Comparison of generalized reflex myoclonic reactions in cats under chloralose anesthesia and under strychnine. *Amer. J. Physiol.*, *176*, 253.

53. KURTZMAN, N. A., ROGERS, P. and HARTER, H. R. (1970): Neurotoxic reaction to penicillin and carbenicillin. *J. Amer. med. Ass.*, *214*, 1320.

54. WENDLAND, K. L. (1969): Myklonien nach Gaben von Carbamazepin. *Nervenarzt*, *39*, 231.

55. GOTTWALD, W. (1968): Transitorisches Abheilen von Psoriasis-Effloreszenzen während Hydantoinvergiftung mit seltener zentralnervöser Symptomatik. *Derm. Wschr.*, *154*, 241.

56. DENNY-BROWN, D. (1960): In discussion of C. M. Fisher. The clinical picture in Creutzfeldt-Jakob disease. *Trans. Amer. neurol. Ass.*, *85*, 147.

57. FAVAREL-GARRIQUES, B. (1972): Two cases of severe poisoning by lithium carbonate. *Ann. méd.-psychol.*, *1*, 253.

58. SCHULZE, B. (1972): Zur Frage Medikamentos induzierter cerebraler Reaktionen: Ein Fall von myoklonischen Status unter Behandlung mit tricyclischen Antidepressiva. *Nervenarzt*, *43*, 332.

59. CHAPTAL, J., JEAN, R., LABAUGE, R., BONNET, H. and AGHAI, E. (1963): Myoclonies oppositionnelles par intoxication à la piperazine. *Arch. franç. Pédiat.*, *20*, 17.

60. PFEIFFER, C. C., JENNEY, E. H. and MARSHALL, W. H. (1956): Experimental seizures in man and animals with acute pyridoxine deficiency produced by hydrazides. *Electroenceph. clin. Neurophysiol.*, *8*, 307.

61. WILLIAMSON, D. A. J. (1968): Fits in utero followed by infantile myoclonic twitchings. *Proc. roy. Soc. Med.*, *61*, 1255.

62. GILBERT, J. J. (1971): Benign myoclonus. *J. Amer. med. Ass.*, *217*, 210.

63. LANDERS, M. B. and KLINTWORTH, G. (1971): Subacute sclerosing panencephalitis (SSPE). *Arch. Ophthal.*, *86*, 156.

64. WALDINGER, C. and BERG, R. B. (1963): Signs of pyridoxine dependency manifest at birth in siblings. *Pediatrics*, *32*, 161.

65. WATSON, C. W. and DENNY-BROWN, D. (1953): Myoclonus epilepsy as a symptom of diffuse neuronal disease. *Arch. Neurol. Psychiat. (Chic.)*, *70*, 151.

66. LUTTRELL, C. N., BANG, F. B. and LUXENBERG, K. (1959): Newcastle disease encephalomyelitis in cats. II. Physiological studies on rhythmic myoclonus. *Arch. Neurol. Psychiat. (Chic.)*, *81*, 285.

67. WOODBURY, D. M., PENRY, J.K. and SCHMIDT, R. P. (1972): *Antiepileptic Drugs*. Raven Press, New York.

68. SYMONDS, C. (1954): Myoclonus. *Med. J. Aust.*, *1*, 765.

69. MATTSON, R. H. (1972): The benzodiazepines in antiepileptic drugs. In: *Antiepileptic Drugs*, pp. 497-516. Editors: D. M. Woodbury, J. K. Penry and R. P. Schmidt. Raven Press, New York.

70. HERSHON, H. I. and PARSONAGE, M. (1969): Comparative trial of diazepam and pheneturide in treatment of epilepsy. *Lancet*, *2*, 859.

71. CAMERMAN, A. and CAMERMAN, N. (1970): Diphenylhydantoin and diazepam: Molecular structure similarities and steric basis of anticonvulsant activity. *Science*, *168*, 1457.

72. RANDALL, L. O., HEISE, G. A., SCHALLEK, W., BAGDON, R. E., BANZIGER, R., BORIS, A., MOE, R. A. and ABRAMS, W. B. (1961): Pharmacological and clinical studies on Valium (T.M.). A new psychotherapeutic agent of the benzodiazepine class. *Curr. ther. Res.*, *3*, 405.

73. HARDIN, J. A. and GRIGGS, R. C. (1971): Diazepam treatment in a case of strychnine poisoning. *Lancet*, *2*, 372.

74. ZBINDEN, G. and RANDALL, L. O. (1967): Pharmacology of benzodiazepines: laboratory and clinical correlations. *Advanc. Pharmacol.*, *5*, 213.

75. VIALA, A., CANO, J. P., DRAVET, C., TASSINARI, C. A. and ROGER, J. (1971): Blood levels of diazepam (Valium) and N-desmethyl diazepam in the epileptic child. *Psychiat. Neurol. Neurochir.*, *74*, 153.

76. ELIAN, M. (1969): The long-term oral use of Valium (diazepam) in epilepsy. *Epilepsia*, *10*, 487.

77. WEINBERG, W. A. and HARWELL, J. L. (1965): Diazepam (Valium) in myoclonic seizures. *Amer. J. Dis. Child.*, *109*, 123.

78. PRENSKY, A. L., RAFF, M. C., MOORE, M. J. and SCHWAB, R. S. (1967): Intravenous diazepam in the treatment of prolonged seizure activity. *New Engl. J. Med.*, *276*, 779.

79. CALDERON-GONZALEZ, R. and MIRELES-GONZALEZ, A. (1968): Management of prolonged motor seizure activity in children. *J. Amer. med. Ass.*, *204*, 544.

80. KLEIN, R. and LIVINGSTON, S. (1950): The effect of adrenocorticotropic hormone in epilepsy. *J. Pediat.*, *37*, 733.

81. SOREL, L. and DUSAUCY-BOULOYE, A. A. (1958): A propos de 21 cas d'hypsarhythmie de Gibbs: Son traitement spectaculaire par l'ACTH. *Acta neurol. belg.*, *58*, 130.

82. LOW, N. L., BOSMA, J. F., ARMSTRONG, M. D. and MADSEN, J. A. (1958): Infantile

spasms with mental retardation. II. Treatment with cortisone and adrenocortico-tropin. *Pediatrics, 22,* 1165.

83. FORSHAM, P. H. and MELMON, K. L. (1968): The adrenals. In: *Textbook of Endo-crinology,* pp. 287-404. Editor: R. H. Williams. W. B. Saunders Co., Philadelphia.

84. SAYERS, G. and TRAVIS, R. H. (1970): Adrenocorticotropic hormone; adreno-cortical steroids and their synthetic analogs. In: *The Pharmacological Basis of Thera-peutics,* pp. 1604-1642. Fourth Edition. Editors: L. S. Goodman and A. Gilman. The MacMillan Co., New York.

85. QUARTON, G. C., CLARK, L. D., COBB, S. and BAUER, W. (1955): Mental distur-bances associated with ACTH and cortisone: A review of explanatory hypotheses. *Medicine (Baltimore), 34,* 13.

86. ROSE, A. and MATSON, D. D. (1967): Benign intracranial hypertension in children. *Pediatrics, 39,* 227.

87. WOODBURY, D. M. (1958): Relation between the adrenal cortex and the central nervous system. *Pharmacol. Rev., 10,* 275.

88. CASO, A. (1953): Effectos del tratamiento de las lesiones cerebrales con ACTH. *Bol. Inst. Estud. méd. biol. (Méx.), 11,* 61.

89. MARTIN, M. M., GABOARDI, F., PODOLSKY, S., RAITI, S. and CALCAGNO, P. L. (1968): Intermittent steroid therapy. Its effect on hypothalamic-pituitary-adrenal function and the response of plasma growth hormone and insulin to stimulation. *New Engl. J. Med., 279,* 273.

90. The Boston Collaborative Drug Surveillance Program (1972): Acute adverse reactions to prednisone in relation to dosage. *Clin. Pharmacol. Ther., 13,* 694.

91. KINSBOURNE, M. (1962): Myoclonic encephalopathy of infants. *J. Neurol. Neurosurg. Psychiat., 25,* 271.

92. HASSLER, R., RIECHERT, T., MUNDINGER, F., UMBACH, W. and GANGELBERGER, J. A. (1960): Physiologic observations in stereotaxic operations in extrapyramidal motor disturbances. *Brain, 83,* 337.

93. HASSLER, R. (1968): Myoclonies extrapyramidales traitées par coagulation stéréo-taxique de la voie dentatothalamique et leur mécanisme physiopathologique. *Rev. neurol. (Paris), 119,* 409.

94. LAITINEN, L. V. (1967): Thalamotomy in progressive myoclonus epilepsy. *Acta neurol. scand., 43, Suppl. 31,* 170.

95. SPIEGEL, E. A., WYCIS, H. T., SZEKELY, E. G., ADAMS, J., FLANAGAN, M. and BAIRD, W. H. (1963): III. Campotomy in various extrapyramidal disorders. *J. Neurosurg., 20,* 871.

96. WYCIS, H. T. and SPIEGEL, E. A. (1969): Campotomy in myoclonia. *J. Neurosurg., 30,* 708.

97. TURTSCHANINOW, P. (1894): Experimentelle Studien über den Ursprungsort einiger klinisch wichtiger toxischer Krampfformen. Cited by H. Gastaut and M. Fisher-Williams (ref. 19). *Naunyn-Schmiedeberg's Arch. exp. Path. Pharmak., 34,* 208.

98. MUSKENS, L. J. (1928): *Epilepsy, Comparative Pathogenesis, Symptoms and Treatment.* Cited by H. Gastaut and M. Fisher-Williams. (ref. 19).

99. ADRIAN, E. D. and MORUZZI, G. (1939): Impulses in the pyramidal tract. *J. Physiol., 97,* 153.

100. LUTTRELL, C. N. and BANG, F. B. (1958): Newcastle disease encephalomyelitis in cats. I. Clinical and pathological features. *Arch. Neurol. Psychiat. (Chic.), 79,* 647.

101. LUTTRELL, C. N., BANG, F. B. and LUXENBERG, K. (1959): Newcastle disease encephalomyelitis in cats: II. Physiological studies on rhythmic myoclonus. *Arch. Neurol. Psychiat. (Chic.), 81,* 285.

102. MILHORAT, T. H. (1967): Experimental myoclonus of thalamic origin. *Arch. Neurol. (Paris)*, *17*, 365.

103. MILHORAT, T. H., BALDWIN, M. and HANTMAN, D. A. (1966): Experimental epilepsy after rostral reticular formation excision. *J. Neurosurg.*, *24*, 595.

104. ZUCKERMAN, E. G. and GLASER, G. H. (1972): Urea-induced myoclonic seizures. An experimental study of site of action and mechanism. *Arch. Neurol. (Chic.)*, *27*, 14.

105. DAUBE, J. R. and PETERS, H. A. (1966): Hereditary essential myoclonus. *Arch. Neurol. (Chic.)*, *15*, 587.

106. MAHLOUDJI, M. and PIKIELNY, T. R. (1967): Hereditary essential myoclonus. *Brain*, *90*, 669.

107. OSWALD, I. (1959): Sudden bodily jerks on falling asleep. *Brain*, *82*, 92.

108. PENFIELD, W. and JASPER, H. (1954): *Epilepsy and the Functional Anatomy of the Human Brain*. Little Brown and Co., Boston, Mass.

109. GREENHOUSE, A. H. (1971): In discussion of R. D. Snyder and O. Appenzeller. Segmental myoclonus in meningomyelocele. *Trans. Amer. neurol. Ass.*, *96*, 97.

110. HOWARD, F. M. (1963): A new and effective drug in the treatment of Stiff-Man syndrome. *Proc. Mayo Clin.*, *38*, 203.

111. SCHUCH, P., STEPHAN, U. and JACOBI, G. (1966): Neurotoxic side-effects of piperazines. *Lancet*, *1*, 1218.

112. JOHNSON, H. C. and WALKER, A. E. (1945): Intraventricular penicillin: A note of warning. *J. Amer. med. Ass.*, *127*, 217.

113. REULING, J. and CRAMER, C. (1947): Intrathecal penicillin. *J. Amer. med. Ass.*, *134*, 16.

114. OLDSTONE, M. B. A. and NELSON, E. (1966): Central nervous system manifestations of penicillin toxicity in man. *Neurology (Minneap.)*, *16*, 693.

115. NEW, P. S. and WELLS, C. E. (1965): Cerebral toxicity associated with massive penicillin therapy. *Neurology (Minneap.)*, *15*, 1053.

116. DOBELL, R. C., WYANT, J. P., SEAMANS, K. B. and GLOOR, P. (1966): Penicillin epilepsy. Studies on the blood-brain barrier during cardiopulmonary bypass. *J. thorac. cardiovasc. Surg.*, *52*, 469.

117. BLOOMER, H. A., BARTON, L. J. and MADDOCK, JR., R. K. (1967): Penicillin-induced encephalopathy in uremic patients. *J. Amer. med. Ass.*, *200*, 121.

118. LERNER, P. I., SMITH, H. and WEINSTEIN, L. (1967): Penicillin neurotoxicity. *Ann. N.Y. Acad. Sci.*, *145*, 310.

119. FISHMAN, R. A. (1964): Active transport and the blood-brain barrier to penicillin and related organic acids. *Trans. Amer. neurol. Ass.*, *89*, 51.

120. DARCOURT, G., FADEUILHE, A., LAVAGNA, J. and CAZAC, A. (1970): Trois cas de myoclonies d'action au cours de traitements par l'imipramine et l'amitriptyline. *Rev. neurol. (Paris)*, *122*, 141.

121. LANCE, J. W. and ADAMS, R. D. (1963): The syndrome of intention or action myoclonus as a sequel to hypoxic encephalopathy. *Brain*, *86*, 111.

122. ROSEN, A. D., BERENYI, K. and LAURENCEAU, V. (1969): Intention myoclonus. Diazepam and phenobarbital treatment. *J. Amer. med. Ass.*, *209*, 772.

123. BOUDOURESQUES, J., ROGER, J., KHALIL, R., VIGOUROUX, R. A., GOSSET, A., PELLISSIER, J. F. and TASSINARI, C. A. (1971): A propos de 2 observations de syndrome de Lance et Adams. Effet therapeutique de Ro-05-4023. *Rev. neurol. (Paris)*, *125*, 306.

124. HIROSE, G., SINGER, P. and BASS, N. H. (1971): Successful treatment of posthypoxic action myoclonus with carbamazepine. *J. Amer. med. Ass.*, *218*, 1432.

125. SHERWIN, I. and REDMON, W. (1969): Successful treatment in action myoclonus. *Neurology (Minneap.)*, *19*, 846.

126. LHERMITTE, F., PETERFALUI, M., MARTEAU, R., GAZENGEL, J. and SERDARU, M. (1971): Analyse pharmacologique d'un cas de myoclonies d'intention et d'action post-anoxiques. *Rev. neurol. (Paris)*, *124*, 21.

127. LHERMITTE, F., MARTEAU, R. and DEGOS, C. F. (1972): Analyse pharmacologique d'un nouveau cas de myoclonies d'intention et d'action post-anoxiques. *Rev. neurol. (Paris)*, *126*, 107.

128. LHERMITTE, F., TALAIRACH, J., BUSER, P., GAUTIER, J. C., BANCAUD, J., GRAS, R. and TRUELLE, J. L. (1971): Myoclonies d'intention et d'action post-anoxiques. Etude stéréotaxique et destruction du noyau ventral latéral du thalamus. *Rev. neurol. (Paris)*, *124*, 5.

129. RESNICK, J., ENGEL, W. K. and SEVER, J. L. (1968): Spontaneous improvement in a patient with elevated measles antibody in blood and spinal fluid. *New Engl. J. Med.*, *279*, 126.

130. COBB, W. A. and MORGAN-HUGHES, J. A. (1968): Non-fatal subacute sclerosing leucoencephalitis. *J. Neurol. Neurosurg. Psychiat.*, *31*, 115.

131. WHITTIER, J. R. (1956): Flexor spasm syndrome in the carnivore. *Amer. J. vet. Res.*, *17*, 720.

132. KOLAR, O., OBRUCNIK, M., BEHOUNKOVA, L., MUSIL, J. and PENICKOVA, V. (1967): Thymectomy in subacute sclerosing leucoencephalitis. *Brit. med. J.*, *3*, 22.

133. CONNOLLY, J. N., ALLEN, I. V., HURWITZ, L. J. and MILAR, J. H. D. (1968): Subacute sclerosing panencephalitis. Clinical pathological epidemiological and virological findings in three patients. *Quart. J. Med.*, *37*, 625.

134. HANISSIAN, A. S., JABBOUR, J. T., DELAMERENS, S., GARCIA, J. H. and HORTA-BARBOSA, L. (1972): Subacute encephalitis and hypogammaglobulinemia. *Amer. J. Dis. Child.*, *123*, 151.

135. DEGIACOMO, P., CAPPIELLO, J. and PERNIOLA, T. (1967): Haloperidol in subacute sclerosing leucoencephalitis. *Lancet*, 2, 1095.

136. CHEN, T. T., WATANABE, I., ZEMAN, W. and MEALEY JR., J. (1969): Subacute sclerosing panencephalitis: Propagation of measles virus from brain biopsy in tissue culture. *Science*, *163*, 1193.

137. HOFFMAN, C. E., NEUMAYER, E. M., HAFF, R. F. and GOLDSBY, R. A. (1965): Mode of action of the antiviral activity of amantadine in tissue culture. *J. Bact.*, *90*, 623.

138. HASLAM, R. H. A., McQUILLEN, M. P. and CLARK, D. B. (1969): Amantadine therapy in subacute sclerosing panencephalitis. *Neurology (Minneap.)*, *19*, 1080.

139. ROBB, R. and WATERS, G. (1970): Ophthalmic manifestations of subacute sclerosing panencephalitis. *Arch. Ophthal.*, *83*, 426.

140. CUTLER, R. W. P., WATTERS, G., HAMMERSTAD, J. P. and MERLER, E. (1967): Origin of cerebrospinal fluid gamma globulin in subacute sclerosing leukoencephalitis. *Arch. Neurol. (Chic.)*, *17*, 620.

141. FREEMAN, J. M. (1969): Treatment of Dawson's encephalitis with 5-bromo-2'-deoxyuridine. *Arch. Neurol. (Chic.)*, *21*, 431.

142. WEAR, D. J. and RAPP, F. (1971): Latent measles virus infection of the hamster central nervous system. *J. Immunol.*, *107*, 1593.

143. FREEMAN, J. M. (1968): Treatment of subacute sclerosing panencephalitis with 5-bromo-2-deoxyuridine and pyran copolymer. *Neurology (Minneap.)*, *18*, 176.

144. DYKEN, P. and KOLAR, O. (1968): Dancing eyes, dancing feet: Infantile polymyoclonia. *Brain*, *91*, 305.

145. COGAN, D. G. (1968): Opsoclonus, body tremulousness, and benign encephalitis. *Arch. Ophthal.*, *79*, 545.

146. BARINGER, J. R., SWEENEY, V. P. and WINKLER, G. F. (1968): An acute syndrome of ocular oscillations and truncal myoclonus. *Brain*, *91*, 473.

147. MOE, P. G. and NELLHAUS, G. (1970): Infantile polymyoclonia-opsoclonus syndrome and neural crest tumors. *Neurology (Minneap.)*, *20*, 756.

148. FORD, F. R. (1966): *Diseases of the Nervous System in Infancy, Childhood, and Adolescence.* Fifth Ed. Charles C. Thomas, Springfield, Ill.

149. LARBRE, F., BETHENOD, M., GUIBAUD, P., MAMELLE, J. C. and GENOUD, J. (1972): Syndrome oculo-cérébello-myoclonique et neuroblastome à propos de deux observations. *Arch. franç. Pédiat.*, *29*, 411.

150. CHRISTOFF, N. (1969): Myoclonic encephalopathy of infants. A report of two cases and observations on related disorders. *Arch. Neurol. (Chic.)*, *21*, 229.

151. JANNY, P., TOURNILHAC, M., MONTRIEUL, B. and PLANE, C. (1970): Encéphalopathie aiguë avec opsoclonus à évolution spontanément régressive. *Rev. neurol. (Paris)*, *122*, 113.

152. FORSTER, C., LENARD, H. G., PACHE, H. D. and VERSMOLD, H. (1971): Die infantile myoklonische Encephalopathie. *Z. Kinderheilk.*, *111*, 67.

153. DESPRESS, P., HEROUIN, C. and SERINGE, P. (1968): Encéphalopathie myoclonique avec opsoclonies. A propos de deux observations. *Ann. Pédiat.*, *15*, 185.

154. ROSS, A. and ZEMAN, W. (1967): Opsoclonus, occult carcinoma, and chemical pathology in dentate nuclei. *Arch. Neurol. (Chic.)*, *17*, 546.

155. ELLENBERGER, C., CAMPA, J. F. and NETSKY, G. (1968): Opsoclonus and parenchymatous degeneration of the cerebellum. *Neurology (Minneap.)*, *18*, 1041.

156. MARTIN, E. S. and GRIFFITH, J. F. (1971): Myoclonic encephalopathy and neuroblastoma. Report of a case with apparent recovery. *Amer. J. Dis. Child.*, *122*, 257.

157. BRISSAUD, H. E. and BEAUVIAS, P. (1969): Opsoclonus and neuroblastoma. *New Engl. J. Med.*, *280*, 1242.

158. SOLOMON, G. E. and CHUTORIAN, A. M. (1968): Opsoclonus and occult neuroblastoma. *New Engl. J. Med.*, *279*, 475.

159. LEONIDAS, J. C., BRILL, C. B. and ARON, A. M. (1972): Neuroblastoma presenting with myoclonic encephalopathy. *Radiology*, *102*, 87.

160. DAVIDSON, M., TOLENTINO, Y. and SAPIR, S. (1968): Opsoclonus and neuroblastoma. *New Engl. J. Med.*, *279*, 948.

161. SANDOK, B. A. and KRANZY, H. (1971): Opsoclonus as the initial manifestation of occult neuroblastoma. *Arch. Ophthal.*, *86*, 235.

162. ELLENBERGER, C. and NETSKY, M. (1970): Anatomic basis and diagnostic value of opsoclonus. *Arch. Ophthal.*, *83*, 307.

163. ALESSI, D. (1940): Lessioni parenchimatose del cervelletto da carcinoma uterino (gliosi carcinotossica?) *Riv. Pat. nerv. ment.*, *55*, 148. Cited by C. Ellenberger and M. Netsky (ref 162).

164. DRUCKMAN, R. and CHAO, D. (1955): Massive spasms in infancy and childhood. *Epilepsia*, *4*, 61.

165. FALCONER, M. A. (1972): Febrile convulsions in early childhood. *Brit. med. J.*, *3*, 292.

166. SCRIVER, C. R. (1967): Vitamin B6 deficiency and dependency in man. *Amer. J. Dis. Child.*, *113*, 109.

167. SWAIMAN, K. F. and MILSTEIN, J. M. (1970): Pyridoxine dependency and penicillamine. *Neurology (Minneap.)*, *20*, 78.

168. FOSSATI, P., PRUVOT, P. M., CARIDROIT, M., BUVAT, J., MONTOIS, R. and LINQUETTE, M. (1972): Carence familiale en pyridoxine chez une diabétique et ses enfants. Encéphalopathie myoclonique infantile avec hypsarythmie guérie par la vitamine B6 chez l'un d'entre eux. *Lille méd., 17,* 719.

169. SCRIVER, C. R. (1960): Vitamin B6 dependency and infantile convulsions. *Pediatrics, 26,* 62.

170. STAMPS, F. W., GIBBS, E. L. and HAASE, E. (1951): Epileptic patients treated with Aureomycin. Clinical and electroencephalographic changes. *Dis. nerv. Syst., 12,* 227.

171. GIBBS, E. L., FLEMING, M. M. and GIBBS, F. (1954): Diagnosis and prognosis of hypsarrhythmia and infantile spasms. *Pediatrics, 13,* 66.

172. GASTAUT, H., SALTIEL, J., RAYBAUD, C., PITOT, M. and MEYNADIER, A. (1959): A propos du traitement par l'ACTH des encéphalites myocloniques de la première enfance avec dysrhythmie majeure (hypsarhythmie). *Pédiatrie, 14,* 35.

173. STAMPS, E. W., GIBBS, E., ROSENTHAL, I. M. and GIBBS, F. A. (1959): Treatment of hypsarrhythmia with ACTH. *J. Amer. med. Ass., 171,* 408.

174. BRAY, P. F. (1963): The influence of adrenal steroids and corticotropin on massive myoclonic seizures in infancy. *Pediatrics, 32,* 169.

175. HARRIS, R. (1964): Some EEG observations in children with infantile spasms treated with ACTH. *Arch. Dis. Childh., 39,* 564.

176. JEAVONS, P. M., HARPER, J. R. and BOWER, B. D. (1970): Long-term prognosis in infantile spasms: A follow-up report on 112 cases. *Develop. Med. Child Neurol., 12,* 413.

177. WILLOUGHBY, J. A., THURSTON, D. L. and HOLOWACH, J. (1966): Infantile myoclonic seizures: an evaluation of ACTH and corticosteroid therapy. *J. Pediat., 69,* 1136.

178. TROJABORG, W. and PLUM, P. (1960): Treatment of 'hypsarrhythmia' with ACTH. *Acta paediat. (Uppsala), 49,* 572.

179. SNYDER, C. H. (1967): Infantile spasms. *J. Amer. med. Ass., 201,* 198.

180. GANDINI, S. and GANDINI-COLLODEL, E. (1967): Trattamento del'encefalopatia mioclonica infantile con ipsaritmia con levoglutamina et ACTH ad alte dosi. *Riv. Neurol., 13,* 311.

181. FARINA, M. and RENSON, L. (1961): Note préliminaire à propos d'une possibilité thérapeutique nouvelle des encéphalopathies myocloniques infantiles avec hypsarhythmie. *Acta neurol. belg., 61,* 1060.

182. MARKHAM, C. H. (1964): The treatment of myoclonic seizures of infancy and childhood with LA-1. *Pediatrics, 34,* 511.

183. GIBBS, F. and ANDERSON, E. (1965): Treatment of hypsarrhythmia and infantile spasms with a Librium analogue. *Neurology (Minneap.), 15,* 1173.

184. MILLICHAP, J. G. and ORTIZ, W. R. (1966): Nitrazepam in myoclonic epilepsies. *Amer. J. Dis. Child., 112,* 242.

185. VÖLZKE, E., DOOSE, H. and STEPHAN, E. (1967): The treatment of infantile spasms and hypsarrhythmia with Mogadon. *Epilepsia, 8,* 64.

186. MARTIN, D. (1970): Die intravenose Anwendung von Nitrazepam (Mogadon) in der Epilepsiebehandlung. *Neuropaediatrie, 2,* 27.

187. HANSON, R. A. and MENKES, J. H. (1970): A new anticonvulsant in the management of minor motor seizures. *Neurology (Minneap.), 20,* 379.

188. LOMBROSO, C. T. and FORSYTHE, I. (1960): A long-term follow-up of acetazolamide (Diamox) in the treatment of epilepsy. *Epilepsia, 1,* 493.

189. TIBBLES, J. A. R. and MCGREAL, D. A. (1963): Trial of amino-oxyacetic acid, an anticonvulsant. *Canad. med. Ass. J., 88,* 881.

190. HUTTENLOCHER, P. R., WILBOURN, A. J. and SIGNORE, J. M. (1971): Medium-chain triglycerides as a therapy for intractable childhood epilepsy. *Neurology (Minneap.)*, *21*, 1097.

191. GASTAUT, H. and VILLENEUVE, A. (1967): The startle disease or hyperekplexia. Pathological surprise reaction. *J. neurol. Sci.*, *5*, 523.

192. COHEN, N. H., McAULIFFE, M. and AIRD, R. B. (1961): Startle epilepsy treated with chlordiazepoxide (Librium). *Dis. nerv. Syst.*, *22*, *Suppl. 7*, 20.

193. KUGELBERG, E. and WIDEN, L. (1954): Epilepsia partialis continua. *Electroenceph. clin. Neurophysiol.*, *6*, 503.

194. HARPER, J. R. (1968): True myoclonic epilepsy in childhood. *Arch. Dis. Childh.*, *43*, 28.

195. SNYDER, C. H. (1968): Myoclonic epilepsy in children: Short-term comparative study of two benzodiazepine derivatives in treatment. *Sth. med. J.*, *61*, 17.

196. KILLIAN, J. M. and FROMM, G. H. (1970): A double-blind comparison of nitrazepam versus diazepam in myoclonic seizure disorders. *Develop. Med. Child Neurol.*, *13*, 32.

197. LINDNER, R. (1970): Diagnostic différentiel du Petit Mal myoclonique-akinétique (syndrome de Lennox) et du syndrome myoclonique observé au cours des lipidoses. *Rev. neurol. (Paris)*, *123*, 327.

198. GASTAUT, H., ROGER, J., SOULAYROL, R., TASSINARI, C. A., REGIS, H. and DRAVET, C. (1966): Childhood epileptic encephalopathy with diffuse slow spike-waves (otherwise known as 'Petit Mal Variant') or Lennox syndrome. *Epilepsia*, *7*, 139.

199. VAN HEYCOP TEN HAM, M. W. and DE JAGER, H. (1963): Progressive myoclonus epilepsy with Lafora bodies. Clinical-pathological features. *Epilepsia*, *4*, 95.

200. RIEHL, J. L., LEE, D. K., ANDREWS, J. M. and BROWN, W. J. (1967): Electrophysiological and neuropharmacological studies in a patient with Unverricht-Lafora's disease. *Neurology (Minneap.)*, *17*, 502.

201. GATH, I., (1969): Effect of drugs on the somatosensory evoked potentials in myoclonic epilepsy. *Arch. Neurol. (Chic.)*, *20*, 354.

202. PETERSEN, I. and HAMBERT, O. (1966): Clinical and electroencephalographic studies of responses to lidocaine and chlormethiazole in progressive myoclonus epilepsy. *Acta psychiat. scand.*, *42*, *Suppl. 192*, 45.

203. HAMBERT, O. and PETERSEN, I. (1970): Clinical electroencephalographical and neuropharmacological studies in syndromes of progressive myoclonus epilepsy. *Acta neurol. scand.*, *46*, 149.

204. DECLERCK, A. (1968): Diagnostic et traitement de l'épilepsie myoclonique progressive type Unverricht-Lundborg. *Acta neurol. belg.*, *68*, 471.

205. KELLY, R. E. and LAURENCE, D. R. (1955): Treatment of progressive myoclonic epilepsy with mephenesin. *Brit. med. J.*, *1*, 456.

206. CACCIARI, E. and SCANABISSI, E. (1968): Contributo allo studio della mioclonoepilepsia progressiva (sindrome di Unverricht e Lundborg). *Clin. pediat. (Bologna)*, *50*, 9.

207. MORRIS, A. A. (1947): Paramyoclonus multiplex (Friedreich). A clinicotherapeutic approach. *Arch. Neurol. Psychiat.*, *57*, 342.

208. GILBERT, G. J., McENTEE III, W. J. and GLASER, G. (1963): Familial myoclonus and ataxia: Pathophysiologic implications. *Neurology (Minneap.)*, *13*, 365.

209. KREINDLER, A., CRIGHEL, E. and POILICI, I. (1959): Clinical and electroencephalographic investigations in myoclonic cerebellar dyssynergia. *J. Neurol. Neurosurg. Psychiat.*, *22*, 232.

210. MAY, D. L. and WHITE, H. H. (1968): Familial myoclonus, cerebellar ataxia, and deafness. Specific genetically determined disease. *Arch. Neurol. (Chic.)*, *19*, 331.

211. JACOBS, H. (1965): Myoclonus and ataxia occurring in a family. *J. Neurol. Neurosurg. Psychiat.*, *28*, 272.

212. RICHARDSON, E. and BORNHOFEN, J. H. (1968): Early childhood cerebral lipidosis with prominent myoclonus. *Arch. Neurol. (Chic.)*, *18*, 34.

213. LANCE, J. W. (1969): Classification and treatment of myoclonus. *Proc. Aust. Ass. Neurol.*, *6*, 61.

214. LOMBROSO, C. T. (1966): Treatment of status epilepticus with diazepam. *Neurology (Minneap.)*, *16*, 629.

215. SAWYER, G. T., WEBSTER, D. D. and SCHUT, L. J. (1968): Treatment of uncontrolled seizure activity with diazepam. *J. Amer. med. Ass.*, *203*, 913.

216. GORDON, N. S. (1966): Treatment of status epilepticus with diazepam. *Develop. Med. Child Neurol.*, *8*, 668.

Subject index

Prepared by E. Dyckhoff, M.D., Nijmegen